PELICAN BOOKS

A199

THE ARCHAEOLOGY OF PALESTINE

WILLIAM FOXWELL ALBRIGHT

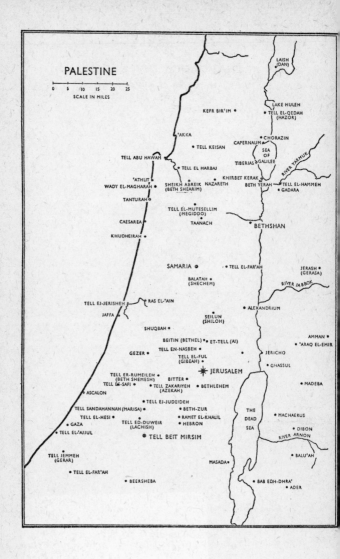

PALESTINE

SCALE IN MILES
0   5   10   15   20   25

LAISH (DAN)

KEFR BIR'IM

LAKE HULEH
TELL EL-QEDAH (HAZOR)

'AKKA

CAPERNAUM   CHORAZIN

TELL KEISAN

SEA OF GALILEE
TIBERIAS

RIVER YARMUK

TELL ABU HAWAM

TELL EL HARBAJ

KHIRBET KERAK

'ATHLIT
WADY EL-MAGHARAH

SHEIKH ABREIK (BETH SHEARIM)

NAZARETH

BETH YERAH

TELL EL-HAMMEH
GADARA

TANTURAH

TELL EL-MUTESELLIM (MEGIDDO)

CAESAREA

TAANACH

BETHSHAN

KHUDHEIRAH

SAMARIA

TELL EL-FAR'AH

JERASH (GERASA)

BALATAH (SHECHEM)

RIVER JABBOK

TELL EJ-JERISHEH
JAFFA

RAS EL-'AIN

ALEXANDRIUM

SEILUN (SHILOH)

SHUQBAH

AMMAN
'ARAQ EL-EMIR

BEITIN (BETHEL)   ET-TELL (AI)

GEZER

TELL EN-NASBEH

JERICHO

TELL EL-FUL (GIBEAH)

JERUSALEM

GHASSUL

TELL ER-RUMEILEH (BETH SHEMESH)
TELL ES-SAFI

BITTER

TELL ZAKARIYEH (AZEKAH)

BETHLEHEM

MADEBA

ASCALON

TELL EJ-JUDEIDEH

TELL SANDAHANNAH (MARISA)

BETH-ZUR

TELL EL-HESI

RAMET EL-KHALIL

MACHAERUS

GAZA

TELL ED-DUWEIR (LACHISH)

HEBRON

THE DEAD SEA

TELL EL-'AJJUL

DIBON

RIVER ARNON

TELL BEIT MIRSIM

TELL JEMMEH (GERAR)

BALU'AH

TELL EL-FAR'AH

MASADA

BEERSHEBA

BAB EDH-DHRA'
ADER

THE ARCHAEOLOGY
OF PALESTINE

—

William Foxwell Albright

PENGUIN BOOKS

Penguin Books Ltd, Harmondsworth, Middlesex
u.s.a.: Penguin Books Inc., 3300 Clipper Mill Road, Baltimore 11, Md
australia: Penguin Books Pty Ltd, 762 Whitehorse Road,
Mitcham, Victoria

—

First published in Pelican Books 1949
Reprinted 1951
Revised and reprinted 1954
Revised and reprinted 1956
Revised and reprinted 1960

Collogravure plates printed by Harrison and Sons Ltd, London
Made and printed in Great Britain
by Richard Clay & Company, Ltd,
Bungay, Suffolk

CONTENTS

Editorial Foreword   6

1. The Art of Excavating a Palestinian Mound   7
2. The Discovery of Ancient Palestine   23
3. Prehistoric Palestine   49
4. Palestine in the Chalcolithic and Early Bronze   65
5. Palestine in the Middle and Late Bronze Ages   80
6. Palestine in the Iron Age   110
     Iron I (Twelfth – Tenth Centuries)   112
     Iron II (Ninth – Early Sixth Centuries   128
     Iron III (c. 550–330 B.C.)   142
7. Palestine in Graeco-Roman Times   146
8. Peoples and Languages, Writing and Literature in Ancient Palestine   177
9. Daily Life in Ancient Palestine   204
     The Time of Jacob: Middle Bronze II   204
     The Time of Elijah: Iron IIA   208
     New Testament Times   212
10. The Old Testament and Archaeology   219
11. The New Testament and Archaeology   238
12. Ancient Palestine in World History   250
Bibliography   256
Acknowledgements   258
List of Plates   259
List of Text Illustrations   260
Index   263

EDITORIAL FOREWORD

PROFESSOR Albright's book on the Archaeology of Ancient Palestine is one of a series of Pelican books planned to describe the beginnings of civilization, from the dawn of history to the first centuries of the present era. In many parts of Asia ancient monuments and remains have, by the caprice of fortune, survived to tell the tale of a remote and long forgotten way of life. The aim of these archaeological books is to present a picture of ancient man chiefly from archaeological evidence, which is pictorial in character. Indeed the attraction of archaeology is that it focuses our attention on a rich variety of objects which we can see, touch, and feel. The evidence may consist of a coin stamped with the portrait of a Caesar; a statue of an Assyrian monarch; or a gracefully painted pot designed by some nameless prehistoric artist: every scrap of evidence takes its place in the ancient mosaic. The fullest records are derived from archaeological excavations in which palaces, temples, cemeteries, houses, and streets have emerged, sometimes more or less complete, from under the ground. Nor can archaeological books afford to neglect the evidence of ancient writings, or the habits and customs of living man, which combine to make the past articulate. Archaeology and history are complementary and interdependent studies.

The wide range of subject-matter covered by Professor Albright in this book demonstrates the close interlocking of archaeology, history, the arts, and the sciences. This treatment has been so successful in attracting the general public as well as the specialist that the book has already been thrice reprinted since its first publication. This latest revision takes account of much recent research in the field of prehistory, especially of Dr Kathleen Kenyon's epoch-making discoveries at Jericho and the collateral evidence for the beginnings of agriculture elsewhere. Other fundamental accretions to knowledge, such as the work of R. de Vaux and its connexion with the discovery of the Dead Sea Scrolls, are witnesses to the extraordinary developments which have occurred in the field during the last decade.

M. E. L. MALLOWAN

Professor of Western Asiatic Archaeology, Institute of Archaeology, University of London. (Professor Mallowan is the general editor of the Pelican series of Near Eastern and Western Asiatic archaeologies.)

CHAPTER 1

The Art of Excavating a Palestinian Mound

—

IT is often easier to gain a clear understanding of any contemporary scene by waiting a few years in order to study it in the light of its history. If we are to see history in perspective, it is equally necessary to study it from the vantage of the contemporary scene. In Chapter Two we shall sketch the history of archaeological exploration and research; in this chapter we will help to give the reader a perspective view of this history by introducing him to the concrete realities of excavation as practised to-day. Excavation is both art and science; the art of good excavation should improve with better archaeological knowledge and method. That art and science sometimes part company is as inevitable as it is regrettable.

One often hears the question, How do sites happen to be chosen for excavation? Possible answers are almost as numerous as excavators. Sometimes they are selected because of some chance find of exceptional importance, as a result of which the call goes out from a government or other highly placed agency for the organization of an expedition. Just this happened in the case of the sensational Syrian excavations at Ras Shamrah and Mari, where discoveries of outstanding interest were made by Schaeffer and Parrot. In Palestine this has often occurred in the case of small digs: for example, clearances of tombs and synagogues or other ancient buildings. Frequently the excavator is attracted by the fame of an ancient site; among many examples are the undertakings in Jerusalem as well as the work of the Germans and Americans at Megiddo, Jericho, Shechem, Samaria, and Bethel. Sometimes a new identification or find attracts somebody's attention; examples are Garstang's soundings at Hazor and the writer's work at Tell Beit Mirsim. Then again, a site is selected mainly because of its accessibility (which is a most important point), as was true of Badè's work at Tell en-Nasbeh and the writer's work at Tell el-Ful (Gibeah). A common reason for digging is the archaeological impressiveness of a site, regardless of its possible history; this led to Petrie's first work at Tell el-Hesi, Garstang's soundings at Tell Keisan and Harbaj, the writer's soundings at Ader.

Of course, there are also some very strange reasons why expeditions are undertaken, not to forget some even stranger reasons why expeditions are projected. An example or two may suffice. When the author was on leave in America in the early summer of 1927, he saw some extraordinary news items and editorials in the provincial U.S. Press about the discovery of the 'Golden Ark' on Mount Nebo by an American explorer. When he returned to the American School in Jerusalem that autumn, one of his first visitors was the 'explorer' in question, who said that he had been referred to the American School by the Palestine Department of Antiquities. It presently appeared that he had visited Nebo once, but was so afraid of the Arabs that he did not dare to return! And this was the extent of the work at Nebo on the strength of which the news of the discovery of the Ark had been cabled to all countries! Far less flamboyant and somehow very touching is the story of the Illinois farmer whom C. C. McCown and the writer met many years ago in a Nazareth hotel. This farmer was superintendent of a rural Baptist Sunday-school, and a neighbour of his was superintendent of a Methodist Sunday-school. One day they got into a discussion about the merits of immersion versus sprinkling. The debate grew intense, and the Methodist advanced what seemed to him a clinching argument against immersion: there was no place in Jerusalem where the whole multitude could have been immersed at Pentecost! So the troubled Baptist proposed to his neighbour that the latter look after his farm while he went to Jerusalem to investigate. He travelled steerage and walked over Palestine in order to save money. He was stabbed and robbed by Arab villagers near Nablus; he nearly died of dysentery contracted in a cheap Jewish hostel at Tiberias. But no matter, his eyes shone as he described the success of his mission and told of measuring the Mamilla Pool at Jerusalem and of estimating that it could have held the entire multitude at Pentecost. Of course, there was no point in telling him that the pool in question is mediaeval, since there undoubtedly were a number of large reservoirs in Jerusalem at that time. His last words as we parted were, 'So I'm going back to convert my Methodist brother!'

A much more important question for the practical excavator than where to dig is generally how to raise the necessary money. Archaeology is a relatively expensive form of research, though far cheaper than astronomy or nuclear physics. Nor is it as costly as suggested by some outstanding examples of 'conspicuous spending'. The wise organizer of excavation looks for a site which can be adequately studied or sampled with available funds. The day has passed when major excavations can be handled by a single archaeologist, as was done at Gezer and Megiddo before the First World War. Modern excavation is far too complex an operation, as we shall see. Of course, a single person may often do admirable work in clearing tombs or excavating very small sites. Sound budgeting and careful disbursal of funds have become almost as important to the success of an archaeological expedition as scientific digging and recording.

Most excavations are undertaken by research organizations and institutions. The Palestine Exploration Fund, which has done the lion's share of all work in Palestine, gathered its funds from regular small contributors and occasional large donors. German and French expeditions are generally supplied with Government funds, at least to cover part of their costs. Men of wealth have frequently shown great generosity;

notable examples are John D. Rockefeller, Sr. and Jr., Jacob Schiff, Sir Charles Marston and Sir Henry Wellcome, Baron Edmond de Rothschild. Often the excavator has raised the necessary funds personally, sometimes employing his patrimony or earning the money by lecturing and writing. Grants may come from endowed institutions and foundations, such as the Rockefeller Foundation or the Carnegie Corporation. There are now many of these endowments in different parts of the English-speaking world, but it is not easy to obtain funds from most of them for archaeological purposes. It is hard to convince the ordinary man that archaeology merits support on a basis similar to that of other scientific undertakings. When individuals or organizations become interested, the interest is usually temporary and is usually focused on the subject of archaeology by the personal enthusiasm of some friend or member, as the case may be.

Raising money for excavation is quite an unpleasant chore. It means that one must become a beggar, going to representatives of endowments and organizations, trying to persuade persons of wealth that the project in question is both worthy and exciting. It is often naïvely thought that it is easier to raise money for excavation in Palestine than for similar work elsewhere. Quite the contrary is generally true. Museum directors and trustees correctly point out that Palestine seldom yields museum objects. Conservative religious folk are likely to show no interest in doing any archaeological work there: since the Bible needs no confirmation there is no object in looking for any more than we already have. The better informed among religiously minded people are likely to scoff at the idea of getting 'human values' from a 'science of potsherds'. Liberals in religion will often say, 'But why dig in Palestine? – you would learn more about the history of religion by excavating in India or China!' Many potential donors have private hobbies which they will insist on importing into excavations. One looks for evidence connecting the

Near East with Middle America through Yucatan. Another demands the use of geophysics or dowsing to locate underground walls and deposits. Neither electro-magnetic apparatus nor willow twigs are of appreciable use in most archaeological enterprises, so such demands may be a serious obstacle to sound method. There are also those who prefer to be guided by a crystal ball (as in the case of the Parker Expedition before the First World War), or by a spiritualistic medium. One patron may insist on publishing the more sensational finds himself, with his own unwarranted interpretations. Another patron may go about discovering new inscriptions and altars of Moloch, to the embarrassment of the sceptical archaeologist whose task is made even more difficult by the enthusiasm which he has himself encouraged!

The main hurdle having been surmounted, the excavator's next task after ensuring the necessary funds is to obtain a concession. The period between the world wars was a halcyon time for the archaeologist working in the Near East. Most of the countries of the Near and Middle East were mandatories of enlightened European governments, which had established departments of antiquities and had drawn up suitable ordinances for the administration of these departments – all in accordance with the provisions of the mandates assigned by the League of Nations. Egypt had had a modern organization of antiquities ever since Sir Gaston Maspero reorganized the service after the death of Mariette Pasha. In all these lands it became easy for a reputable archaeologist, backed by a responsible organization, to obtain permission to excavate and to secure a fair division of objects at the end of a campaign. Since the Second World War it has become much more difficult to obtain permission to excavate from the independent states which have replaced the mandatories. At best it must be expected in future that antiquities will have to remain in the museums or warehouses of the country or province in which the excavation is undertaken;

this has been the law for decades in Italy, Greece, and Turkey. At worst it must be expected that one or more countries of the East will make it impossible for foreigners to excavate there at all, except possibly in collaboration with native institutions or scholars. When native archaeologists of ability are developed, as is already true of Turkey, Iraq, and Egypt, this should not be a bad idea at all – quite the reverse. The future of Palestine is politically obscure, but there is no reason why native and foreign archaeologists should not continue to make important discoveries for a long time to come.

While negotiations are going on with donors and governments, the excavator must gather a staff together. The staff need not have much archaeological training at the beginning of the work, since necessary special training can in large measure be obtained in the course of the excavation. One museum head used to insist that all members of the staffs of archaeological expeditions be trained men, presumably leaving to others the task of training them. Such selfishness generally avenges itself before long. The wise organizer of an excavation must find a director who is both competent and able to get along with people. The excavator of a mound should try to assemble a staff with varied skills, if possible; there should be a competent architect or surveyor, or architects and surveyors, according to the nature of the site. There should be a full-time photographer, who may well be a good amateur, since talented amateurs often get better results than professional photographers unused to this particular type of work. There should be one or more draughtsmen and one or more recorders. A specialist in Palestinian pottery is much more necessary than an epigrapher. A number of these jobs can be taken by students from universities or archaeological institutes. Native surveyors and draughtsmen can be employed to great advantage; it is now possible to find every conceivable type of useful skill in Palestine. For example, there is no longer the slightest excuse for any excavation to be undertaken without enrolling a competent pottery expert on its staff. On an excavation all sorts of talents – even minor ones – prove valuable. A talent for wrestling may fascinate the local *mukhtar* and help to keep him friendly. Some knowledge of first aid and nursing will be of the greatest utility, and the presence of a trained physician in camp may be of incalculable value in keeping up the health of the expedition and ensuring the good will of the native community. A very modest repertory of airs and songs will help to keep the younger – and older – members of a staff happy. And so on.

Women often make the best archaeologists, as is attested by a growing list of eminent women archaeologists. However, it is often wise to separate the sexes in excavating, since the presence of a mixed group in a camp far from a town greatly increases the expense of maintenance. In small expeditions it is difficult to mix the sexes unless the undertaking is very brief or is amply provided with funds. Some of the finest archaeological expeditions in the Near and Middle East have been all-women enterprises; excellent examples are provided by much of the work of Dorothy Garrod, Gertrude Caton Thompson, and Hetty Goldman. Where expeditions are mixed it is highly desirable to have the director's wife present, both to provide a feminine social arbiter and to avert scandal – which has brought not a few expeditions to grief. Lady Petrie and Mrs Garstang were invaluable members of their husbands' expeditions.

While the staff is being gathered, the excavator must not neglect to procure the necessary equipment. Much equipment can be hired or borrowed from other expeditions, especially if the proposed excavation is correlated with others sponsored by a single large institution or organization. Surveyors' instruments are, of course, a prime necessity; they should include a good theodolite or transit, a dumpy level and rod, a plane table and alidade, besides quantities of draughting equipment. All surveying and draughting equipment should be first class; inferior equipment will exact compound interest in annoyance and cheapening of results. Good cameras and plenty of photographic materials are also essential. Most photographic and draughting equipment can now be purchased in Palestine, though it will cost more; on the other hand, it is difficult to gauge the requirements of an expedition in advance. The expedition will require a car and perhaps a light truck; the experience of the war has introduced the invaluable jeep into archaeological practice. Tents and camping equipment, such as folding beds and chairs, will be found necessary, unless the expedition plans to build more permanent quarters. In this connexion, it may be noted that the semi-permanent houses of the Lachish, Gaza, and Isbeita expeditions were destroyed during the disorders of 1936-9; it may perhaps seem less advisable in future than in the past to build permanent houses.

The premonitory headaches of the archaeologist are, however, by no means over. He must also arrange some sort of lease with the native owners of a site. Where property is owned in common, he may be in for interminable negotiations and difficulties. Only an expedition organized for many years of work and with ample funds can hope to be quit of these troubles by Government expropriation, at the excavators' expense. Such expropriation was undertaken in the case of the Megiddo expedition of the University of Chicago (Pl. 4), but the process lasted for a long time. The exactions of the owners, especially when supported by local officials, may be ruinous, as happened once to the Ophel excavation of the Palestine Exploration Fund and more than once to the German Shechem expedition. The author was once haled into court by some of the owners of Tell el-Ful; needless to say, he was exonerated, but the business was time-consuming. The intricate devices thought up by the owners of Tell Beit Mirsim to extract more money from the excavators would be amusing if they were not disconcerting in their lack of community spirit, since each part owner wanted to obtain as much as possible for himself at the expense of the others.

Finally the day arrives when work on the mound can begin. In theory, the site should already have been completely surveyed, with a contour map of the mound, and a

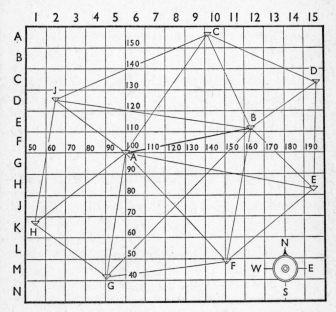

Fig. 1. Triangulation for a co-ordinate grid (after A. H. Detweiler).

co-ordinate grid superimposed on a triangulation grid (Figs. 1, 2). The initial triangulation is required for precision, and the co-ordinate grid is necessary for the location of walls and 'rooms' (*loci*) in the excavation. In practice, digging can generally begin immediately, and the survey can be carried on simultaneously. In small sites, or for provisional purposes, careful use of the plane table may be quite sufficient, without resorting to elaborate triangulation or contour surveying.

A Palestinian mound, or *tell*, as it is called by the Arabs in accordance with immemorial Semitic usage, generally looks like a low truncated cone, with flat top and sloping sides. This peculiar shape, characteristic of the *tell*, *hüyük*, or *tepe* of the Near and Middle East, is produced by the following

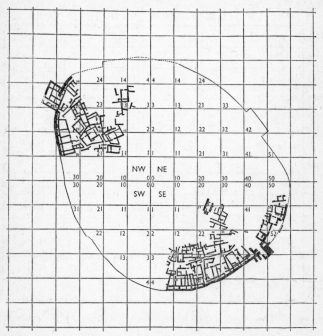

Fig. 2. Schematic plan of Stratum A at Tell Beit Mirsim.

occupational history. At some time in the past, settlers occupied a hill-top near some spring or other source of fresh water. The hill was probably easy by nature to defend, and it probably also had a relatively flat top which made it convenient for settlement. Around it was constructed some kind of rampart, either of rubble or of mud brick. In course of time, after an interval which might range anywhere between

a few years and several centuries, the town or fortress was
destroyed and the place lay unoccupied for an equally unpredictable period. During this period of abandonment, the
rain, driven by the prevailing west wind, washed the debris
of house walls and roofs off the site until further erosion was
checked by the substructure of the fortifications, which remained standing under the debris of the superstructure. The
natural advantages of the site attracted new settlers, sometimes after a long period of neglect. As the centuries rolled
round successive occupations followed one another on the
tell, each marked by its own stratum, like the layers of a cake

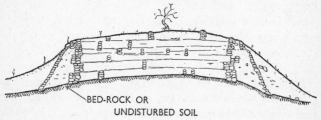

BED-ROCK OR
UNDISTURBED SOIL

Fig. 3. Vertical cross section of typical mound (after A. H. Detweiler).

(Fig. 3). With each new settlement the area available for
building was likely to decrease (though sometimes the reverse
occurred), and the peculiar *tell* shape grew more and more
obvious. The debris of occupation may reach surprising
height (or depth): 21.50 metres (over 70 feet) at Beth-shan and
nearly as much at Megiddo. The depth of debris at Jericho
seems to have been about 20 metres; at Tell el-Hesi it was
reported as 60 feet, but the depth in the centre of the site was
certainly less. Such depths do not compare with the depth of
some Mesopotamian sites, such as Susa, where occupation
was much longer and the consistent use of sun-dried brick
made each stratum thicker, on the average. The number of
strata in a *tell* may vary from one or two to several dozen in
extreme cases. Moreover, many strata contain several clear

phases, and each phase may include a varying number of floor-levels in different buildings. The reader may be reminded that Palestinian *tells* differ in some respects from Mesopotamian *tells* in spite of the fact that their very name is derived from Babylonian *tillu*, 'ruin-heap'. In particular, Mesopotamian mounds are usually artificial accumulations, the original settlement having been founded on the plain instead of on a hill.

Most *tells* are small – more like sites of fortresses than of towns. The area of the Israelite walled 'town' of Tell el-Hesi (Eglon?) was less than a hectare (2.5 acres); the extent of Tell Beit Mirsim, which may rate as an Israelite town of greater than average size, was about 3 hectares inside the walls (7.5 acres). Megiddo is often taken as standard; within the Solomonic walls it was a little over 5 hectares (about 13 acres) in extent; the Bronze Age site was, however, larger. On the other hand, Gezer had an area of some 9 hectares and the great Middle Bronze city of Hazor enclosed nearly 40 hectares inside the rampart of beaten earth (*pisé*). The Middle Bronze town at Tell el-'Ajjul covered some 12 hectares.

Mounds must be excavated with hand labour, since any mechanical device such as bull-dozers or steam shovels would destroy the archaeologist's evidence. Small sites can be dug more economically without any mechanical aids at all, but larger sites require the use of light railways and chutes for debris. Native labour is abundant and generally cheap (relative to the cost of labour in Europe and especially in America); Arab peasants are so poor and so chronically under-nourished that they are very glad of an opportunity to earn good wages in agricultural off-seasons. Jewish labour is much more expensive, but also much better educated and easier to interest in the scientific aims of archaeology. It is very important to have good native foremen, either Palestinian or Egyptian; Egyptian foremen from Guft (Coptus), trained directly or indirectly by Reisner, are the best as a group. Nothing is more important than strict honesty and fairness (which requires generosity) in dealing with Arab labourers, who respond much more quickly to a firm and kindly attitude than do labourers in many other parts of the world. It has been found wise to reward labourers systematically for the finding of objects or the preservation of pottery, while penalizing them for infractions of rules or carelessness in digging out pottery.   Where attempts are made to 'salt' a dig or to get *bakhshish* for objects coming from elsewhere, immediate dismissal seems to be the best way to deal with adults, while children should as a rule be let off with a warning and a small fine.

As the topmost stratum is being cleared, walls and rooms emerge. All walls and permanent installations are carefully planned and photographed; details of masonry and peculiar installations are examined and tested where necessary, with detailed note-book description of anything unusual or hard to picture adequately by plans or photographs. Rooms are numbered serially and with reference to the co-ordinate grid, composed of elements 10, 20, or 25 metres square. Everything found in a given 'locus' is recorded as such. Broken pottery comes in daily in basketfuls, sometimes as many as fifty or a hundred baskets in a single day, each recorded as to provenance and, where desirable, as to level within a stratum. Where possible the sherds are sorted out and vases are wholly or partly reconstructed from the debris. Since pottery forms the basis on which the chronology of a site is constructed, accurate recording, restoration, and description with the aid of profile drawings and photographs are exceedingly important. When small objects of value begin to appear, sieves are brought out, and all the earth in the locus is sifted. Sometimes broken ivories or other delicate objects demand use of paraffin or plaster of Paris. While Palestinian excavations may not yield many museum objects, they are not monotonous, since there is far from being the same unifor-

mity in them that characterizes the normal dig in Egypt or
Babylonia. The late Clarence Stanley Fisher, who had excavated in all three countries, used to state his preference for
Palestine in no uncertain terms: one day, he remarked, one
might find new types of Palestinian pottery of special
chronological value; another day one might find Egyptian
amulets or scarabs – or even a stele covered with hieroglyphs; the next day would perhaps yield a cylinder-seal or
cuneiform tablet. Instead of coming upon mud-brick or stone
walls, the excavator in Palestine is likely to find both; when
he grows tired of the relative simplicity of tracing stone
foundations he may find himself in a stratum of mud-brick,
where all his skill and patience scarcely avail to save the
precious sun-dried brick from being cleared away with the
matrix of debris in which it is imbedded. More than one case
is known where an excavator cleared away what he thought
was a narrow room only to find that he had removed the
wall, leaving rectangular masses of fallen brick in the space
previously occupied by rooms! Or there is the case of an
eminent archaeologist of the old school, who dug to find
tablets and museum pieces. On one occasion he visited the
chantier of another excavator of the contemporary school,
who had carefully cleared his mud-brick walls and left them
standing; as he gazed he exclaimed in surprise, '*Tiens! Vous
avez des murailles!*'

Finally the archaeologist completes the task of clearing all
or part of a given stratum. Then he sadly – or sadistically, if
so disposed – gives the order to remove the walls. As walls
are removed, reconstructions often appear; objects are found
inside walls or under floors. So the chronological interest of
this period of destruction is usually no less than that of the
preceding phase of clearing the debris between walls. When
the task is finished, the co-ordinate grid is dropped to the new
level with the aid of previously fixed points and lines, and
the process of clearing a stratum is repeated. This cycle of

digging and recording strata may go on until the excavator wonders where it will stop. And sometimes it continues down into deposits older than any stratified remains previously recorded. Such was the author's experience during the third campaign at Tell Beit Mirsim (1930) (Pl. 5); this was later the experience of FitzGerald at Beth-shan (1933) and of Garstang at Jericho (1935). Such a thrill must be experienced to be appreciated.

In 1952–8 Miss Kathleen Kenyon applied Sir Mortimer Wheeler's improved trenching method to the excavation of Jericho with such brilliant results that this method is rapidly taking the place of the Reisner–Fisher technique described in this chapter. Actually the latter is supplemented, not displaced, but the Wheeler–Kenyon techniques have come to stay. Essentially they involve careful use of test trenches in order to determine exact stratification before digging an area, followed by additional test trenches at right angles to walls as they are cleared. The sides of these trenches (which are usually less than a metre in depth) are smoothed with a trowel, and all signs of floors, ash levels, deposits of débris, filling, etc., are drawn to scale and used to guide further excavation. In mud-brick sites this method has become indispensable.

When an excavation is finished and the antiquities have been divided, then begins the arduous work of preparing the material for publication. The archaeologist must see to it that everything is properly drawn or photographed, and that as much information has been extracted from objects as possible, if necessary with the aid of chemists, petrographers, wood experts, etc. The plans must be copied, photographs and drawings must be assembled and selected, and the text of the definitive publication must be prepared. It is to be regretted that many archaeologists, including the author, have been guilty of serious procrastination with regard to publication. In the pressure of daily affairs and professional duties it is often hard to find time for the detailed tabulating and indexing which form such a large part of any expedition report. And yet this is most important, since without it the results of excavation are almost useless to scholars and the contribution of an excavator to the progress of archaeology is greatly reduced. In spite of the haste and frequent lack of care with which Sir Flinders Petrie published his results, his promptness was always a great asset. As the Latin proverb has it, *Bis dat qui cito dat*.

POSTSCRIPT

THE first announcement of the successful use of radiocarbon dating for archaeological purposes followed the last revision of the proofs of the first edition. A postscript was added in the 1951 reprint, and is now presented in revised form. The original method employed by W. F. Libby was based on solid carbon samples; this technique was largely replaced by gaseous samples, particularly in the acetylene method of H. Suess. Since 1958 the use of 'enriched' samples has been introduced by H. de Vries and his associates. Radiocarbon (carbon isotope 14) has a half-life of some 5,600 years, and the rate of disintegration appears to be remarkably stable, though factors of uncertainty undoubtedly exist – mostly due to human weaknesses but also of chemical origin. Statistical uncertainty, on the other hand, may be considerably reduced by longer periods of counting radiation from a sample. The period covered has been gradually extended from 15,000–20,000 years to over 70,000. New methods of estimating age (e.g., the potassium–argon method) and correlations with data obtained from the use of oxygen isotopes to date core samples from ancient sea-bottoms (Emiliani) are steadily widening and clarifying the chronological picture. The best recent dates are presupposed in the 1960 reprint.

CHAPTER 2
The Discovery of Ancient Palestine
—

PALESTINE has a unique place among lands of archaeological significance. It is the Jewish Zion, the Christian Holy Land, and the second holiest country of the Muslims. It was not only the cradle of Judaism and Christianity, but through the influence of both on Islam it also became the ultimate geographical home of the latter. Devout Christians and Jews are glad to have light on the persons and places of the Bible; historians welcome new information about the background from which the Bible emerged. Historians of Western civilization turn to Palestine for data bearing on its origins; cultural anthropologists and archaeologists turn to it because of its importance as a geographical bridge between continents and cultural areas.

The extraordinary religious, political, and cultural phenomenon which we call the 'Crusades' left Europe with continuing interest in the Holy Land. The flow of pilgrims was soon resumed, since it was too satisfactory a source of Muslim income to be suppressed, and it swelled with the advent of modern times. Most accounts by contemporary visitors carried on the mediaeval tradition, but the new spirit of inquiry appeared in the description by the Swiss Dominican, Felix Schmid (Fabri), of his journeys to Palestine in 1480 and 1483 (not published until three quarters of a century later). A modern atmosphere breathes from the pages of the German physician, Leonhard Rauchwolff (Rauwolf), whose visit to Palestine in 1575 yielded the first systematic observations in natural history, especially botany. Interest in architecture and archaeology already appears in the drawings of the Fleming, Johann Zuallart (1586), and the accurate descriptions of the Dutchman, Johann van Kootwyck (Cotovicus), in the last years of the sixteenth century.

In the seventeenth and eighteenth centuries scholarly interest in Palestine developed steadily, fed by the periodical appearance of important works. The learned account of the holy places by Quaresmius, based on prolonged and exact, though uncritical study, appeared in 1639; in 1650 came the well-written description of the travels of the Roman, Pietro della Valle, which contained more novel archaeological data than any precursor; in 1679 the French Jesuit, Michael Nau, brought out a valuable, though uncritical, account of his experiences in Palestine; in 1703 the English Protestant chaplain, Henry Maundrell, followed with an excellent account of his travels, containing much new archaeological material. Bishop Pococke's journey in 1738 was still more significant, since he often left the beaten track and published more plans, drawings, and copies of inscriptions than anyone had done before him. There can be no doubt that the publication in 1709 by the Dutchman, Adrian Reland, of his monumental handbook, *Palaestina ex monumentis veteribus illustrata* ('Palestine Illustrated by Ancient Monuments'), had revolutionized scholarly approach to ancient Palestine. For the first time Reland had collected all the pertinent information from extant ancient and modern sources, digesting it critically. The full value of his work was not adequately realized – much less utilized – until the nineteenth century.

As travellers swarmed into Palestine and accounts of their travels multiplied, the proportion of original contributions of relative merit naturally decreased. But with the first quarter of the nineteenth century came a number of first-class scholarly explorers, including particularly the German, Ulrich Jasper Seetzen (1805–7), the Swiss, Johann Ludwig Burckhardt (1801–12), and the Englishmen, C. L. Irby and James Mangles (1817–18). Seetzen was the first to explore Transjordan scientifically; he discovered Caesarea Philippi and especially 'Amman and Gerasa (Jerash). Burckhardt discovered Petra and was the first to record Arabic place-names correctly throughout; his enthusiasm for Arabian exploration was so great that he became a Muslim, travelling as Sheikh Ibrahim. He was thus able to visit such sites as the traditional Tomb of Aaron and to copy inscriptions and make plans in comparative safety. The tomb of this great scholar is in a Muslim cemetery in Cairo. Irby and Mangles discovered 'Araq el-Emir and made valuable archaeological observations. Much of what other scholars had discovered was first published by a somewhat over-ambitious traveller, John Silk Buckingham, in 1821; however, he deserves credit for his publication of the first plans of the important ruins at Jerash and elsewhere.

The year 1838 brought a complete revolution in the surface exploration of Palestine. In that year the American theologian, Edward Robinson (Pl. 1), spent some three months in the Holy Land, crossing and recrossing in various directions with his pupil and friend, Eli Smith. He himself had received a German training in Semitic languages under Gesenius and Rödiger and in geography under the incomparable Ritter; Eli Smith was at home in Arabic and among the Arabs, having spent years as a missionary in Beirut. The two companions, abandoning the beaten trail and recording names, time, compass bearings, etc., as they rode, identified scores of biblical places for the first time. On May 4th, for example, Robinson discovered several ancient towns under nearly the same Arabic names, within a few hours' ride north-east and north of Jerusalem itself. On May 10th he correctly identified no fewer than eight towns in southern Judah. And so it went over the entire country. Robinson's chief competitor, the Swiss Titus Tobler, who began his own valuable topographical researches three years earlier, wrote in 1867: 'The works of Robinson and Smith alone surpass the total of all previous contributions to Palestinian geography from the time of Eusebius and Jerome to the early nineteenth century'.

A century later, at the celebration of the centenary of Robinson's first trip, the two most distinguished European authorities, Père F. M. Abel and Albrecht Alt, expressed themselves similarly. Not being a historical architect or epigrapher, Robinson's contributions to archaeology in the narrow sense were much less significant, but even here he made such important discoveries as that of the line of the Third or Agrippan Wall of Jerusalem, which has recently been confirmed by excavations.

In spite of the increased tempo of exploration and publication in the generation following Robinson's first visit to Palestine, little of permanent value was accomplished, even by such indefatigable explorers as Victor Guérin. The great pioneer's work seemed so thoroughly accomplished that nothing was left for his successors but gleanings. In 1850–1 and 1863 F. de Saulcy explored and excavated in various places; since his enterprise exceeded his knowledge and his vanity exceeded both, there was little to show for his work except some interesting antiquities (now in the Louvre) and the useful clearance of the so-called Tombs of the Kings near Jerusalem. So little was then known about the history of architectural carving and epigraphy that he dated the mausoleum and its contents to the end of the Kingdom of Judah instead of to the last two decades before the end of the Second Temple – about 650 years too early! However, de Saulcy remains the first modern excavator of a Palestinian site.

In 1865 the Palestine Exploration Fund was established. Two years later Charles Warren, a young British ordnance officer, was sent out with ample funds to excavate at Jerusalem. The task proved to be far greater than anyone then dreamed it could be, and the absence of reliable criteria for dating masonry and pottery made the results unsatisfactory from the standpoint of the historian. Warren dated the Herodian masonry of the great retaining wall of the Temple Enclosure to the time of Solomon instead of to the reign of

Herod the Great; on the other hand, he took the Maccabaean fortress of Tell el-Ful (Gibeah) to be a work of the Crusaders. Like Robinson and Guérin he was inclined to consider true mounds as purely natural formations. Yet a great deal of valuable clearance was carried out; and Warren, with the aid of the ordnance survey which was shortly afterwards completed by Captain Charles Wilson, laid the foundations for all subsequent work on the topography and history of Jerusalem.

At the same time that these elaborate operations were being organized by the British, a young Frenchman, Charles Clermont-Ganneau, made numerous brilliant discoveries, as well as a great many minor finds, on his own account. His career, like that of Robinson, illustrates the fact that a single man of genius may advance the sum of knowledge in a given field more than a whole generation of inferior investigators or a treasury full of money for a costly series of undertakings. Coming to the French consular service in Palestine as a young man of twenty-one, it was barely three years before he had recovered the famous Mesha Stone from the Arabs and sent it to the Louvre (1870). The following year he discovered the famous inscription prohibiting the admission of Gentiles into the court of the Temple. The list of his finds and observations is far too long to be presented here. Nor have we space to describe his brilliant *exposés* of the sensational 'Moabite' forgeries which successively deceived some of the most prominent specialists of Europe.

Meanwhile, the Palestine Exploration Fund was not being idle. From 1872 to 1878 it kept a British expedition in the field, making a thorough inch-to-a-mile survey of Western Palestine under the able leadership of C. R. Conder and H. H. Kitchener (Lord Kitchener of Khartoum). This survey has now been superseded in some respects by the cadastral survey of the Palestine Government, but it remains indispensable for the archaeologist and topographer. It is surprising how few significant ruins were overlooked by the surveyors of the expedition. To be sure, many of the identifications by which Conder, in particular, thought that the topography of biblical Palestine was settled for good, have proved to be wrong. But errors and omissions are remarkably few when we consider the scope and speed of the undertaking.

In 1870 the American Palestine Exploration Society was founded on the model of the British organization. After some negotiation it was decided that the American society should undertake the survey of Transjordan to complement the British survey of Western Palestine. Two expeditions were actually sent out to survey the country, but they encountered so many obstacles and suffered such chronic shortage of funds that the project was finally abandoned with very little to show for it. Selah Merrill undertook several expeditions under the same auspices to study the antiquities of Transjordan. However, he was no Robinson, much less a Clermont-Ganneau, and the results of his work were also insignificant. In 1884 G. Schumacher began a cartographic and archaeological survey of Hauran and northern Transjordan which covered a good many years and led to excellent results. Schumacher was a member of the Tempelgesellschaft and had known the country from childhood. He knew how to deal with the Arabs and with Turkish officials; it was thus far easier for him to secure worth-while results than it would have been for any party from abroad.

All these expeditions, including the excavations of Guthe (1881) and Maudsley (1884) in Jerusalem, lacked any means of dating their finds, aside from rare inscriptions. Masonry was then virtually undatable, and inscriptions were subject to differences of opinion which seem incredible in retrospect. Until there was a science of stratigraphy there was no hope for a scientific archaeology. Even Schliemann's discoveries at Troy from 1870 on failed to stimulate Palestinologists to investigate their mounds. For one thing, Schliemann and Dörpfeld had indeed recognized that a mound represented an accumulation of layers of occupations, but they paid little attention to the possibilities of pottery for dating purposes. And it is doubtful whether any man working in Palestine knew much beyond vague hearsay about the discoveries at Troy. So Palestine had to await a third genius of the stature of Robinson and Clermont-Ganneau.

In 1890 the missing genius appeared on the scene, in the person of Flinders Petrie (Pl. 2), a brilliant Englishman of thirty-seven. In spite of his comparative youth he had already spent a decade working in Egypt, where he had begun to introduce systematic recording of all finds, no matter how small, as well as the use of pottery for dating purposes. A decade later he was to discover the fundamental principle of sequence-dating, thanks to which it is possible to extend relative chronology into periods where there are no stratified remains for direct comparison. Petrie worked for six weeks at the mound of Tell el-Hesi in south-western Palestine, making vertical sections and noting the exact level at which every characteristic potsherd was found. As a result he was able to state positively that each period had its own typical pottery, which could be distinguished by a trained eye from corresponding pottery of earlier or later periods. In particular, he succeeded in giving rough absolute dates to several of his pottery periods by identifying certain wares with wares already found in datable Egyptian burials. Though Conder and others scoffed at the new pottery criterion, it was proved by F. J. Bliss, an American scholar who followed Petrie at Tell el-Hesi for three years, that the latter was absolutely right. Scarabs and inscriptions made it possible to date the strata quite closely. The Petrie–Bliss chronology of 1894 was correct almost to the century as far back as about 1500 B.C.; before that the dates were much too low. Had Bliss realized the importance of recording the shapes of the most typical potsherds in each stratum, the essentials of Palestinian pottery chronology might have been fixed for good. As it happened, he failed to publish a correlation of Petrie's detailed treatment of sherds with his own stratigraphic results, and his own publication was much too chary of detail to advance the subject appreciably. The next two decades brought many expeditions and numerous important discoveries; the net gain in improvement of technique was much greater than the gain in chronology and historical interpretation. In fact, the archaeological chronology of Palestine was in some respects more obscure in 1914 than it had been two decades earlier.

During these two decades the Palestine Exploration Fund continued to excavate in Palestine with scarcely any inter-ruption. From 1894 to 1897, Bliss and his architect, A. C. Dickie, worked in Jerusalem, doing a workmanlike job, in which both the archaeological and the architectural side were well handled. This was followed by two prolonged cam-paigns in no fewer than four mounds of the Shephelah, or low hill-country of Judah, in which Bliss was assisted by a brilliant young Irish archaeologist, R. A. S. Macalister. The publication of their results in 1902 represented the highest level of competence attained before the publication of the excavations at Jericho (1913) and Samaria (1924). Exciting historical results from these soundings were few, but the stratification of the four mounds was roughly determined and a quantity of correctly dated pottery was published. All the early pottery from the excavations was included in four rough divisions, covering a lapse of time which we should now date from about 3000 to the first century B.C. To illustrate the relative correctness of this chronology of 1902, we append the following table:

PERIODS	BLISS—MACALISTER	PRESENT DATING
Early Pre-Israelite .	c. ? –1500 B.C.	c. 3000–1800 B.C.
Late Pre-Israelite .	c. 1500–800	c. 1800–1000
Jewish . . .	c. 800–300	c. 1000–587
Seleucidan . . .	c. 300–	Fourth–first centuries

The bulk of the pottery from the last three periods is correctly dated; the principal errors in the chronology of 1902 are due to the fact that pottery from the eighteenth–fifteenth and the sixth–fourth centuries is scarcely represented at all in the plates.

Owing to increasing friction between the two heads of the expedition, as well as to decrease of the Fund's income, the following excavation of Gezer (1902–9) was directed by Macalister, who worked alone except for his efficient fore-man, Yusif Kan'an. The Gezer excavation was a model of economy, but it proved impossible for even the industrious Macalister to do everything. Hence stratigraphy and photo-graphy were neglected; surveying and levelling were utterly inadequate; the architectural aspects of the dig were dealt with only sketchily. After several campaigns Macalister felt himself compelled to change the Bliss–Macalister chronology rather drastically, by pushing the end of the 'Late Pre-Israelite' (his Third and Fourth Semitic) down to 500 B.C., more than four centuries too late, thus dating the pottery and other remains of the later monarchy of Judah in the Persian and Hellenistic ages. The reason for this unfortunate shift was simple: there happens to be an almost complete gap in the history of occupation at Gezer between the tenth and the fifth centuries, but Macalister not unnaturally assumed continuous occupation, trying to fill the great gap with pottery from the immediately preceding phase. When the three massive volumes of his publication appeared in 1912, they were justly hailed as a monumental achievement – 'a monument of bee-like industry', wrote the German excava-tor of Jericho. But almost everything in them has had to be redated and re-interpreted; for instance, a fragment of a cuneiform tablet from about 1400 B.C. was dated about the sixth century, while the famous Gezer Calendar was dated several centuries too late because of the erroneous ceramic chronology. On the other hand, there were many advances over older views. The characteristic pottery of the later Middle Bronze was separated from Late Bronze pottery, under the name 'Second Semitic', dated *c*. 1800–1400 B.C. (which is nearly correct). A mass of objects was classified and described, thus furnishing later students with valuable comparative material.

In 1909 Macalister was called to the chair of Celtic Archaeology at Dublin, and Duncan Mackenzie was invited by the Palestine Exploration Fund to direct the projected excavation of Beth-shemesh. Having a first-hand knowledge of Aegean pottery, Mackenzie was able to appreciate the full significance of the Philistine pottery (first named by Hermann Thiersch in 1908) which turned up in abundance at this site. It is not surprising that his dates for Iron Age pottery were in general correct – even too high in part – and that he reversed Macalister's tendency to date 'Jewish' pottery too late. After three short campaigns, work here was abandoned for lack of funds. And then the First World War broke out, compelling plans for new undertakings to be cancelled.

German and Austrian scholars had been looking longingly towards Palestine for many years. At the turn of the century, relations between Germany and Austria on the one side and Turkey on the other improved to the point where it was judged politically expedient to inaugurate excavations. In 1898 the Deutsche Orient-Gesellschaft was founded under the patronage of the German Emperor. In 1901 the energetic young German biblical scholar, Ernst Sellin, who was then teaching in Vienna, organized an expedition to excavate the splendid mound of Taanach, five miles south-east of Megiddo. He made extensive soundings (1901–4) and discovered numerous important objects, among them a dozen cuneiform tablets and fragments from the century preceding the Amarna period. Unfortunately, the undertaking was inadequately staffed and the stratigraphy of the site was neglected. Schumacher, who had long been engaged in surface explorations, got his initial experience of actual excavation with Sellin, and was presently placed in command of a German expedition to excavate the great site of Megiddo (1903–5). However, he worked single-handed, just as Macalister was doing at Gezer. As a trained draughtsman he produced much better plans and drawings than the latter, but they proved so inaccurate that the surveyors of the Oriental Institute found it impossible to incorporate them into their own survey or ground plans. In fact, certain trenches indicated on Schumacher's plans could not be identified at all with any trenches which he had actually dug. Schumacher's ignorance of the ceramic index to chronology vitiated his stratigraphy to such an extent that little of it has proved serviceable. Yet his work had considerable intrinsic value, and it undoubtedly played an important part in the development of Palestinian archaeology into a well-consolidated discipline.

In 1907 a joint German–Austrian mission began work at Jericho, in the southern valley of the Jordan; it continued until 1909 under the direction of Sellin and Carl Watzinger, assisted by a staff of architects. For the first time in our story we meet with a properly staffed major excavation. When the excavation report was issued in 1913, expectations were fulfilled: plans and photographs were superb, and the pottery was adequately published with drawings and photographs to illustrate a detailed text. The construction of the splendid Middle Bronze wall was fully and competently described. The stratigraphy of the site was well handled, though the excavation barely penetrated strata of the third millennium. On the other hand, the chronology was far from being correct, since the excavators neglected to acquaint themselves with the results of the British excavations and substituted a new system of their own. This new system was based mainly on a hypothesis of Sellin's with regard to the identity of the wall supposed to have fallen before the Israelites and of a

wall inferred from the Bible to have been built by Hiel the
Bethelite in the ninth century B.C. Actually the wall which he
supposed to have collapsed at the Israelite siege had been
destroyed early in the Middle Bronze Age, while the supposed Hielite wall was built not later than the seventeenth
century, a good eight centuries before the time of Hiel!

The year 1908 may be said to mark a decisive advance in
the technical aspect of Palestinian archaeology, since it was
then that the actual work of excavation (aside from preliminary soundings) began at both Jericho and Samaria. For
the first time since scientific excavation began there were
trained staffs on hand to take care of all important phases of
the work. No longer was the arduous task of digging and
recording left to one or two men. The Harvard excavation of
Samaria, under the direction of George Andrew Reisner,
aided particularly by C. S. Fisher, continued through three
campaigns. Thanks to the generosity of a wealthy American
banker, Jacob Schiff, the then magnificent sum of $60,000
was available for the undertaking, so it never suffered from
the usual chronic want of funds. Moreover, Reisner was himself an archaeological genius worthy of standing beside
Robinson, Clermont-Ganneau, and Petrie. He had already
spent a decade in Egypt, where he had developed a new
archaeological technique which has since become standard – a
combination of the British methods of Petrie, the German
methods of Dörpfeld and Koldewey, and his native Middle-
Western American practicality and knack for large-scale
organization. Fortunately he was also in command of the
necessary funds for work, funds which he never wasted but
always put to good use. Reisner employed all the resources
of accurate surveying, competent architectural analysis, complete photographic records, and systematic filing cabinets;
nothing was left to chance and nothing was considered as too
insignificant to merit serious consideration. Since the two
massive volumes of the Samaria publication did not appear

until 1924, the full impact of the new methods reached Palestinian archaeology through the work of Reisner's pupil, Fisher, himself an archaeological genius of no mean quality.

Passing over numerous minor undertakings and meritorious surface explorations from the period before the First World War, we come to the year 1920, when the British Mandatory Government in Palestine set up a modern Department of Antiquities, headed by an experienced archaeologist, John Garstang of the University of Liverpool. Under the new liberal policy towards foreign excavators, archaeology flourished as never before. During the fifteen halcyon years from 1921 to 1936, after which the outbreak of disorders in Palestine slowed excavation down to a walk, no year passed without several excavations. The number of archaeological enterprises increased steadily until it reached its climax in the early thirties. The author counts himself fortunate to have been in Palestine from 1920 to 1935, taking an active part in excavation and interpretation. These were stimulating years, when every month saw some distinct progress towards our remote goal of a complete archaeological history of Palestine. With an almost entirely new lot of archaeologists at work, we had to begin at the very bottom, building up our discipline inductively without accepting any of the earlier results as established until our independent research corroborated them. Instead of the almost total lack of contact between the Germans and British which had been the order of the day, and instead of the repeated breaks in continuity which had appeared whenever a new archaeologist came to Palestine, there was a splendid attitude of co-operation. *Facile princeps* was the French Dominican, L. H. Vincent, who had studied the excavations since the late nineties and had published an admirable survey of results in 1907. Père Vincent was the tutor of all; he spared no pains to induct the neophyte into the mysteries of his discipline. His knowledge of pottery was unrivalled, though he shared in many of the misapprehensions of the earlier excavators and was scarcely successful in his efforts to produce a chronological synthesis from the widely divergent results of Macalister and Watzinger. New military roads and Ford cars made travel incomparably easier than it had been. Archaeologists visited each other's excavations and met at the Palestine Museum or in the meetings of the Palestine Oriental Society to exchange views and results. Small wonder that progress became relatively steady!

Of course, this does not mean that there were no set-backs. Men with established reputations sometimes came in from abroad and showed themselves unwilling or unable to learn the elements of Palestinian pottery chronology. A supposed sanctuary was discovered on the slopes of Gerizim and was dated by its excavator to the time of Gideon, about 1100 B.C., whereas it was really a villa, and its pottery was later recognized by specialists as typically Middle Bronze; the excavator was wrong by some five centuries, simply because he did not consider it in keeping with his dignity to consult other scholars. A chalcolithic village from the early fourth millennium was discovered and partly excavated; the eminent director of the work was led through a curious series of misunderstandings to date it fifteen hundred years too late, and having once adopted the low date he adhered to it until his untimely decease. An Iron Age tomb was dated by another excavator five hundred years too early, owing to similar misunderstandings.

We will not strain the reader's tolerance by cataloguing all the excavations in Palestine and Transjordan since 1920, but will limit ourselves to a general survey of progress in the field, with a paragraph for each of the more significant undertakings or groups of projects. We shall often be obliged to write non-committally, either because the excavator is still active or because the publication of his results is not yet complete. Only after an excavation has been finished, and all significant details published, is it really safe to attempt a broad historical appraisal.

The most extraordinary advance in Palestinian archaeology has certainly been in the field of prehistory. In 1920 this branch of our science was wholly undeveloped. Surface explorations and a few soundings in caves had brought to light flint artifacts which closely resembled Chellean, Mousterian, and Aurignacian flints from the Palaeolithic of Western Europe. But there was no stratigraphy and there was no independent evidence as to the fauna and flora, the geology and geochronology, or the type of man associated with any given type of flint tool. In 1925 a young Englishman, F. Turville-Petre, excavated in two caves above the Sea of Galilee and discovered the first stratified deposits in Palestine, in one of which he found the first remains of prehistoric man. The main find was part of a typically Neanderthal skull, in an equally typical Mousterian context, thus proving that the correlation previously set up between the Mousterian of France and that of Palestine was substantially correct (Pl. 7). In 1928 Miss Dorothy Garrod, the eminent pre-historian of Cambridge University, began a long series of campaigns in Palestinian caves, which continued until 1934 under the joint auspices of the British School of Archaeology in Jerusalem and the American School of Prehistoric Research. Among the outstanding discoveries made by her expedition were the new Natufian culture and nearly a dozen complete and fragmentary skeletons of fossil men. The French were also active at the same time; a consular official of note, René Neuville, undertook a series of productive excavations in caves elsewhere in Palestine.

The lead in Palestinian archaeology between the wars was taken by British organizations, often in co-operation with American groups or individuals. The Palestine Exploration Fund and the British School of Archaeology undertook a whole series of minor excavations and soundings, beginning with some work at Ascalon under the direction of Garstang and W. J. Phythian-Adams. Between 1923 and 1928 a series of campaigns was undertaken on the Ophel hill in Jerusalem, headed successively by Macalister, J. Garrow Duncan, and J. W. Crowfoot. Enough masonry and pottery of the Bronze and Iron Ages were found to make it certain that this was the real nucleus of the 'City of David'.

The excavation of Jericho, begun by the Germans, was continued by Garstang in 1929–36, and especially by Kathleen Kenyon in 1952–8. Garstang failed to establish the date of the fall of the last Canaanite town, but he discovered the first pre-pottery Neolithic urban culture. His failure to obtain clear evidence of an urban installation in Late Bronze was due to drastic erosion of the mud-brick débris of the site during the four centuries or so between the latest pre-Israelite occupation and the rebuilding of the Israelite town in the early ninth century B.C. The effect of wind and rain on such sites has tended to be overlooked. However, he did find remains of a Late Bronze fortress, dated by pottery, as well as near-by burials of the fourteenth–thirteenth centuries B.C. Miss Kenyon has not been able to add substantially to Garstang's evidence for the latest pre-Israelite occupation, but her work has clarified chronology throughout, and has yielded sensational results for pre-pottery Neolithic.

The revered Nestor of archaeologists, Flinders Petrie, returned to Palestine in 1927, after a lapse of thirty-seven years. Ever the independent investigator, Petrie decided to pay no attention to the results of other scholars, but to make his own chronological inferences as his work developed. In theory, these inferences were based on typological comparisons of local objects with similar objects found in Egypt. In practice, the material often proved too scanty to justify reliable conclusions, since he refused to pay any attention to the accumulated results of other specialists in the field. Thus when he presented his chronology of Tell el-'Ajjul ('Ancient Gaza'), he dated the earliest remains there about 3500–3200 B.C. instead of about 2000, correlating them with the Fifth Egyptian Dynasty instead of with the Eleventh; the most important city on the site he dated about 2600–2400 instead of about 1500, correlating it with the Twelfth Dynasty instead of with the Eighteenth! Nor is this reduction of Petrie's dates merely the personal opinion of the writer; it is based on clear-cut identifications of pottery forms which can be verified by any intelligent visitor to the Palestine Museum or by any student with the patience to examine the latest publications. Besides the work at Tell el-'Ajjul (1930–4) briefer excavations were undertaken at two other sites of the Negeb (Tell Jemmeh, south of Gaza, and Tell el-Far'ah, probably Sharuhen). Minor digs at Anthedon and Petra in 1935–7 rounded out the Palestinian phase of the operations of the British School of Archaeology in Egypt, which Petrie had founded forty years before.

Two very important British excavations remain to be considered: the joint British–American–Hebrew-University project at Samaria (1931–5) and the Wellcome–Marston expedition at Lachish (Tell ed-Duweir), from 1932 to 1938. The Samaria excavation continued under J. W. Crowfoot where Reisner had left off, and cleared up numerous persistent chronological uncertainties. Thanks to the tremendous progress in dating potsherds during these twenty years it was possible to correct a number of unavoidable errors made by Reisner: the round towers lining the acropolis proved to be Hellenistic instead of Israelite, being thus reduced nearly five centuries in date; the 'Herodian' street of columns turned out to belong to the third or fourth century A.D. Reisner's most remarkable discovery, some seventy inscribed sherds (ostraca) belonging to the early eighth century B.C. (not ninth, as he supposed), has been matched by more ostraca and a fine collection of carved and inlaid ivories from the ninth or eighth century. The Lachish expedition was brilliantly directed by J. L. Starkey (Pl. 3), who had learned his craft under Petrie; if he had not been treacherously murdered in January 1938, he might now well rank with the outstanding geniuses of archaeology. Starkey possessed extraordinary promotional flair, combined with a keen instinct for archaeological analysis. At the same time he demonstrated unusual talent for engineering operations and organization of archaeological work. With the aid of an excellent staff he did full justice to every aspect of his excavation, including surveying, photography, pottery, and epigraphy. The sensational find in 1935 and 1938 of more than a score of Hebrew ostraca, a third of which were quite legible, has dwarfed all other finds on the site. Lachish was a very important fortress at different periods, and Starkey's elaborate preparations have greatly simplified the task of the next excavator. There can be little doubt that the excavation of the latest Canaanite strata will yield many inscribed objects in cuneiform and other scripts, and will go a long way towards settling the vexed problem of the date of the Israelite conquest of Canaan.

The first American expedition to be organized in the period between the wars was the excavation of the great citadel of Beth-shan (Pl. 6) under the auspices of the University of Pennsylvania Museum and the successive direction of C. S. Fisher, Alan Rowe, and G. M. FitzGerald. In all there were ten campaigns here between 1921 and 1933. Fisher was a trained architect and archaeologist of the Reisner school, and the Beth-shan undertaking was beautifully planned and executed. Since both Rowe and FitzGerald had been trained by Fisher there was no real discontinuity in the succession of excavators. The outstanding feature of the excavation was the partial clearance of several superimposed Egyptian fortresses from the fourteenth–twelfth centuries; in them were found several Egyptian stelae and a number of shrines of considerable interest for the history of Canaanite religion. FitzGerald's soundings to bed-rock recovered a valuable stratigraphic sequence going back to the middle of the fourth millennium.

In 1925 Fisher left the service of the University of Pennsylvania and joined the staff of the Oriental Institute of the University of Chicago, in order to direct the excavation of Megiddo. This famous ancient town had already been trenched by the Germans (see above), who had found little of exceptional interest. The new expedition was, however, far better organized, with resources which dwarfed all preceding archaeological enterprises. From 1925 to the last campaign in 1939 the expedition must have cost nearly a million dollars (including the cost of publication). Unhappily Fisher's health broke down and he had to withdraw; he was followed successively by P. L. O. Guy and Gordon Loud, neither of whom possessed their predecessor's experience or flair for pottery. The initial plan to dig the great site systematically, stratum after stratum, fortunately had to be abandoned because of the prohibitive expense. Our use of the adverb 'fortunately' may seem strange, but it must be realized that the very best technique of to-day will probably seem primitive a century hence, and that it is a sad mistake to exhaust the possibilities of any important site like Megiddo. Actually only a fraction of the great mound has been removed, and there is ample room for correcting chronology and making important discoveries. The most interesting results so far are the extensive stables of the Israelite kings, which were first built in the time of Solomon, and the astonishing hoard of carved ivories from the twelfth century B.C. Also of considerable interest are the soundings in the fifteen or more strata which preceded the Israelite occupation, going back to the beginning of the fourth millennium or earlier.

The American School of Oriental Research in Jerusalem, though founded in 1900, had never had funds enough to attempt any but very minor excavations. In 1926 it launched a series of co-operative excavations, all more or less loosely affiliated. C. S. Fisher had been attached, in an advisory capacity, to its staff, and his assistance proved invaluable.

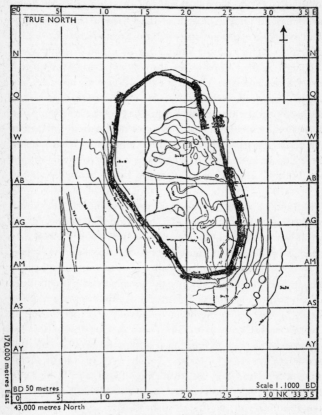

Fig. 4. Schematic plan of Tell en-Nasbeh.

The first of these expeditions to get under way was the excavation of Tell en-Nasbeh (Fig. 4), on the high road north of Jerusalem, which is generally identified with biblical Mizpah. In five campaigns (1926–35) the site was almost completely excavated, a feat made possible by the fact that the centre of the hill had been completely denuded and that there was little stratification. The organizer and director of the undertaking, W. F. Badè, followed Fisher's methods closely, and even the smallest objects were carefully recorded. The publication, in two massive volumes, edited by C. C. McCown (1947), is a model of what such publications should be. The same month a second project was launched by M. G. Kyle and the present writer, who directed the work; this was the excavation of Tell Beit Mirsim, south-west of Hebron, generally regarded as biblical Kiriath-sepher or Debir. In four campaigns (1926–32) the site was partly dug, proving to have been occupied through some ten or eleven periods of occupation, from the late third millennium to about 589 B.C. The chief importance of this work was the care devoted to the pottery sequence, which was promptly published and has become a standard basis of comparison for Palestinian archaeologists. The stratum of the Jewish Monarchy reveals the only well-preserved town of Judah so far excavated; the plans and contents of scores of houses have been published and give, for the first time, a clear picture of the way in which the people of Judah lived at the time of Isaiah and Jeremiah. Two years later Elihu Grant launched a third project at Beth-shemesh, also with the aid of Fisher. In five campaigns (1928–33) a considerable part of the mound was removed, and numerous interesting finds were made. The principal value of the work is in the light shed on the early Israelite occupation between the twelfth and the ninth centuries. With the competent aid of G. E. Wright the chronology of the site was thoroughly clarified before the publication was completed. It is interesting to note that the work of these three expeditions has been completely published in a dozen volumes and numerous shorter studies. Unhappily the same cannot be said of some far costlier projects of the same period.

Besides these three prolonged excavations, numerous

shorter projects were undertaken by the American School of Oriental Research in Jerusalem. Including only the more significant, we mention the work at Beth-zur (1931), directed by O. R. Sellers, with the assistance of the present writer, and at Bethel (1934), directed by the present writer and J. L. Kelso. Both were productive; the excavation of Bethel was resumed by Kelso in 1954. But the most remarkable undertaking of all was not launched until 1933, when Nelson Glueck began a systematic archaeological survey of Transjordan, resumed year after year until 1946. The whole of the land, from 'Aqabah to the Syrian border, was carefully examined, and many hundreds of previously unknown ancient sites were recorded and dated by the sherds which strew their surfaces. Since there are scarcely any true mounds in this region, the results are generally definitive, so far as broad outlines of occupation history are concerned. Glueck has succeeded in establishing the remarkable fact that most of Transjordan (except the Jordan Valley and the extreme north) was occupied only in relatively short periods, separated by long periods of nomadism. The most important two phases of nomadic occupation, during which there was little or no settlement, lasted from the twentieth century to the thirteenth, and roughly from the sixth to the first century B.C. In addition to his valuable survey, Glueck directed small, but very productive digs at a Nabataean temple of the first two centuries A.D. and at Tell el-Kheleifeh, ancient Ezion-geber on the Gulf of 'Aqabah (1937–40). Three short campaigns at the latter brought to light stratified remains of copper refineries going back to the tenth century B.C. and the reign of Solomon.

During the years 1933–8 the Colt expedition, directed by H. Dunscombe Colt with the aid of T. J. Colin Baly, undertook the archaeological examination of four large towns in the Negeb, south of Judah: Sbeitah (ancient Subeta), 'Auja el-Hafir (Nessana), Khalasah (Elusa), and 'Abdeh (Eboda).

Though the results were, strictly speaking, almost entirely outside the scope of the present book, they were very important, as will become clear after they have been fully published. One significant discovery was that the towns alternated in importance and did not all flourish simultaneously, as had been taken for granted by previous explorers. The most sensational find was a quantity of Greek and Arabic papyri from the sixth and seventh centuries A.D., discovered at Nessana. Quite aside from their unusual historical significance is the fact that their very preservation encourages us to hope for additional documents from even earlier periods.

Though British and American scholars have done most of the excavating in Palestine since the First World War, they have been ably seconded by numerous projects organized by European and Palestinian archaeologists. Most of the excavations undertaken by Catholic organizations belong to a survey of Byzantine and mediaeval architecture; they are thus too late for our scope and must be omitted here. The excavation of Teleilat el-Ghassul, in the Jordan Valley south-east of Jericho, was continued by the Jesuit fathers for eight campaigns, from 1929 to 1938. Here Father Alexis Mallon and others cleared part of the two upper levels of a chalcolithic site from the first half of the fourth millennium. The new Ghassulian culture was at first dated much too low by the excavators, but the date was duly corrected by the later excavators, Fathers Koeppel, Mahan, and Murphy. The careful excavation of this site and the recovery of mural frescoes in several colours have enormously enhanced our appreciation of the level of culture in Palestine nearly six thousand years ago.

In 1934 H. Steckeweh brought the German work at Shechem (Balatah) to a provisional close after a most chequered history. Work had been begun here by Ernst Sellin in 1913 and had been resumed by him in 1926. Unfortunately, none of the archaeologists sent out before the last campaign was willing to study Palestinian pottery before-hand, or even to ask the advice of experts already in the country. Moreover, a quarrel broke out between Sellin and the expedition archaeologist, G. Welter, who was able to force the former out of the excavation until he had himself mismanaged the work so badly that he had to be recalled. It is a very great pity, since the site was exceptionally important and was protected by some of the most remarkable fortifications of the Bronze Age which have yet been found in Palestine. But virtually no attention was paid to pottery chronology or stratification until the last campaign, when Steckeweh cleared up more stratigraphy in a few weeks, at a very low cost, than all the expensive work of the preceding years had been able to do. In archaeology, as in other things, no amount of 'front' will replace knowledge.

In 1933–4 Mme Judith Marquet-Krause undertook a most important excavation at Ai, just east of Bethel. Here extra-ordinary remains of the third millennium came to light, but continuation of the work was interrupted after two campaigns by the untimely death of Mme Marquet. The French expect to resume work here at an early opportunity. Another French excavation was launched in 1946 under the direction of the brilliant young Dominican, Roland de Vaux, at Tell el-Farʿah, a large mound north-east of Nablus. Owing to the great inflation since the Second World War, the cost of digging has increased between three and four times, so Père de Vaux has had to limit his work to small dimensions, when compared with the size of many excavations between the wars. However, the stratigraphic analysis of an excavation often gains when archaeologists are not overwhelmed by a large force of native diggers and a continuous flood of material that must be recorded. The stratification of Tell el-Farʿah is largely Chalcolithic, so this site will contribute greatly to the task of defining the successive phases of culture in the fourth millennium.

As Jewish Palestine has increased in population and resources, there has been an almost unparalleled development of higher culture, from which archaeology has not been the last field to benefit. When the writer first came to Palestine at the end of 1919 he found no lack of interest, but both trained men and resources were lacking. Numerous small projects were undertaken by Jewish organizations and agencies even in those difficult years. When the Hebrew University was opened in 1925 archaeological activity began to develop, and it was not long before enthusiastic youths obtained the necessary training and found the funds with which to dig. By 1948 there were many competent Jewish archaeologists, and the number has continued to increase steadily. Foremost among the earlier excavators was E. L. Sukenik (father of Yigael Yadin), who worked in many sites of different periods and became the leading authority on the Jewish tombs and synagogues of Palestine. Sukenik's first important undertaking was the excavation (chiefly with L. A. Mayer) of the line of the Third Wall of Jerusalem, at intervals from 1925 to 1940. This line had been correctly pointed out by Robinson nearly a century earlier, but owing to a series of misunderstandings and not a little dogmatism, its existence was gradually ignored and its rediscovery proved a sensation in archaeological circles. Sukenik then devoted himself increasingly to the study of Jewish tombs and synagogues, where his discoveries have been outstanding. Thanks to his efforts the number of Jewish tomb inscriptions from the last century of the Second Temple (c. 30 B.C.–A.D. 70) has been more than doubled. Through his excavations and studies of Jewish synagogues (el-Hammeh, Beit Ilfa, etc.), many vexed problems have found solution; in particular a clear division has been set up between the early synagogues of the second and third centuries A.D. and a later group of the fourth–sixth centuries.

In 1936–40 the Jewish Palestine Exploration Society

undertook systematic excavations at Sheikh Abreik, ancient Beth-shearim. Here B. Maisler and his colleagues found an important Jewish cemetery from the third and fourth centuries A.D., containing many inscriptions and much painted decoration. In some ways this is the closest parallel yet found to the Jewish catacombs of contemporary Rome. A well-built synagogue of the early fourth century was also found.

A great many major and minor excavations have been undertaken in both Jordan and Israel since 1948. Besides those already mentioned (e.g., Jericho, Beth-shearim, Bethel), we must stress the importance of the work carried out at Hazor in Galilee by Y. Yadin and his colleagues (1955–8), at Shechem (Balatah) by G. E. Wright and others (1956–), and at Gibeon by J. B. Pritchard (since 1956). Hazor, in particular, has yielded epoch-making data for Middle and Late Bronze, the date of the Israelite occupation, and the age of Solomon. Shechem has now been dated stratigraphically for the first time. Gibeon has been identified with el-Jib by the discovery of dozens of inscribed jar-handles bearing its name. Among other important undertakings have been the excavations of the American School in Jerusalem at Dibon in Moab (since 1950), the work at Roman Jericho carried out by J. L. Kelso and J. B. Pritchard in 1950 and 1951, as well as the uninterrupted series of campaigns at Dothan directed by J. P. Free since 1953. Since 1949 numerous campaigns under the direction of R. de Vaux have uncovered the Essene settlements at Khirbet Qumran and Ain Feshkhah. In Israel (besides the work of Maisler-Mazar and Yadin mentioned above) there have been exceptionally significant prehistoric undertakings in the Beersheba area and at Eynan near Lake Huleh (Jean Perrot and others), the work at Beth-yerah (Khirbet Kerak, begun in 1944) on the Sea of Galilee, excavations at Qasileh (Mazar), Sheikh Ahmed el-'Areini ('Gath'), at Nahariyah, Jaffa, etc.

CHAPTER 3

Prehistoric Palestine

—

OWING to the great increase of surface exploration in Palestine in the middle decades of the nineteenth century, it was not long before the geologist Louis Lartet, followed by Abbé Richard, discovered the first flint artifacts (1864). Lartet understood what they were, since nearly twenty years had elapsed since Boucher de Perthes's revolutionary publication and four years had passed since Edouard Lartet had begun the excavation of prehistoric cave deposits. But the good abbé thought that his flint tools dated from the time of Joshua, who had used them to circumcise the Israelites! Thanks particularly to extensive soundings made by the Jesuit fathers Zumoffen and Bovier-Lapierre in the caves of Phoenicia and to the surface explorations of Père Germer-Durand in Palestine, it was possible for Paul Karge (a Catholic secular priest) to include all the data obtained before the First World War in a synthesis entitled *Rephaim* (1917). In spite of the absence of any stratigraphical researches Karge's chronological arrangement of finds was on the whole correct, since he followed the typological method of comparing the flint artifacts of Palestine and Syria with corresponding artifacts of France which could be stratigraphically dated.

In Chapter 1 we have briefly mentioned the systematic excavation of Palestinian caves by F. Turville-Petre, Dorothy Garrod, and René Neuville, since 1925. Others have joined this small group, and to-day our knowledge has developed far beyond the level of Karge, being now based on systematic stratigraphy as well as on typology. Geologists, archaeologists, and anthropologists have joined forces, assisted by specialists in many other disciplines. Palestine was for a number of years second only to France in its value for pre-historians; it is only fair to add that South Africa has now stolen the limelight from both countries.

In the Cretaceous period of the Mesozoic Age, Palestine was submerged by the advancing waters of the Tethys Sea. Though Palestine remained a continental shelf, just off the shore, the marine sediments of the Cretaceous period reach a maximum thickness of nearly a mile in central Palestine. While these deposits were slowly rising at the bottom of the sea, millions of years elapsed. Then, over fifty million years ago, the Tertiary Age began, and before many million years had passed, Palestine rose above the sea and after much oscillation attained what were roughly its present boundaries. At that time there was no Jordan Valley nor Dead Sea, and land-levels were very different. It was not until less than two million years ago that the tectonic movements in the earth's crust which characterized the Tertiary Age culminated in the great cleft which we know in its modified form of to-day as the Jordan Valley. The appearance of this north-south cleft was accompanied by upheavals of rock deposits which created the hill-country of Western Palestine.

According to the Milankovitch–Köppen–Zeuner correlation of the curve of solar radiation with the phases of the Pleistocene, this geological period, to which belong all hitherto identified traces of fossil man and his implements, began less than a million years ago. The Pleistocene was characterized by four cold and wet phases, separated by three warm and dry phases. The cold phases are called 'glacial periods' in northern latitudes and 'pluvial periods' in the latitude of Palestine, where there was no glaciation, but instead a greatly increased rainfall. Following the ter-minology of Alpine geologists, the glacial periods are termed Günz–Mindel–Riss–Würm, in the same alphabetic and chronological order, while the interglacial periods are the Günz–Mindel, the Mindel–Riss, and the Riss–Würm. No consistent terminology has up to the present time been developed for the pluvial and interpluvial phases of more southerly latitudes. The whole question is enormously complicated by the fact that there were many advances and recessions of the ice in Europe, so there were successive phases of each period of glaciation. In other words, geologists speak of two phases of Günz, three phases of Würm, etc. In pluvial Palestine, where there was no glaciation, the climatic cycle may have been even more complex. According to the Zeuner theory of geochronology the Günz glaciation ended slightly less than 550,000 years ago; so that even if we assume a considerable lag, we can scarcely come down much below half a million years ago for its end. During the pluvial periods there was a large lake or bay of the Mediterranean in the Jordan Valley; in the interpluvial phases the marine connexion with the sea was interrupted and the lake shrank to minor size, like the Dead Sea to-day. Some day, when the marl terraces of the Jordan Valley have been studied in detail, we shall have confirmation or correction of the solar-radiation chronology by an exact count of the annual laminations of these terraces. One estimate of the time required to deposit the thickest of these terraces, the Lisan Terrace, is 40,000 years.

Meanwhile, however, the progress of radiocarbon dating since 1949 (above, p. 22) has proved that the last (Würm–Wisconsin) glaciation came to an end about 11,000 years ago and began some 60,000 years ago (or even less), thus cutting the solar chronology in half. Views on the date of the oldest well-defined artifacts (Abbevillian) have oscillated between the third and the first interglacial, with current opinion favouring the second. Until there has been substantial progress in correlating the river terraces and gravel beds of Western Europe with the glacial moraines of the Alps, it is unlikely that geological opinion will be stabilized. Meanwhile we may provisionally accept the Günz–Mindel correlation; to it belong the French Abbevillian, the Chellean, and the older phases of Acheulian, all of which have been found mainly in river-terraces and open-air stations; it was not until the later Acheulian that the first cave deposits appear. This means that weather conditions had become so unfavourable that men took refuge in caves and soon began to live in them regularly, at least during the inclement part of each year. In Palestine we find exactly the same situation; in open-air stations we find hand-axes of distinct Chellean or early Acheulian appearance (Fig. 5), and it is not until we reach the latest phases of Acheulian that cave deposits are found.

The oldest flint industry so far represented in the caves excavated by Miss Garrod and M. Neuville is closely parallel to the French Tayacian (Fig. 6). This industry was followed in the Palestinian caves by several phases of Acheulian, the earliest being associated with fauna characteristic of a wet, tropical climate. This stage corresponded roughly to the Riss glaciation, dated by Zeuner about 230,000–180,000 years ago, but probably much more recent. After this wet Acheulian came several more phases of the same culture, during which the climate tended to shift towards drier conditions in the interpluvial age equated roughly with the Riss-Würm interglacial period. With this period the Lower Palaeolithic came to an end. We do not yet know what sub-species of man was responsible for making these tools and weapons, with the aid of which he maintained his existence in the conflict against monstrous rhinoceroses, hippopotami, elephants, cave-oxen, whose bones are found in the same levels.

To the Middle Palaeolithic belong a series of closely related flint cultures from a number of excavated caves in different parts of Palestine (Fig. 7). These cultures resemble both the French Mousterian and Levalloisian, but are not identical with either; the excavators have, accordingly, called them Levalloiso–Mousterian (Fig. 8). In this period flake tools

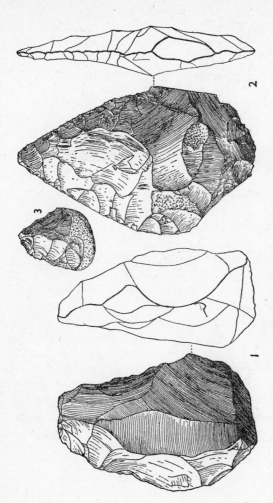

Fig. 5. Hand-axes: (1) Chellean; (2) Acheulian (after René Neuville).

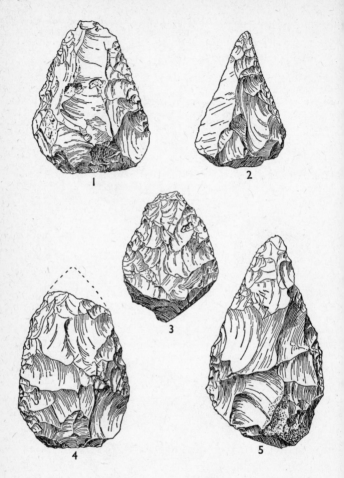

Fig. 6. Upper Acheulian hand-axes (after Dorothy Garrod).

superseded hand-axes, and there was an extraordinary development of skill in flaking. The climate of the early Levalloiso–Mousterian was dry and warm; there were large swamps

(not rivers), where crocodiles flourished. In a slightly later deposit (first dated 150,000–120,000 years ago, but now placed roughly between 50,000 and 40,000 B.P.) Miss Garrod and T. D. McCown found a dozen fossil human skeletons; more were later found by Neuville in Galilee. To

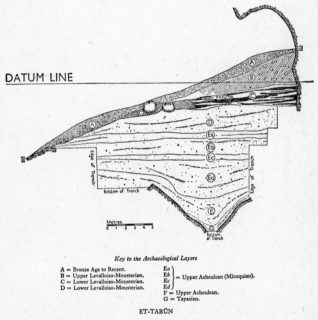

DATUM LINE

Key to the Archaeological Layers

A = Bronze Age to Recent.
B = Upper Levalloiso-Mousterian.
C = Lower Levalloiso-Mousterian.
D = Lower Levalloiso-Mousterian.

Ea
Eb } = Upper Acheulean (Micoquian).
Ec
Ed

F = Upper Acheulean.
G = Tayacian.

ET-TABŪN

Fig. 7. Stratified section through Tabun Excavation.

the astonishment of the scientific world, the Carmel individuals proved to represent a mixed race, intermediate between palaeanthropic man (*Homo neanderthalensis*) and neanthropic man (*Homo sapiens*) and reflecting several stages between the two extremes. In view of the exclusively Neanderthaloid character of the dozens of Mousterian skeletons hitherto found in Europe, this mixture of races can be explained only by the fact that Palestine is an inter-continental bridge, where a mixture of types is to be expected, *a priori*. It would appear that

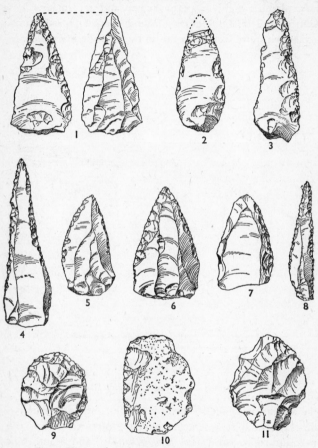

Fig. 8. Flint artifacts from Lower Levalloiso-Mousterian
(after Dorothy Garrod).

Homo sapiens came from the south-east into Europe, driving Neanderthaloid man before him, and interbreeding with the conquered foe at the same time. Incidentally, one result of this discovery has been to strengthen the hands of geneticists, who insist that it is an error to label the principal types of prehistoric man as different species. Since it is now clear that they interbred freely, they were at most sub-species of a single species of the genus *Homo*. It is by no means clear that the term 'race' is not better than 'sub-species', especially when we bear in mind that the polytypism now known to be characteristic of early man is equally characteristic of dogs, whose classification as a single species is not disputed by zoologists. There is no place for pride of species or race in science. Yet when Franz Weidenreich said jokingly, at a congress of physical anthropologists in Copenhagen just before the Second World War, that *Homo sapiens* apparently came from Palestine to northern Europe, the Nazi delegation rose and walked out of the room!

The Levalloiso–Mousterian continued into a cold, wet period which may be confidently correlated with the last glacial of Europe, the Würm phase. During this period it was replaced by the Aurignacian culture of the Upper Palaeolithic. Meanwhile Palestine passed through striking climatic changes during three successive Würm phases, which would now be dated between about 60,000 and 11,000 years ago. The Aurignacian flint culture was much richer in flint forms than the Mousterian. From the latter part of the European Aurignacian have come down marvellous cave paintings of pre-historic beasts, which continued into the Magdalenian Age at the end of the European Palaeolithic. Nothing like these cave paintings has yet been discovered in Palestine or neighbouring lands; it is, therefore, impossible to say whether their non-appearance is accidental or not. For a time it was believed that there was a frieze of prehistoric animals at Umm el-Qatafah, but this turned out to be an illusion, much to the relief of geologists who were worried by the collocation of beasts from different periods and climatic conditions.

The Aurignacian of Palestine did not last nearly as long as the Aurignacian of Europe. Probably long before the Solutrean had replaced the Aurignacian in Europe the Middle Aurignacian of Palestine was replaced by an inferior flint culture, which Miss Garrod has dubbed 'Atlitian'; the latter has much in common with the Upper Aurignacian of Europe. It was formerly believed by most prehistorians that there was a yawning gap between the Aurignacian of Palestine and the upper phases of the Mesolithic (known from surface finds made by Père Germer-Durand and others), in which cultures similar to the European Solutrean and Magdalenian would be found. The gap was, however, being filled up rapidly in the years before World War II, and nothing resembling these European cultures has yet been discovered. The material culture of Palestine was simply different in those ages from that of Europe, and it was not until much more recent times that closer cultural parallelism was restored. In this period radiocarbon dating is now introducing much greater chronological precision, confirmed by previously known but often disregarded evidence from the Scandinavian varve series. The Aurignacian of Palestine must be dated in the latter part of the Würm glaciation, between 35,000 and 15,000 years ago. It may well have been culturally ahead of the European Aurignacian, since it was probably nearer the focus of cultural diffusion.

The Epipalaeolithic or Early Mesolithic of Palestine is being gradually filled out, though the lack of detailed publication of finds makes it difficult to be sure of our ground. Neuville reports the discovery of an industry (Magharet el-Khiyam G-F) which appears to have been intermediate between the Atlitian and the contemporary Capsian of North Africa; he ranges it definitely with the Capsian and considers it as no longer Palaeolithic. Then comes the Kebaran of Turville-Petre, which continues and intensifies the microlithic tradition of the Capsian. These industries may perhaps be dated somewhere between 12,000 and 9000 B.C.; they were presumably coeval with the Magdalenian and Azilian of Europe. Probably soon after the retreat of the last glaciation in Europe, the characteristic Mesolithic of Palestine, termed 'Natufian' by Miss Garrod, made its appearance. Since the typical lunates of the Natufian appear also in the Mesolithic of Europe (Tardenoisian), but even more characteristically in Mesolithic South Africa, it is still quite impossible to determine its source. A closely related culture has been located at Helwan south of Cairo, and the University of California Sinai Expedition located a station in the desert, 70 miles east of Ismailiyeh, in 1947. The Natufian of Palestine was a thorough-going microlithic culture, consisting largely of flint blades and points, most typical of which is the so-called lunate, a crescent or arc-shaped blade, probably used to tip reed arrows (Fig. 9). In addition there are many gravers (*burins*), with a point end. Among large flint artifacts the most noteworthy are sickle-blades and 'picks', which point to the agricultural character of Natufian culture. The latter was already familiar with the reaping of grain, for which regular sickles were used. Miss Garrod and Turville-Petre have discovered complete and broken sickle-hafts of bone, with carved animal heads decorating the handles of long blades, in which were set flint edges, end to end. In the course of time the appearance of the sickle became modified, but the same principle was still employed in Palestine as late as the threshold of the Iron Age. Some of the so-called picks are rather hoes, used to break up the ground before sowing grain. It follows that the earliest Natufians whom we can trace were already cultivators of grain, though doubtless in the most primitive stage of hoe-culture (*Hackbau*). They were thus food-producers as well as food-gatherers. On the other hand, there is no hint that any animals were domesticated except the dog, a fine skull of which was recovered. This canine was of medium size, and seems to have been a comparatively recent domestication from an extinct type of jackal.

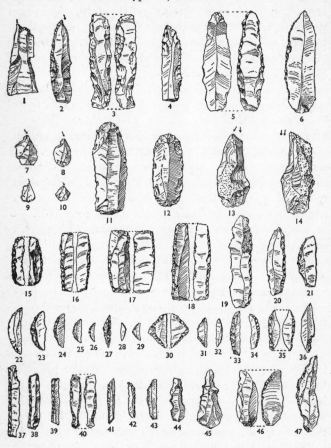

Fig. 9. Lower Natufian artifacts (after Dorothy Garrod).

The Natufians themselves were typical early Mediterraneans, with slender bony structure, long-headed (dolichocephalic) and delicate of features; the men averaged only a little over 5 feet in height (Pl. 8). Since very similar human skeletons have been found in the Badarian of Egypt as well as in late chalcolithic Gezer and Byblus, it seems to follow that these folk belonged to the ancestral Semito-Hamitic stock, which had not yet become as sharply differentiated into linguistic and national groups as later. The only marked physical change was in height, but it is now well known that improvement in nutrition over a very few generations brings pronounced increase in height. The Natufians were still essentially food-gatherers, in spite of their discovery of the cultivation of grain; we are entirely safe in assuming that most of their food came from fishing and hunting. But harpooning fish and hunting gazelle with dogs do not produce a very steady diet for a rapidly increasing population. The Natufians were already well aware of the principal uses of bone which we find in subsequent archaeological ages; they already possessed bone pins and awls, pendants and beads, etc. We have alluded above to their remarkable carved-bone handles of sickle-hafts, one of which represents a young fawn (Pl. 10). Pestles and mortars of stone were also found; they were clearly used in part, at least, for preparing grain.

Jean Perrot's excavations at Eynan near Lake Huleh since 1956 have shown that the men of the Early Natufian were already building houses with stone substructures and pavements, and using elaborate burial practices and installations. Similar remains have also been found by Kathleen Kenyon under the Neolithic levels of Jericho; radiocarbon yields a date for them ±7800 B.C. Since the earliest date for the pre-pottery Neolithic of Jericho is only about a thousand years later, the Upper Natufian levels reported by R. Neuville from his caves, may be tentatively placed in the seventh millennium B.C. Here also comes the proto-Neolithic of Miss Kenyon, which is more closely related to the earlier Natufian than to the Tahunian.

This age was followed by pre-pottery Neolithic, which

represents a completely new phase of culture, unknown before Garstang's first discovery of it at Jericho in 1935, and not widely accepted until Miss Kenyon's sensational finds twenty years later. Jericho proves to have been a well-built town, surrounded by stone fortifications, during much of the seventh and sixth millennia B.C. Two phases of pre-pottery Neolithic were distinguished, each of which must have lasted for centuries. The first was characterized by mud-bricks shaped like the backs of pigs ('hog-back' bricks); the second offered a succession of plaster floors – no fewer than fourteen in one area. Many radiocarbon datings establish the age of these successive installations, the second of which appears to have been abandoned in the middle centuries of the sixth millennium. Since Europe was still in the Mesolithic Age during most of pre-pottery Jericho, we must assume a very considerable lag between Palestine and contemporary Europe.

Jericho is the first pre-pottery Neolithic settlement of 'urban' character to be discovered in the Old World, but there can be no doubt that similar cultures were scattered widely over the Near and Middle East between about 7000 and 5000 B.C. A number of pre-pottery villages have been located in north-eastern Iraq, and one of them (Qal'at Jarmo) has been excavated by R. J. Braidwood. Similar sites have been located all the way from Pakistan to Thessaly. Khirokitia in Cyprus is also a pre-pottery Neolithic site, which must presumably go back to a period at least a thousand years earlier than the excavator's date c. 3700–3400 B.C. In most places pre-pottery Neolithic is probably buried deep under the alluvium of the river valleys, but at Jericho the occupation site lay outside the irrigated area fed by the water of 'Ain es-Sultan, and it was thus possible to excavate to bed-marl without reaching ground-water.

At Jericho we find the earliest known permanent houses and sanctuaries, with walls of beaten earth or of small, rounded mud-bricks. The shrine contained a portico originally supported by six wooden posts, a wide ante-chamber, and a large inner room. In and around this structure were no ordinary household objects, but instead there were many animal figurines (sheep, large cattle, goats, pigs), as well as plastic models of the male organs, etc. It may be recalled that the Natufian of Magharet el-Wad yielded a well-carved flint phallus, so the cult of the male organ was already ancient in Palestine.

The most extraordinary finds in the pre-pottery phase of neolithic Jericho were plastic statues of human beings, apparently occurring in groups with a man, woman, and child in each group. These plastic statues were made by smearing *hawarah* (native lime marl) on a framework of reeds, which formed a kind of skeleton; they were of normal proportions, about two-thirds life-size *en face*, but very thin in profile. The published examples look like nothing else known, either from earlier or from later periods (Pl. 9).

Scattered through Palestine, especially in Transjordan, are numerous large and small dolmen fields. The dolmen (from Breton words meaning 'stone' and 'table') consists essentially of massive stone slabs set up end to end to form the walls of a chamber, or corridor, or series of chambers, with other massive slabs laid over them to form the roof. The whole structure was often buried under a tumulus of earth or stone. There are also rows of great stones (menhirs), and stone-circles, etc. A few massive fortifications of the same type of masonry have been discovered. Characteristic of all these constructions so far studied is the absence of pottery, either whole or in sherds. A few vases of various later periods and some relatively modern sherds have been found in or near open dolmens, but they do not prove anything about the date of the latter. Megalithic stone constructions, principally dolmens, occur in many parts of Eurasia; in north-western Europe they can be dated between the fifth and the third millennium, while megalithic stone sanctuaries, such as Stonehenge, may come down into the second millennium. Since the Palestinian structures belong typologically with the Neolithic rather than with the Bronze Age dolmens of Europe, we may confidently date them in the Palestinian Neolithic, that is between 7000 and 4000 (possibly 4500) B.C. Of course, these dolmens are imitations of the houses in which people had lived. This has been suggested from time to time, but can now be proved beyond reasonable doubt by the work of J. d'A. Waechter and V. M. Seton-Williams in Wadi Dhobai south-east of 'Amman (1937-8). Here they found a stone industry like that of the Tahunian of pre-pottery Jericho, together with huts made by setting limestone slabs on edge to make rough circles. Moreover, in 1947 Garstang discovered in the post-pottery neolithic levels of Mersin in Cilicia, 'megalithic' buildings made by laying heavy blocks of stone side by side and piling one on another to make walls. Rooms and corridors were constructed in this fashion; individual stones might weigh several tons. If further evidence to support the early date of the Palestinian dolmens were needed, it would be easy to produce. For example, it cannot be accidental that the Ghassulian graves excavated by Stekelis were dug in the ground and lined with stones, which were then covered with small slabs in essentially megalithic pattern – but the stones are small and can easily be handled by a single man. The pre-pottery Neolithic of Palestine was followed by a pottery-using Neolithic, best known from Jericho IX and especially from the excavations of Stekelis in the Yarmuk Valley, where he has isolated very interesting remains of the Yarmukian of Sha'ar ha-Golan culture, dating from the middle centuries of the fifth millennium. The pottery is often decorated with a distinctive herring-bone design, and crudely carved stone figurines are found in some quantity.

CHAPTER 4

Palestine in the Chalcolithic and Early Bronze

—

WE derive our knowledge of the Chalcolithic Age of Palestine largely from the excavations of the Jesuit Fathers at Teleilat el-Ghassul between 1929 and 1938 (see above). It is true that there was at first a vigorous controversy among archaeologists as to the relative date of this culture. However, the question was settled before the beginning of the Second World War by several discoveries of Ghassulian pottery below levels belonging to the Late Chalcolithic and the Early Bronze. We can now divide the Chalcolithic into three principal phases: Early (including especially Jericho VIII and several sites in the Wadi Ghazzeh at the southern end of Palestine), Middle (Ghassulian), and Late (especially Esdraelon and the late Chalcolithic of Beersheba). It is still not certain where the line between Neolithic and Early Chalcolithic is to be drawn, and there are good reasons for opposing the now standard extension of Early Bronze to include the last century or two of the third millennium. There are also objections to the name 'Chalcolithic', which means 'copper (or bronze)-(and)-stone'; actually flint continued in use for making knives until the end of the third millennium, and sickle-edges of flint were still used down to the beginning of the Iron Age. Some scholars are inclined to think that copper was known even in the early Neolithic, but this seems improbable to the present writer. At some time in the course of the fifth millennium, perhaps about 4500 B.C., copper made its first appearance. After a few centuries, however, copper became more abundant, and stone was replaced by copper as a material for axe-heads and arrow-heads; arrow-heads of stone disappeared before the Ghassulian

Period, and stone axe-heads with ground edges in the neolithic tradition vanished after Ghassulian (though completely
polished stone axe-heads remained in occasional use until
late in the Bronze Age).

Until the lower levels of other river-valley mounds have
been excavated, the oldest clear Chalcolithic stratum must
probably remain Jericho VIII, which we may provisionally
date toward the end of the fifth millennium. The ware of this
level contrasts sharply with that of the older Neolithic
(Jericho IX); in the latter chopped straw was mixed with
clay to serve as temper (*dégraissant*), whereas in Jericho VIII
we find that large and small stone grit had already replaced
chopped straw. The flint industry of Jericho VIII is characteristically Neolithic in type, with flint arrow-heads still
numerous. Even in the lower, still unexcavated, strata of
Ghassul arrow-heads are few and of poor quality; when we
reach the upper two levels of the same site they vanish
entirely (see above). Most of Megiddo XX, some of the early
settlements in the Wadi Ghazzeh, and the industry of flint
and pottery excavated by Stekelis in Magharet Abu 'Usbah
are also probably examples of pre-Ghassulian Chalcolithic.
In 1946–7 R. de Vaux discovered early Chalcolithic deposits
of the same pre-Ghassulian (sic) date in the lowest stratum
of Tell el-Far'ah in north-central Palestine.

We may date the Ghassulian in the middle centuries of
the fourth millennium, with the two strata so far excavated
at Ghassul itself falling relatively late in the period, but before
3400 B.C. The civilization of this age, which may be correlated
roughly with the earliest Amratian (S.D. 30) of Egypt and
late Halafian or early Obeidian in northern Mesopotamia,
was in some respects highly developed. The people of
Ghassul lived in well-constructed houses, some of them
built of hand-moulded sun-dried bricks on a foundation of
field stones, some built entirely of such bricks; they were
roofed with wood, which collapsed when the town was

Fig. 10. Polychrome fresco from Ghassul.

destroyed by fire. Many of the mud-brick walls had been covered with fresco paintings in several colours, some of which were partly recovered by the excavators. It is a striking fact that the art of painting elaborate geometrical designs reached a higher pitch of achievement in the early fourth millennium in Palestine, Syria, and Mesopotamia than it did for thousands of years thereafter. The variety of polychrome designs inside shallow bowls and platters of Halafian times prepares us for the amazingly intricate polychrome painting of an eight-pointed star on a fresco at Teleilat el-Ghassul (Fig. 10). Around the star were fragments of an intricate field containing stylized dragons and geometric figures. Another, well-preserved, fresco represents a bird, painted with a naturalistic attention to detail which can scarcely be paralleled in subsequent early periods except in Egypt. Still another, damaged, fresco seems to portray a reception of some kind, in which a man faces right, while in front of him are seated two human figures, each with feet placed on a four-legged footstool, just as in later times. Since the first of these two figures wears embroidered shoes, it may represent a patrician lady or a goddess. No building can yet be identified as a sanctuary. The cemetery of Ghassul was partly excavated by Stekelis; it contained cist graves, lined and covered with stones whose shape and position are strongly reminiscent of megalithic dolmens (see above), though very much smaller.

In 1934 Sukenik excavated a cave burial-place near Khudheirah in the Plain of Sharon; in it he discovered clay chests, pottery, and a number of painted caskets of clay, shaped like houses (Fig. 11). The chests and house-urns were all intended to receive the bones of deceased persons after their flesh had decayed. The pottery was closely related to Ghassulian ware. The house-urns stand on four feet like the house-urns of Bronze Age Germany, with which they have other features in common. However, rectangular pile-dwellings with ridged roofs and doors were common in different regions and periods, so there is no reason to establish a direct connexion between them. In the early fourth millennium, just as in the much earlier Natufian, Sharon was doubtless extremely marshy, and was thus not suited for the type of dwelling

which was most practical in the dry valley north of the Dead
Sea. It would be interesting to know just what were the
changes in climate which led to the abandonment of sites like
Ghassul, situated far out in the Jordan plain where the soil
could not be irrigated without prohibitive effort. It seems
reasonably certain that there were more lateral streams flow-

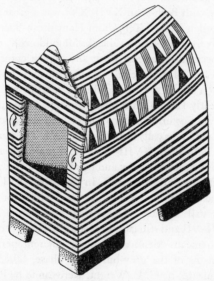

Fig. 11. House-urn burial from the Chalcolithic of Khudheirah.

ing into the Jordan than there are to-day, and that they
flowed longer before going dry. After this age we find that
settlements in the Jordan Valley were nearly always established at the entrances of the valleys, near perennial streams
and springs which are still sources of water. Curiously
enough, well-watered Jericho seems to have remained unoccupied for most of the fourth millennium.

After the final abandonment of Ghassul, which may have
been due to a general devastation of the country before 3400

B.C., some time may have elapsed before men began to settle down again. New settlements then sprang up in places like Beth-shan, athwart the road from Megiddo to the Jordan, where Stratum XVIII may go back to the end of Ghassul. The latter culture continued in modified form at Beersheba in the south, where Perrot and Aharoni have found villages dated by radiocarbon to the 34th or 33rd century. Contemporary with Beth-shan XVII–XVI was a great site in the central Jordan Valley, Tell Umm Hamad esh-Sherqi, which was discovered by Nelson Glueck. Megiddo XX, the lowest level of occupation at that great site, which commands the western Plain of Esdraelon, is unfortunately not a single phase, but a mixed stratum exhibiting remains which extend from an early Chalcolithic phase through Ghassulian or an immediately posterior occupation (which shares clay horns or *cornets* with Ghassul) to Beth-shan XVI. The Late Chalcolithic of Beth-shan XVIII–XVI (*c.* 3400–3200 B.C.) concluded with a phase of grey and black-burnished ware which continued into Early Bronze I. In Beth-shan XVI we find a house type of roughly rectangular plan, with a rounded end, which we call 'apsidal'. The apsidal house appears later in Jericho VI–VII and still later in Megiddo. However, the plans are by no means identical in these different periods. The finest remains of the grey-burnished phase, called the 'Esdraelon culture' by G. E. Wright, were found by R. de Vaux in 1947 at Tell el-Far'ah.

In Egypt Mustafa 'Amr Bey has discovered Palestinian pottery in some quantity at Ma'adeh, south of Cairo. Here there was a large village and cemetery of Middle Gerzean date, which must precede the last century of the fourth millennium. This pottery has some striking affinities with the Esdraelon ware of the 33rd–32nd centuries B.C.

About the thirty-first century B.C. we arrive at the threshold of the Early Bronze Age. This long enigmatic age may now be subdivided with great confidence, thanks especially to the well-stratified sequences of Megiddo, Beth-shan, and Jericho, to which have recently been added Beth-Yerah and Tell el-Far'ah near Shechem. Moreover, it is possible to date each phase according to Egyptian dynastic chronology: Early Bronze I (thirty-first to twenty-ninth century) was contemporary with the latest predynastic period in Egypt; Early Bronze II (twenty-ninth to twenty-sixth century) was coeval with the latter part of the First Dynasty; Early Bronze III (twenty-sixth to twenty-third century) corresponds to the Pyramid Age, from the Third to the Fifth Dynasty; Early Bronze IV (or III B) is a transitional phase lasting down into the twenty-first century B.C. It is to be noted that these dates are based on a minimal Egyptian chronology, in which we assume that the lowest practicable dates for the first ten dynasties are approximately correct. With every upward shift of Egyptian dates there must be a corresponding upward revision of our Early Bronze and Chalcolithic chronology.

In the transitional period which led from Late Chalcolithic into Early Bronze I, about the thirty-second or thirty-first century B.C., may be placed Stages VII–V/IV on the eastern slope of Megiddo. This phase must be interpolated between Beth-shan XV and XIII, and corresponds to Stratum XIX of the Megiddo mound proper. In Stage V were discovered a number of sherds impressed before baking by cylinder seals with animal and floral designs. They were first attributed by Frankfort to the Early Dynastic I or II of Mesopotamia, but in 1945 Dunand published some thirty similar impressions from the lowest urban level of Byblus which have altered the picture. There can be no question that Dunand is substantially right in correlating them with the Jemdet Nasr period of Mesopotamia (c. 3100–2900 B.C.). Towards the end of the fourth millennium there must have been an exceedingly intensive transfusion of culture going on in the Near and Middle East. Syria and Palestine naturally became the cultural intermediaries through which Mesopotamian influences streamed into Egypt in the period just before the First Dynasty, as has been demonstrated particularly by Frankfort and Scharff.

In the period which we now call conventionally Early Bronze I there was a bifurcation of pottery culture, dividing northern and southern Palestine on both sides of the Jordan into two districts which had much in common but still diverged more than in later periods. In northern Palestine we find vast quantities of jars decorated with band slip (or grain wash, as it is also rather unhappily called). These jars are covered with parallel or criss-cross (lattice) patterns made by bands of slip, usually on the smoothed natural surface of the vessel. The best example of the civilization of this period (about the thirty-first to thirtieth centuries B.C.) is found at Beth-Yerah II, which was excavated by Stekelis and his collaborators in 1945–6. In that period the city was surrounded by a mud-brick wall no less than 8 metres thick; the wall was built in three parts, with a vertical section in the middle and sloping additions on both sides. The roughly contemporary Stratum XV at Beth-shan is also characterized by rectangular mud-bricks and straight walls, which replace the apsidal buildings of Beth-shan XVI.

Approximately contemporary with the band-slip ware in the north of Palestine was the painted pottery of the south (Fig. 12). Here we find extensive use of bands of parallel or wavy lines painted over the whole surface of the vase in red or brown paint. Frequently a lattice or network of painted lines covers the entire vase. This period is well represented by such groups as Tomb 3 of Ophel (Jerusalem), the Gezer caves, the Ai necropolis, Jericho VI–VII, the early burials of Tell en Nasbeh. On the whole it seems to represent the beginnings of town building in the hill-country of southern Palestine. Vases from this period were imported into Egypt, where they appear at Abusir el-Meleq and elsewhere in sites from the latest predynastic age, about 3000 B.C. according to the lowest possible dating.

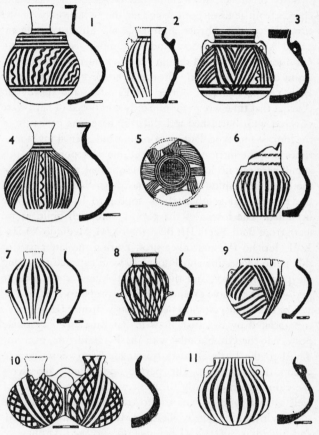

Fig. 12. Early Bronze I pottery in Palestine Museum.

About the twenty-ninth century (the latest possible 'minimal' date) while the First Dynasty was being established in Egypt, we note the emergence in Palestine of the pottery culture which we call 'Early Bronze II'. There can be no doubt whatever about the correlation of this period with the dynasty of Menes, since numerous characteristic vases and sherds from it have been found in the royal tombs of the First Dynasty at Abydos and Saqqarah. Moreover, the so-called Abydos vase, a one-handled stump-based pitcher with curvilinear red painted design on a buff surface, has turned up in characteristic Early Bronze II context in a tomb near Beth-Yerah. The finer pottery of Palestine and the Syrian coast at that time was predominantly composed of hard ware covered with burnished red slip; the base was generally of the high-stump type. Pattern-combing and burnishing, some-times in quite intricate designs, became very popular in this age. There can no longer be any doubt that this was one of the most flourishing periods of northern Palestine, though the central and southern hills appear to have been little occupied. The towns of the period were well built, as we learn from Beth-Yerah III, Beth-shan XIII, Megiddo XVIII–XVI, Jericho IV, and other sites. During the latter part of this period Palestine and Phoenicia were exposed to strong Egyptian influence, and the powerful kings of the Thinite period seem to have extended their empire into Asia.

The next archaeological period, Early Bronze III (Fig. 13), is correlated by Egyptian finds in Palestine and Palestinian pottery in the Gizeh tombs with the Pyramid Age, from the Third to the Fifth Dynasty (minimal date twenty-sixth to twenty-third century). This period undoubtedly represents the culmination of Early Bronze civilization in Palestine as well as in Egypt. Towns and fortresses were still scattered sparsely in the hill-country; Tell Beit Mirsim was not yet settled, and Megiddo XVII–XVI belongs only to the first phase of the period. But there was a flourishing city at Beth-Yerah, in which the accumulated debris of successive phases reached an average depth of 2 metres; the city was then destroyed and was not resettled for over two thousand years. Beth-Yerah

was surrounded by a 4-metre thick wall of lava boulders and
was further protected on the outside by a glacis of beaten

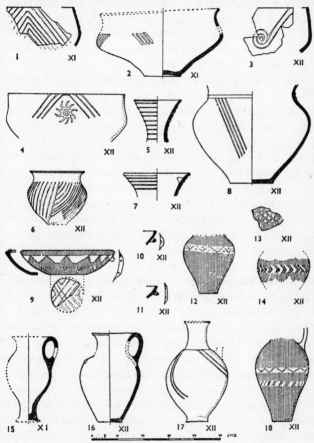

Fig. 13. Early Bronze III pottery from Beth-shan.

earth (*terre pisée*). Beth-shan (XII–XI) and Jericho (III) were
also occupied during this period. The most interesting town
of the age which has yet been excavated was undoubtedly Ai

(et-Tell east of Bethel), where Mme Marquet discovered a temple (erroneously termed 'palace' by the excavators). In this temple, which was rectangular, with the main door on one of the long sides (broad-house type), the walls were laid in regular courses of hammer-dressed masonry, while the roof was supported by wooden pillars standing on well-hewn column bases. The structure itself is roughly intermediate in type between a rectangular sanctuary of Megiddo XIX, dating from about 3000 B.C., and three similar structures of about the nineteenth century from Megiddo XV; to judge from the stratification of neighbouring areas the Ai temple may have been erected about the twenty-sixth century B.C. Near by, in a small shrine, was found a quantity of broken bowls and trays of Egyptian calcite (alabaster), of types which characterized the beginning of the Pyramid Age (Third Dynasty). A tomb, excavated at Taanach, south-east of Megiddo, copied Egyptian stone workmanship of the period of Djoser; the sherds found in it point to the end of Early Bronze II or the early part of III, i.e., about the twenty-sixth century.

The most interesting new pottery of this age is the lustrous red and black burnished 'Khirbet Kerak' ware, which first became known at the site which bore this name, ancient Beth-Yerah, at the south-west corner of the Sea of Galilee. The exterior of these vases is usually ornamented with geometrical forms, spirals, and curves of plastic origin; it is often elaborately ribbed or fluted. Add to these features the graceful shape of the vases, and we have some of the most beautiful pottery ever made in Palestine. Braidwood's work in northern Syria has proved that virtually identical pottery was common there in Stratum XI of Tell ej-Judeideh, which was characterized by Mesopotamian cylinder-seals of Early Dynastic type, while below it, in Stratum XII, were found Jemdet Nasr seals. This would leave us a scope of four centuries or more, between about 2800 and 2400 B.C., but the

Palestinian evidence points clearly to a period of not over two centuries (c. 2600–2400) for the popularity of this pottery style in Palestine. It is doubtful whether we are justified in concluding from the fact that this pottery has only appeared in a very few sites in Palestine that it did not spread far southward. A few sherds from Jericho which FitzGerald identified as of this type, are sufficient to show that it did spread into southern Palestine. The southern hill-country, however, was not well settled in Early Bronze III, so our evidence is essentially negative. Unfortunately for our documentation, sites in the plains and river valleys were generally settled much earlier than the hill towns; in consequence Early Bronze strata are often so deep that few excavators reach them, at least over a sufficient area to produce satisfactory sampling of their contents.

The following period, Early Bronze IV (or III B), is essentially a supplementary phase of the preceding; we need not allow it a duration of over two hundred years (twenty-third to twenty-first century B.C.). There are no really new pottery types; the last clear traces of stump-bases vanish and the quality of red burnishing rapidly declines. A good many · towns in the southern hill-country were first settled in this period (or the latter part of Early Bronze III); examples are Tell Beit Mirsim and Beth-shemesh. In Transjordan we find a rapid increase in the density of occupation, as we know from Nelson Glueck's exploration, confirmed by soundings at Ader and Bab edh-Dhra'. This is the period of the Sixth Dynasty and the beginning of the First Intermediate in Egypt, during which the commencement of West Semitic expansion into Egypt is attested by hieratic documents.

No well-preserved constructions of Early Bronze IV have yet been discovered, so our knowledge of its culture must remain a ceramic fragment for the present. The most remarkable remains of this period are probably constituted by a series of open-air monuments in Transjordan. At Bab edh-

Dhra', overlooking the Dead Sea from an eastern terrace, is a great open-air enclosure, defended by a wall of large field stones. Inside the enclosure and around it are many ancient hearths, with quantities of sherds from about the twenty-third to twenty-first centuries B.C. Outside, at a greater distance, are many graves dug in the ground and surrounded with small stones arranged in such a way as to resemble megalithic dolmens superficially (except for the great difference in the size of the stones and some other rather fundamental divergences). Most of the graves were covered by shallow tumuli. At a little distance is a group of fallen menhirs (*masseboth*), which seem originally to have numbered seven. At Lejjun and Ader are other alignments of high standing stones, also in association with occupied sites from Early Bronze IV, during which this type of cultic installation appears to have been popular.

The pottery of the Early Bronze did not, of course, come abruptly to an end; there was a transitional stage in the twenty-first century B.C. (possibly beginning in the twenty-second century). This stage was first illustrated by Tell Beit Mirsim I ('eye'), where envelope ledge-handles were found to characterize it. Since 1930 the same phase has been isolated at Megiddo and elsewhere. A very fine example of it was recently discovered by Nelson Glueck at Tell Umm Hamad el-Gharbi in the Jordan Valley. The pottery of this phase was characterized by improved processes of manufacture, leading to better levigated ware and harder baking; the potter's wheel came again into use to shape the necks and rims of vessels. The most easily identifiable criterion for dating is, as indicated above, the envelope ledge-handle. This name, given it by P. L. O. Guy, is derived from the fact that the laps of the pushed-up ledge-handle, which had been characteristic of previous periods since Early Bronze II, are now folded over and fastened down as neatly as though each lap were the flap of an envelope.

Two remarkable stelae from Moab appear to belong to the latter part of the Early Bronze Age: the stele of Shihan, discovered by F. de Saulcy and now in the Louvre (Pl. 11); the stele of Balu'ah, now in the 'Amman museum (Pl. 12). The former does not bear an inscription and the archaic egyptianizing garb points to Egyptian influence during the Pyramid Age. The Balu'ah stele was re-used in the twelfth (or possibly eleventh) century B.C., but the form of the stele and the remains of the original inscription above the late panel both suggest a date towards the end of the third millennium (see Chapter 8). If these two stelae are correctly attributed to this period, they throw welcome light on the little-known higher culture of Palestine at that time.

CHAPTER 5

Palestine in the Middle and Late Bronze Ages

—

IN the course of the twenty-first century B.C. the pottery culture of the Early Bronze gave way to that of Middle Bronze I (twenty-first to nineteenth century B.C.). This ceramic culture came down from Syria, where it is known as 'caliciform', because of the tendency of potters to prefer the calyx form of vases to any other. In Hamath on the Orontes, Harald Ingholt was able to differentiate four successive phases of this ware, which may be dated roughly between the twenty-second and the nineteenth centuries (the original date between 2400 and 2000 must be reduced in keeping with the general reduction of Mesopotamian dates). Even allowing a certain time lag in the southward movement of this pottery, it certainly reached Palestine during the twenty-first century, though it seems never to have displaced the earlier types completely in southern Transjordan. It is not necessary to suppose that this ceramic movement was connected with any shift of peoples; it seems rather to have been a cultural drift associated with the diffusion of the Syro-Mesopotamian culture of the period immediately preceding the Third Dynasty of Ur (*c.* 2070–1960 B.C.).

However, Palestine was at that time in the throes of tribal upheaval, and there was much destruction and abandonment of towns. Until recently the first phase of the Middle Bronze Age was one of the least-known times in the early archaeological history of Palestine. Though discovered by Watzinger at Jericho (where it was erroneously labelled 'Late Canaanite') in 1908, this pottery was commonly neglected by archaeologists, most of whom assumed that Middle Bronze II pottery of the Hyksos period had been immediately pre-

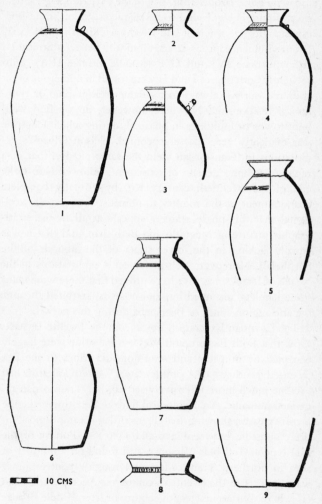

Fig. 14. Pottery of Stratum H (Middle Bronze I) at Tell Beit Mirsim (*c.* 1900 B.C.).

10 CMS

ceded by Early Bronze (Fig. 14). In the 1930 campaign at Tell
Beit Mirsim it was found to be characteristic of Strata I–H,
especially of H, where it had freed itself from typical Early
Bronze influence; it lay stratigraphically between Stratum J
(Early Bronze IV) and G–F (Middle Bronze II A). Subsequently both phases I and H were found in numerous other
sites and burials, always in the same stratigraphic or typological relationship. Nowhere, however, do we find well-
built towns or buildings in phase H, during which Palestine
was evidently very sparsely peopled. Nelson Glueck's explorations in Transjordan yield the same picture, that of a
rapidly declining density of settlement, followed before the
end of the twentieth century B.C. by virtually complete
abandonment of the country to nomads. It is scarcely accidental that this phase scarcely appears at all in the stratigraphic picture of Megiddo and Beth-shan, and that it was
equally lacking in the lower strata of the mounds of the
Shephelah. Moreover, Nelson Glueck's explorations in the
Negeb of Israel since 1952 have proved that there were many
stone hamlets, occupied by semi-nomads, scattered through
the arid region south of Beersheba during this period.

The Egyptian Execration Texts from the Twelfth Dynasty
show that both Eastern and Western Palestine were largely
occupied by nomadic and semi-nomadic tribes in the late
twentieth century B.C. A century later, Western Palestine had
become much more intensively settled, but Transjordan remained nomadic. Archaeological finds in Palestine make the
picture clearer, showing that Transjordan became almost entirely nomadic between 2000 and 1800 B.C. Pottery of the
I–H type at Tell Beit Mirsim is still found on a number of
sites in northern Transjordan, and roughly contemporary
ware appears in the twentieth century at Ader in Moab and
elsewhere. But no nineteenth century or later Middle Bronze
pottery has yet been found anywhere in Transjordan outside
of the Jordan Valley and the extreme north. What this means

is not hard to deduce from the evidence of the Execration Texts. These curious documents are vases and statuettes, inscribed in extremely cursive hieratic with the names of actual or potential rebels in Egypt and neighbouring lands, who were thus supposed to be at the mercy of Pharaoh. If threatened by rebellion the latter had only to break the objects on which were written the names and accompanying formulae, to the accompaniment of a magical ceremony, and – presto – the rebels would somehow come to grief! Two important groups of these objects have hitherto been published, a group of vases from Berlin by Kurt Sethe (1926) and a collection of statuettes at Brussels by G. Posener (1940). The former probably date from the end of the twentieth century, the latter from the late nineteenth; they show a considerable decrease in the relative number of tribal units and a corresponding increase in the number of city-states, in full accord with the evidence of pottery distribution.

The Middle Bronze Age corresponds to the Patriarchal Age of the Bible, though it is not yet possible to date the migration of Abram from Mesopotamia or of Jacob into Egypt precisely. In the writer's present opinion the Terachid movement from Ur to Harran and westward may have taken place in the twentieth and nineteenth centuries, and Jacob's migration to Egypt may have fallen somewhere in the eighteenth or more likely the seventeenth century, in connexion with the Hyksos movement. See Chapter 10 for further details about the light shed by archaeology on the Patriarchal Age.

The relative chronology of Middle Bronze II and the first phase of Late Bronze was not cleared up completely until the excavations of 1928–32 at Tell Beit Mirsim, confirmed and supplemented by the results of deep excavations at Megiddo in 1935–7. Since these two well-stratified sites, one in the north and the other in the south, agree surprisingly well in their succession of pottery types, there can be no doubt that the joint results of both excavations yield a standard picture for the whole country. This may be illustrated by the following table (with dates given in centuries):

PERIOD	TELL BEIT MIRSIM	MEGIDDO	REMARKS AND PARALLELS
Late Bronze I A	Gap	IX (1550–1479)	Tell el-ʿAjjul II
Middle Bronze II C	D	X (17th–16th)	Last Hyksos phase
Middle Bronze II B	E_2	XI (17th)	Middle Hyksos
	E_1	XII (18th–17th)	Early Hyksos
Middle Bronze II A	F	XIII (18th)	Thirteenth Dynasty
	G	XIV (19th–18th)	Late Twelfth Dynasty
Middle Bronze I, II A	I, G	XV {(19th) (21st–20th)}	(composite stratum)

Since Egyptian chronology is now fixed within a decade or two for the entire period included in this chapter, our dates are approximately certain wherever we can establish a good correlation with Egyptian cultural history. Thanks to scarabs and inscriptional evidence, this is quite possible. For example, Tombs I and II of Byblus, discovered by Pierre Montet, were contemporary with Amenemmes III and IV, respectively, and must accordingly be dated towards the end of the nineteenth century B.C. The pottery which they contain is in general similar to (and often identical with) our Palestinian Middle Bronze II A, though there are a few divergent forms. It follows that the appearance of this ceramic phase at Byblus must antedate the middle of the nineteenth century and probably goes back to about 1900 B.C. The still later Tombs III and IV of Byblus also contain the same pottery, and a large 'foundation jar' from the temple area exhibits the same characteristics. The scarabs found in this jar are typical of Egypt at the end of the nineteenth and the beginning of the eighteenth century B.C. Thanks to these and other lines of evidence the shift from Middle Bronze II A to II B can be placed somewhere in the second half of the eighteenth century B.C. Similar material makes it possible to date the remaining phases of Middle Bronze II and Late Bronze I according to the indications of our table.

Before surveying the more important aspects of the material civilization of Middle Bronze II (which will be called 'Middle Bronze' for convenience in the rest of the chapter), we shall sketch the outlines of the political history of the period. During phase A (Megiddo XV–XIII, Tell Beit Mirsim G–F) Western Palestine, Phoenicia, and parts of Syria were dominated by Egyptian power and material culture (Pl. 13). Monuments attesting to direct connexions with the Egyptian Court as far back as the early nineteenth century B.C., have been found far north at Ugarit and far east at Qatna, north-east of Hums. The finds at Byblus give a vivid idea of the extent to which the art and craftsmanship of Phoenicia were influenced by Egypt. The Execration Texts (see above) even enable us to draw the boundary of the direct sphere of Egyptian control across central Syria north of Damascus to the Eleutherus Valley in central Phoenicia. The people of Transjordan became almost entirely nomadic in this period. After the downfall of the Twelfth Dynasty the Asiatic provinces became independent, though a brief revival of Egyptian central power about 1750 B.C. led to partial restoration of Pharaonic influence at Byblus and possibly elsewhere. However, Egypt was much too weak to consolidate her empire, so the north-western Semites, who then occupied most of Syria and Palestine, were free to develop economic and military strength without outside interference. The contemporary letters and economic tablets from Mari on the Middle Euphrates mention numerous states and towns in Syria, including Byblus and the Damascene (Apum). They refer only to the town of Hazor in Palestine, which was not only more remote but also much poorer than Syria. However, it was probably from Palestine that the first Semitic precursors of the Hyksos irruption came, well before the end of the eighteenth century B.C. How far these chieftains penetrated Egypt we do not know, but they had apparently overrun Lower Egypt and perhaps Middle Egypt before the invasion of the Hyksos princes of the Fifteenth Dynasty, early in the seventeenth century.

The movements of the early seventeenth century are still exceedingly obscure, but it seems increasingly probable that a great southward migration of Indo-Aryans and Horites (Hurrians) took place then. There is no trace of these racial elements in Palestine and southern Syria during the nineteenth or eighteenth centuries, yet by the fifteenth century Indo-Aryan and Horite princes and nobles were established almost everywhere. Some sort of mass migration of these peoples southward must have occurred meanwhile. By this time horse-drawn chariotry had been introduced as the most important instrument of warfare, and we must picture the northern hordes as sweeping through Palestine and Egypt in swift chariots, with footmen playing a strictly subordinate role. A concomitant of the introduction of chariotry into warfare was the spread of the art of building great fortifications of beaten earth (*terre pisée*), usually rectangular in plan. Such earthwork fortifications are first mentioned in Babylonian sources in the early seventeenth century, and whereever there is pottery evidence in Syria and Palestine for the time of construction, we find the early Hyksos date indicated. Good Palestinian examples are Laish (Dan) and Hazor in the Upper Jordan Valley. *Pisé* fortifications also occur at this time in many other places: Tell Keisan, Shechem, Lachish, Tell Beit Mirsim, Tell el-'Ajjul, etc.

In the seventeenth century Palestine was the centre of a North-west-Semitic 'empire' controlled from the Hyksos capital at Avaris in the north-eastern corner of the Nile Delta. At its height under Apophis and Khayana, this Hyksos state may have ruled from the Euphrates to southern Nubia. Its principal extant monuments are thousands of scarabs used by its officials and notables for sealing documents and jars; at no period in Palestinian history do we find as many scarabs as during the Hyksos period, from about 1700 to about 1550

B.C. (Pl. 15). This was a time of great local prosperity; the number of settlements and tombs increased steadily, and the luxurious funerary appointments of Middle Bronze II B–C exceed anything else known in the history of the country. We are reduced to conjecture about the sources of the wealth of Hyksos Palestine, but our guesses can scarcely be appreciably wrong. It is only reasonable to suppose that the flourishing commerce of the age was mainly responsible; Palestine had become a high road of trade between Africa and Asia. But the preponderance of weapons and ornaments made in Egypt, or made after Egyptian models, suggests that much of the wealth was brought back to Palestine by warriors who had fought in Egypt on behalf of the Hyksos.

After the end of the Fifteenth Dynasty in the early sixteenth century, the Hyksos Empire seems to have broken up rapidly. Before the end of the reign of Amosis I the Hyksos had been driven out of Egypt, and the southernmost fortresses of Palestine had been stormed after bitter resistance. The stubbornness with which the Hyksos princes of Palestine resisted the Egyptian and Nubian armies is illustrated by the Egyptian account of the three-year blockade of the fortress of Sharuhen (probably Tell el-Far'ah on the edge of the southern desert), as well as by the scenes of devastation which meet the eye of the excavator who penetrates to the destruction levels belonging to the middle of the sixteenth century. Tell Beit Mirsim, Megiddo, and probably Beth-zur and Jericho illustrate the ferocity of the Egyptian onslaught. With the Egyptian conquest of Palestine in the reigns of Amosis I and Amenophis I we are on the threshold of the Late Bronze Age, on which see below.

If all the city walls and gates of the Middle Bronze Age which have been discovered were adequately published, it would be possible to describe the evolution of the art of fortification in considerable detail. To judge from the walls of the third millennium and the early centuries of the second so far recovered, the older native practice had been to construct vertical walls in Egyptian fashion, without an exterior revetment or a sloping glacis to protect them against besiegers. Though we find at Jericho and Ai double or triple lines of wall, following Mesopotamian usage, single lines of vertical wall remain the most common type of fortification. In Tell Beit Mirsim G (nineteenth century B.C.) we have a wall about 3·25 metres (nearly 11 feet) wide, strengthened by towers which average 10 metres or a little more in length and 6 metres or more in width. In Stratum F we find the same wall continuing in use, but widened at weak points. These walls, like the earlier ones at Ai, were built of comparatively small stones, laid in rough courses. Following them we have the interlude in which fortifications were constructed largely of beaten earth, as described above. From the later phases of Middle Bronze II come both vertical stone walls and battered (sloping) walls (Pl. 14). Shechem and Jericho have yielded magnificent examples of battered walls, in which a substructure of massive polygonal masonry is erected, with the outer face sloping (often with a bulge), while the inner face is vertical. On the flat top of this sloping substructure was a vertical superstructure of mud-brick. The masonry of these walls was of the polygonal type known as cyclopean, in which great boulders of irregular outlines were fitted to one another and the chinks were filled in with small stones, after which the outside face was roughly hammer-dressed. Some of the stones in these walls are over 2 metres across. The great battered wall of Shechem was found standing to an extreme height of 10 metres; behind it was found an older sloping wall of polygonal masonry. The date of the two great structures we have described was somewhere in the seventeenth or early sixteenth centuries B.C. Sometimes the battered structure was replaced by a sloping stone glacis of similar construction, which was backed up against older walls or simply against the debris of older occupation; the wall of

Stratum D at Tell Beit Mirsim, which seems to have been built in the late seventeenth century, was in part of this type. We also find vertical walls without revetment, following the older tradition; a good example is the Middle Bronze wall of Beth-zur, which was built of massive polygonal masonry, but was only about 2·50 metres wide, with a tower about 10 by 5 metres, like the older wall of Tell Beit Mirsim G; it may have been built in the late seventeenth century. Many of these fortifications were so solidly constructed that they remained standing for centuries and were repaired when necessary. It would seem that the battered wall and glacis types of construction came from Asia Minor to Palestine, since they are first found in the north much earlier than in Palestine; excellent examples appear at Alalakh (Tell 'Atshaneh) and Ugarit in northern Syria.

Another extremely interesting peculiarity of Middle Bronze II fortifications is the fortress gate with two or three gateways, each flanked by a pair of massive piers; all four or six of the piers were of the same size and were symmetrically disposed in two parallel alignments. This type of gateway, which had a long history and gradually changed to new derived types after the sixteenth century, originated in Mesopotamia, where it appears in the great palace of Zimri-Lim in Mari in the eighteenth century B.C. It is found in Middle Bronze strata all over Palestine, and particularly good examples of the triple type have been excavated at Shechem and Megiddo (Fig. 15). These monumental gateways were not only impressive, but they must also have been effective in defence or the type would not have persisted so long. As a rule they seem to have been built with flanking towers; access to them was gained by a ramp leading up from the valley outside. It is hardly necessary to point out that the vogue of the double or triple gateway was closely connected with the introduction of horse-drawn chariots; the narrowest ones, as at Tell Beit Mirsim, were wide enough for a single chariot, and the widest ones known were spacious enough to permit two chariots to pass in the doorways.

We have already referred to the wealth of the country in Middle Bronze II. This relative state of prosperity does not, however, mean that the land was at peace or that the common man was necessarily well off. On the contrary, at no other

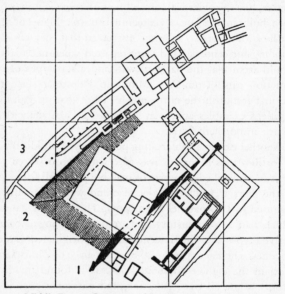

Fig. 15. Middle Bronze Gateway and Late Bronze Temple at Shechem.

period in the history of Palestine was there such lack of public security. At Tell Beit Mirsim, for instance, there were at least four general destructions and four more partial ones in two centuries and a half (1800–1550 B.C.). At Megiddo in the same period there were at least five general destructions; the number of partial ones is not yet known. Some of these 'partial' destructions certainly followed a military débacle, but they were not followed by abandonment and deposit of a new stratum of debris. Occasionally they reflect a catastrophic

earthquake, as once in Bethel. The country was in the hands
of chieftains who were constantly at war with one another,
and who therefore surrounded their residences with massive
fortifications like the great battered walls of Shechem and

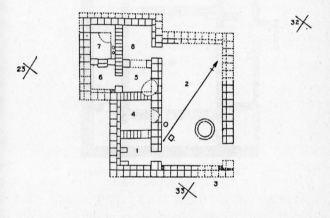

TEL BEIT MIRSIM
SECTION SE
LEVEL D

Scale 0 2 4 6 8 10 Metres

Fig. 16. Patrician house of Stratum D at Tell Beit Mirsim (*c.* 1600 B.C.).

Jericho. At no other time in the history of Palestine do we
find as many strongly fortified settlements, which often re-
mind one more of castles than of towns. These Canaanite
chieftains were surrounded by patrician kinsmen and
retainers; the mass of half-free serfs must have lived
wretchedly, judging from the contrast between the mansions
of the nobles and the hovels of the common man. In the Late

Bronze Age we find ample documentary illustration of this same social gulf between the patricians and their serfs.

A good many palaces and patrician houses of the Middle Bronze have now been excavated in whole or in part. The best-preserved one comes from Stratum D at Tell Beit Mirsim (Fig. 16); it may have been built in the late seventeenth century and have been rebuilt after a complete destruction in the first half of the following century, not long before the Egyptian conquest. Similar, but larger, buildings have been

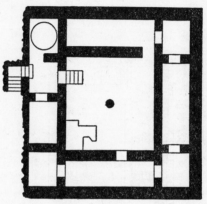

Fig. 17. Middle Bronze villa at the foot of Mount
Gerizim (c. 1600 B.C.).

found at Megiddo and Bethel, near Shechem, at Jericho, and elsewhere (Fig. 17). The largest palace of this age yet discovered comes from the seventeenth–sixteenth century stratum at Tell el-'Ajjul. Including the interior court it occupied about 2000 square metres, or half an acre; its exterior wall was 2 metres thick, built of mud-brick on the high stone socle which was so characteristic of this age. Tell el-'Ajjul was situated near the Palestine end of the desert road which connected the Hyksos capital at Avaris with the Asiatic portion of the empire; it is thus not surprising that it was strongly fortified and provided with a palace of princely dimensions.

All these palaces and noble houses consisted of a court and a row or rows of rooms communicating with it; living quarters for the patrons were in a second storey, as was demonstrated by our observations at Tell Beit Mirsim.

Most of the objects in our museums from this age were found in tombs, which were generally family graves in subterranean caverns, sometimes occupied for generations on end. We also find tombs of individuals, generally consisting of a vertical shaft sunk from the surface of the ground to an underground chamber, with which it communicated by a lower door. Costly weapons and jewellery were generally buried with wealthy nobles and their women folk; the cavern graves were apparently not limited to any one class, as may be inferred from the great variation between the value of the objects deposited in different caves and with different skeletons. Pottery is, of course, always found in great abundance in these tombs (Fig. 18).

A distinctive feature of the pottery from Middle Bronze II is the fact that it is virtually all wheel-made, shaping by hand being restricted to the cheapest type of cooking pot and similar ware. Shapes are generally very graceful, with beautifully proportioned curves. Sharp carination points unmistakably to metallic prototypes, which were imitated faithfully in clay. The metallic illusion was heightened by smearing thick coats of red or cream slip over the surface of the better vases while they were leather hard, that is, after they had been allowed to dry slowly in the shade, but before they had been baked. This slip was then carefully burnished all over with a spatula of stone or bone until it shone like copper or silver. Beautiful though this pottery was, it was seldom exported to other countries, since the potter's art had also reached a high pitch of excellence there, and metal or calcite (alabaster) vases were vastly preferred to cheaper pottery. There was nothing in Palestine like the delicate Kamares ware of Middle Bronze Crete, which was in great demand in Egypt. One of the best-known pottery types of our age is the so-called Tell el-Yahudiyeh jug, a one-handled, pear-shaped (piriform) vase with a button base and a double handle, decorated at the top

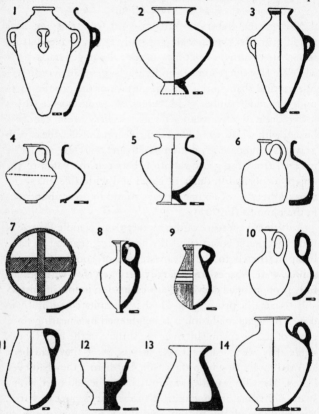

Fig. 18. Pottery of Middle Bronze II in Palestine Museum.

with a vestigial rivet (a skeuomorphic inheritance from metallic prototypes). The surface of these vases was generally highly burnished black, decorated by chalk-filled punctured ornament arranged in simple geometric designs. These small vases were used for perfume, and they became diffused very widely through trade channels. Hence they have long been employed by archaeologists as criteria of Hyksos date (though they came into use before the Hyksos period).

We know a good deal about Middle Bronze art, but much less than we may expect to know after excavating undisturbed destruction levels of this period in some of the more important Canaanite cities in Phoenicia and Syria. The

Fig. 19. Running fawns on inlay of Middle Bronze from Tell Beit Mirsim (c. 1600 B.C.).

finds already made in Palestine and at Byblus in Phoenicia have proved that Canaanite art depended heavily on Egyptian sources of inspiration. This was notably true in the closing decades of the Middle Empire in Egypt (nineteenth to eighteenth centuries), as we know from Byblus. In the Hyksos Age we find more originality. At the same time that Egyptian scarabs, pectorals, and calcite vases were imitated and manufactured locally, we find the beginnings of an independent high art. This art is illustrated at present by beautifully carved metal work, such as toggle pins used in holding garments together; it appears also in ivory and bone inlay, and more rarely in stelae like the serpent goddess of Tell Beit Mirsim (Figs. 19, 20). The Canaanites already excelled in textile manufacture, dyeing woollen cloth rich red or blue colours with a dye prepared from a shell-fish known as murex. Unfortunately no samples of cloth have survived the oxidizing agencies of thirty-five centuries.

The Egyptian conquest of Palestine about the middle of the sixteenth century ushers us into the Late Bronze Age. There is still some confusion between the first phase, which we may term 'Late Bronze I A', and the preceding Middle Bronze, to which its most characteristic wares were long referred. However, a division at this point is more satisfactory to the ceramic expert than any other that has yet been devised. Between 1550 and the middle of the following century we find great quantities of an exceedingly homogeneous type of pottery with bichrome painted ornament, characterized by friezes divided into panels like architectural metopes (Fig. 21). This panelled ornament runs heavily to birds, fishes, and stereotyped geometric patterns (e.g., the so-called 'union jack'). Especially popular were deep bowls and various kinds of pitchers and jars. This ware dominates the ceramic picture in Tell el-'Ajjul II and Megiddo IX; it is wholly missing at Tell Beit Mirsim, unquestionably because of a gap at that site between the Egyptian destruction about 1550 B.C. and the reoccupation of Stratum C several generations later. It was very popular on the Canaanite seaboard, where it was introduced from Cyprus; from Canaan it was further exported to Egypt and the hinterland. The total absence of this ware and contemporary types from Jericho so far is a strong argument for a gap in the sequence of periods there, just as at contemporary Tell Beit Mirsim.

Until the recent publication of the 'Fosse Temple' at Lachish, the following phase, Late Bronze I B, was something of a step-child, since it was known from tombs rather than from stratified deposits. Most of the pottery from

Fig. 20. Reconstructed Stele of serpent goddess
from Tell Beit Mirsim (16th century B.C.).

Stratum I of the Fosse Temple is characteristically I B in type, though the structure must have been built before the end of the sixteenth century. The earliest Late Bronze level at Beth-

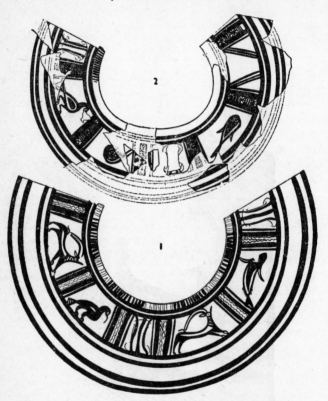

Fig. 21. Decoration on bichrome ware of Late Bronze I A (Lachish, *c.* 1500 B.C.).

shan, Stratum IX, was first attributed to the fifteenth century ('Thothmes III'), but the pottery has proved to date from the following century (which does not exclude a fifteenth-century date for the foundation of the Egyptian fortress on

this site). The C_1 stratum at Tell Beit Mirsim and the contemporary Late Bronze occupation of Jericho are both
chiefly fourteenth century, not fifteenth as was first supposed.

The second phase of Late Bronze is hard to subdivide with
accuracy. However, despite many common features there are
also differences enough to enable us to subdivide it with
caution into Late Bronze II A (roughly fourteenth century)
and II B (roughly thirteenth century). The former represents
the Amarna Age and the shift from the Eighteenth to the
Nineteenth Dynasty in Egypt; the latter reflects the Ramesside period. Where there is an abundance of varied pottery
from a single deposit of homogeneous character (all items of
the deposit belonging to about the same time), a few simple
rules will help to place a Late Bronze deposit chronologically.
The presence of any Mycenaean ware from Greek lands
suggests a date between 1400 and 1230, soon after which
importation of this ware ceased. Aside from a very few
examples of earlier Mycenaean importations, virtually every
piece of Aegean origin found in Palestine belongs to Late
Mycenaean (Late Helladic III) (Fig. 22). Base-ring ware from
Cyprus (generally black, dark brown, or dark grey, with a
metallic ring when struck) is seldom later than II A, since it
died out rapidly after the beginning of the thirteenth century.
Cyprian wishbone-handled bowls, generally creamy or
bluish grey, with a black or dark brown 'ladder' design, run
through II A and B, and were relatively common in II B.

The civilization of Palestine in Late Bronze continued to be
a poor relation of the much richer Canaanite culture of
Phoenicia and southern Syria. Had it not been for the influence from the north, Palestine might easily have lost its
own culture and have become a barbaric reflection of
Egyptian civilization. During this whole period Palestine
remained an integral part of the Egyptian Empire; there is no
evidence that any of the frequent rebellions lasted for more
than a few years at most. There is ample testimony from our

sources, fragmentary though they are, to the frequency of
rebellion. Tell el-Hesi was destroyed three times within the
period in question – four, if we count the destruction of

Fig. 22. Mycenaean Vases from Late Bronze II (1375–1225 B.C.).

Stratum IV at the end of our period. Megiddo was destroyed
twice. The Egyptian fortress at Beth-shan, probably built in
the fifteenth century, was destroyed at least twice before the
middle of the thirteenth century. Of course, the frequency of
destruction in the age of the *pax Aegyptiaca* was much less
than in the preceding Middle Bronze and the following Early

Iron. There was some stability, and the city-states were as a rule protected against invasions from outside. But in return for this limited measure of security the natives paid dearly, since Egyptian exactions were untiring and often brutally oppressive. It is scarcely surprising that the wealth and culture of southern Canaan decreased rather steadily under foreign misrule, until it reached an extremely low ebb in the thirteenth century as compared with its high point at the end of the Middle Bronze, before the Hyksos had been expelled from Egypt.

As has been intimated above, the art of fortification changed but little during the Late Bronze Age. The same may be said of the construction of patrician houses, which still consisted of rows of rooms, single or double, around a large court. Good examples have been found at Taanach, Megiddo, Bethel, and elsewhere. At Bethel was found a remarkably well-constructed system of stone-lined drains, which ran under the plaster floors of patrician

Fig. 23. Representation of Astarte on seal-cylinder from Bethel (c. 1300 B.C.).

houses and discharged rain-water and drainage outside the city wall (Fig. 23).

In one respect we note a considerable advance during the period of Egyptian occupation: writing came more and more into use (cf. Chapter 8). The Canaanites of the Late Bronze Age were familiar with at least four, probably five systems of writing, all of which they employed on occasion in order to write their own language. These five scripts were: (1) Accadian (Mesopotamian) cuneiform; (2) Egyptian hieroglyphs; (3) the linear alphabet from which our own ultimately descends; (4) the cuneiform alphabet of Ugarit (Fig. 24); (5) the syllabic script of Byblus (though this may have gone out of use during Late Bronze). There is, however, no evidence that any of these except Nos. 3 and 4 were used regularly for writing Canaanite; Nos. 1 and 2 were used only occasionally for this purpose. Fortunately for us, the Canaanites of this

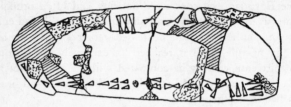

Fig. 24. Tablet from Beth-shemesh in Ugaritic alphabet.

age wrote largely in the Accadian script and language, borrowed from Mesopotamia in the Middle Bronze Age; since cuneiform was written on clay tablets, many of them

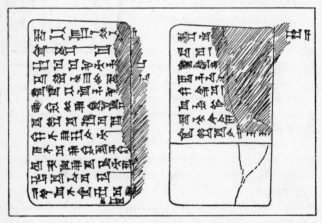

Fig. 25. Cuneiform Letter to Birashshena (Shechem, c. 1400 B.C.).

have resisted the ravages of time and have been dug up by archaeologists. About a score of cuneiform tablets from the fifteenth and fourteenth centuries have hitherto been discovered in Palestinian excavations, twelve of them at Taanach, the rest at Tell el-Hesi, Gezer, Shechem (Fig. 25), Jericho, and Megiddo (1955). With them we must include nearly a hundred and fifty of the cuneiform tablets found at Tell el-Amarna in Middle Egypt since 1887; some two hundred other tablets of the same group were written elsewhere, mostly in Syria and Phoenicia. Under favourable conditions these tablets are almost indestructible; when Bliss found the first tablet in Palestine (1892) he thought it to be of stone. The Amarna letters to the Egyptian Court from Canaanite vassals throw a flood of light on the life and politics of the day. The tablets found in Palestine include letters, business documents, and administrative lists. Accident may at any time reveal a whole Palestinian archive from this period. Nor is it improbable that Canaanite religious texts written in the cuneiform alphabet, like the documents from the fifteenth and fourteenth centuries at Ugarit, may also be found in Palestine (see Chapter 8).

Egyptian stelae and statues were set up in many towns and fortresses of Palestine. Beth-shan, which was an Egyptian garrison town, has already yielded three royal Egyptian stelae and a fragment of a fourth, a royal statue, private stelae, and other hieroglyphic inscriptions (Fig. 26). A fragment of a stele of Tuthmosis III or Amenophis II was discovered at Chinnereth (Tell el-'Oreimeh). Other Egyptian inscriptions have been found at various places occupied during this period. There can be no doubt that there is much historically significant inscribed material still buried in the mounds of Palestine.

Temples, sanctuaries, and religious objects from the Late Bronze Age are now numerous. At Lachish a sanctuary of the period 1500–1230 B.C. has been discovered; it was rebuilt twice within the period, and the contents of each phase have great chronological value (see above). At Megiddo a temple with three successive phases was found in Strata VIII–VII A (*c.* 1400–1150). At Beth-shan at least two Late Bronze temples were uncovered in Strata IX and VII; they belong to the fourteenth (not fifteenth, as first thought) and the thirteenth (not fourteenth) centuries B.C., respectively, and the three remaining temples belong to the Iron Age (see below). Thanks to similar temple plans found by Schaeffer at Ugarit it is now possible to identify the massive structure at the North Gate of Shechem, which Welter dated about the fourteenth century, as a temple; it had been the object of a controversy between Sellin and Welter. This structure was about 25 by 21 metres in size, and was provided with massive exterior walls, 5 metres (nearly 17 feet) thick; the entrance was flanked by towers. In the interior there had been two rows of columns, each row containing three columns. The stone structure which was excavated must originally have supported two or more stories of mud-brick. At Ugarit and in Megiddo similar ground plans show corresponding thickness of walls, so there must have been a whole class of Canaanite temples in several stories. These structures are no doubt reflected by the later many-storied house-shrines at Beth-shan.

On the other hand, there is no longer any reason to consider the so-called Gezer high place, which was still in use in Late Bronze though apparently founded towards the end of Early Bronze (see above), as a sanctuary in the strict sense of the term. It seems rather to have been a mortuary shrine, and the alignment of standing stones is to be compared with contemporary *masseboth* (menhirs) in the temple of Dagon at Ugarit and in the stele field of Assur. The 'high places' of the following Iron Age, mentioned frequently in the Bible, were also open-air installations like the Nabataean 'high places' of Petra (see Chapter 7).

One of the commonest classes of religious objects found in Late Bronze levels is constituted by the so-called 'Astarte' plaques (Fig. 27). These are pottery plaques, generally oval in shape, on which were impressed (from a pottery or metal

Fig. 26. Stele of Sethos I from Beth-shan (*c.* 1318 B.C.).

mould) a figure of the nude goddess Asherah, *en face* with her arms upraised, grasping lily stalks or serpents, or both, in her hands. The goddess's head is adorned with two long spiral ringlets identical with the Egyptian Hathor ringlets. These plaques were borrowed from Mesopotamia, where they have a long prehistory in the Early Bronze Age. Other types of naked goddess, both plaques and figurines, also occur.

Fewer examples of Canaanite art have been found in strata of the Late Bronze than commonly thought, since much that was formerly believed to belong to this age is now known to be more recent. To Iron I belong the incense-stands and anthropoid sarcophagi of Beth-shan, the ivory box-lid from Tell el-Far'ah, and (in Phoenicia) the sarcophagus of Ahiram. Most (though not all) of the ivories in the great cache at Megiddo belong to the twelfth century (see below) (Pls. 16, 18). Thanks to the rich archaeological booty yielded by Late Bronze Ugarit we know that the art of Canaan was much richer than might be supposed from the excavations in Palestine. The two fine repoussé golden bowls from the fifteenth or fourteenth centuries, found by Schaeffer at Ugarit, are a vivid illustration of the kind of Canaanite art which we must expect in richer centres. Most Palestine sites of this period were the homes of very poor chieftains, who suffered constantly under Egyptian exactions (see above); art treasures cannot be expected from them. Moreover, since Palestine was so near Egypt, its art was subjected to continuous Egyptian influence and most artistic productions were crude imitations of Egyptian originals. This influence appears vividly in Beth-shan and Lachish, where we find both Egyptian importations and local imitations, often very inferior in artistic merit (Fig. 28). There is much foreign influence from the Aegean, especially in pottery. A good example of import from Syria is the fourteenth- (not fifteenth-) century basalt orthostate from Beth-shan, showing two scenes of combat between a lion and a large mastiff; the slab may have been

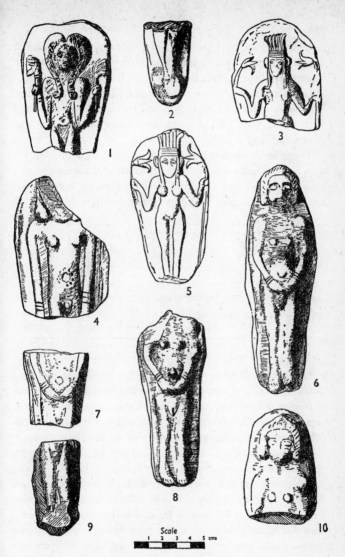

Fig. 27. *Astarte* plaques from Tell Beit Mirsim (Nos. 1–5 are Late Bronze; 6–10 are Iron I).

part of the Egyptian spoils of war. The sculptures found at Ugarit show a pronounced decline in artistic skill between the fifteenth and the thirteenth centuries. The same artistic retrogression appears in Palestine; it is well illustrated by the unbelievably crude limestone lion and shallow bowl decorated with lions, both dating from the thirteenth century, discovered at Tell Beit Mirsim (Pl. 17).

These last two objects were discovered in a rubbish pit near a still unexcavated building (presumably a temple) from the end of Stratum C (fifteenth to late thirteenth century). All around were traces of the violent destruction by fire to which

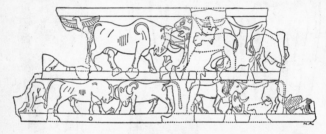

Fig. 28. Ivory inlay from Lachish (13th century B.C.).

the latest Canaanite town on this site (probably the Debir of Josh. x, 39) had been subjected by the invading Israelites. A similar destruction was the fate of contemporary Lachish, at a time which cannot have preceded the fourth year of Marniptah, son and successor of Ramesses II. These destructions about 1220 B.C. were preceded by the destruction of Jericho and Bethel by the incoming Israelites. Unfortunately, we can date these latter two destructions only by the fact that they followed a period in which Mycenaean pottery was being imported and imitated. In neither site do we find many scattered sherds to help us with our dating; nearly all the rooms were absolutely empty, and the sherds from the stratum in question may often reflect a time decades before the final destruction. At present the evidence points to a date in the thirteenth century for the fall of Bethel. The problem of Jericho has become more obscure since Miss Kenyon's work, which showed that the Late Bronze level was almost completely denuded by wind and rain during the long abandonment after the Conquest.

During the Middle and Late Bronze Ages, the coast from Mt. Casius, near Antioch in northern Syria, to the extreme south of Palestine had been occupied by a people of mixed race, speaking closely related North-west Semitic dialects and sharing a common material and religious culture. In southern Syria and Palestine their territory once extended eastward to the edge of sedentary occupation. In spite of local differences, these 'Canaanites' (as they were called by their neighbours and ultimately called themselves) were fully as homogeneous as the Hittites or the early Greeks. As we have seen, Canaanite civilization was in some ways highly developed, in others startlingly crude.

With the invasion of the Israelites in the thirteenth century and the invasion of the Sea Peoples at the beginning of the twelfth, the history of Canaanite Palestine comes virtually to a close, though the river valleys and plains of northern Palestine were occupied for two centuries more by Canaanite city-states. However, the Canaanites had exhausted the cultural energy which had hitherto sustained them; after a long eclipse and a fresh transfusion of blood they were to emerge as a vital new people, the Phoenicians, who shared with Israel the material achievements of Iron Age Palestine.

CHAPTER 6

Palestine in the Iron Age

—

It is sometimes assumed that there was a sudden change from
the dominance of copper and bronze to that of iron as
material for tools and weapons. It is also sometimes thought
that the change was very slow. Neither extreme view is
correct. Meteoric iron was known as far back as predynastic
Egypt and was utilized for tools and weapons in the third
millennium. Not only can such iron be easily distinguished
from terrestrial iron by the presence of a small amount of
nickel, which is very rarely found in our native planetary
ore, but its meteoric origin is directly implied by the Egyptian name ('metal of heaven') and the cuneiform ideogram.
It was not until the fourteenth century B.C. that iron began to
be used rather extensively for weapons (daggers, axe-heads,
swords); in the following century iron occurs still more
frequently, and a cuneiform letter from the Hittite capital in
Asia Minor shows that the Hittites exploited the metal under
monopolistic conditions. This Hittite monopoly of iron was
not broken until the destruction of the Hittite Empire, about
1200 B.C. Thereafter we find iron displacing copper and
bronze for tools and weapons, and by the tenth century it was
the principal metal for plough-tips and sickles, as well as for
weapons. Petrie's date in the fourteenth century for the
general introduction of iron into Palestine is based on his
erroneous absolute dates; a careful survey of all iron finds in
the light of their context shows clearly that the Philistines
first used iron in the twelfth and eleventh centuries (Tell el-
Far'ah tombs), and that the Israelites adopted it more
slowly, being hindered by the Philistine iron monopoly (I
Sam. xiii, 19 ff.).

The chronological situation in the Iron Age was badly

confused by the excavators of Gezer and Jericho, and more recently it has been obscured by conflicting nomenclature. We have described briefly in Chapter II how Macalister was led to depress the date of Iron I by trying to fill an unrecognized occupational gap of several centuries at Gezer, and how Watzinger was misled by Sellin's identification of the great battered wall of the Middle Bronze with a wall alleged to have been built by Hiel the Bethelite in the ninth century B.C. (cf. I Kings xvi, 34). In spite of the correct reaction of Mackenzie at Beth-shemesh, the archaeological chronology of Palestine was in a state of indescribable confusion when the author began digging at Gibeah of Saul (Tell el-Ful) in 1922. Since then the absolute chronology has been greatly clarified, thanks to Phythian-Adams' work at Ascalon (1920) and Hamilton's excavation of Tell Abu Hawam (1933–4), the writer's work at Gibeah, Tell Beit Mirsim (1926–), and Bethel (1934), the work of Reisner (published in 1924), Crowfoot and Miss Kenyon at Samaria, the work of Shipton and others at Megiddo (1925–), etc. It must be emphasized that the dating of sufficiently characteristic groups of homogeneous pottery from the Iron Age, between the twelfth and the seventh centuries, is now fixed to within narrow limits. The high points in this sequence will be described below; meanwhile attention may be called to the comparative uselessness of archaeological work in Palestine for biblical scholars until the pottery chronology of the Old Testament period had been worked out in detail. Under these conditions it is scarcely surprising that most biblical historians of the generation before us gave up any attempt to utilize archaeological data, except in the case of inscriptions or outstanding architectural monuments or museum objects.

Just as the pottery chronology was being fixed, new confusion was introduced into the archaeology of the Iron Age by a conflict of nomenclature. In 1921 the three official schools of archaeology in Jerusalem (British, French, and

American), in co-operation with the Department of Antiquities, drew up a system of archaeological periods in which the Iron Age was classified as follows:

> (i) Early Iron (Palestinian) – 1200–600 B.C.
>   (a) Philistine; (b) Israelite
> (ii) Middle Iron (Palestinian) – 600–100 B.C.
>   (a) Jewish; (b) Hellenistic

In his early excavations the author kept this official system, subdividing it into 'Early Iron I' (1200–900 B.C.) and 'Early Iron II' (900–600 B.C.), but later he introduced 'Early Iron III' to cover the Babylonian and Persian periods. Subsequently Clarence S. Fisher replaced the original official system with 'Early Iron' (1200–900), 'Middle Iron' (900–600), and 'Late Iron' (600–300 B.C.). As a result of this shift the Megiddo excavators, for instance, were employing 'Early Iron II' to designate the period between 1050 and 900 while the writer was using the same distinctive term for the whole period from c. 900 to c. 600 B.C. This confusion could lead only to chaos unless the use of centuries was substituted for that of periods. For this reason the writer has given up the use of the terms 'early – middle – late' entirely, replacing them by 'I – II – III'. In this chapter we shall use the following terminology for the successive phases of the Iron Age before Hellenistic times:

PERIODS	CHRONOLOGY	BIBLICAL HISTORY
Iron I	Twelfth–tenth centuries inclusive	Judges and United Monarchy
Iron II	Ninth century to beginning of sixth	Divided Monarchy
Iron III	c. 550–330 B.C.	Exile and Restoration

IRON I
Twelfth–tenth Centuries

At the end of the preceding chapter we described briefly the chronological evidence from the destruction levels which separated the last Canaanite occupation from the earliest Israelite. Reoccupation by the Israelites was apparently slow at first (e.g., Jericho), and was gradually speeded up (after a considerable gap at Bethel, but with little or no gap at Tell Beit Mirsim). By the end of the thirteenth century they were probably in the process of settling down throughout the hill-country on both sides of Jordan. However, they were not able to break through the Canaanite chariotry in order to storm the strongly fortified towns in the plains and river-valleys; we know from the excavations at Megiddo and Beth-shan that these towns resisted the Israelites for generations. On the other hand, the Israelite population increased rapidly in the hills. Thanks to the rapid spread of the art, then recent, of constructing cisterns and lining them with waterproof lime plaster instead of the previously used limy marl or raw-lime plaster, the Israelites were able to settle in any site where there was rain, whereas their earlier Canaanite precursors had been forced to restrict their occupation in general to sites near springs or perennial streams.

At the beginning of the twelfth century B.C. the coasts of Palestine were inundated by a flood of seafaring peoples from the islands and shores of the northern Mediterranean. The entire coastal plain of Palestine seems to have been occupied by the Sea Peoples, best known among whom are the Philistines and the Tjikal, who occupied the district between Gaza and Ekron and the coast south of Carmel, respectively. The Philistines brought their own culture with them, but they soon amalgamated with the Canaanites whom they had conquered, and since they possessed the richest tract of land in Palestine it was not long before they were able to dominate the other Sea Peoples. About the middle of the eleventh century the Philistines defeated the Israelites at Ebenezer, captured the Ark, and destroyed Shiloh. Evidences of destruction in other towns of Judah about the same time indicate that they also devastated much of Western Palestine, reducing the Israelites to subjection. Saul threw off the Philistine yoke at the beginning of his reign (c. 1020 B.C.), but after his death on Gilboa the Philistines regained control of the country, which they did not lose until well along in the reign of David (c. 990 B.C.). From that time on they played only a very secondary role, mainly commercial.

Hitherto our knowledge of Philistine culture has been obtained almost wholly from sites outside of the Philistine Plain, owing to the fact that the five cities of the Pentapolis continued to be occupied in subsequent ages and that the accumulated depth of debris is now formidable, as Garstang and Phythian-Adams discovered at Ascalon and Gaza. What we know from archaeology about Philistine material culture comes largely from excavations in the Shephelah and the Negeb. A very distinctive type of pottery emerged in the Philistine Plain during the first decades of the twelfth century, continuing in use until the late eleventh century, after which it seems to have survived only in traces. Since this 'Philistine' ware is abundant in all levels and deposits of this period in Philistia itself, and is also found in abundance in the adjacent sites of the Negeb and the Shephelah between c. 1150 B.C. and the late eleventh century, its title to be called 'Philistine' seems excellent. Moreover, the ware in question decreases relatively as one moves away from Philistia; it still occurs in deposits of the same age at Beth-zur, Tell en-Nasbeh, and Bethel, and is found very sparingly at Megiddo. It has not yet, however, been discovered at Beth-shan or Tell Abu Hawam, although there was continuous occupation of these sites throughout this period. From the standpoint of geographical distribution alone the term 'Philistine' is thus perfectly correct.

Our knowledge of the prehistory of the biblical Philistines has been greatly increased by the excavations of A. Furumark, C. F. A. Schaeffer, and P. Dikaios since 1947 at Sinda and Enkomi in eastern Cyprus. In a hitherto unknown phase, to be dated between c. 1225 and 1175 B.C., Furumark found locally made pottery of Mycenaean III C 1 b style,

which was almost identical with the earliest Philistine pottery
of Palestine. This Cypriote pottery resembles the Mycenaean
ware of Argos, and must have come from Greece. When
these settlers, who may have been Pelasgians (see p. 185),
invaded Palestine about 1175 B.C., they continued to manufacture this same ware as 'Philistine' pottery. The main
types of the latter are craters (two-handled bowls) and
jugs, generally buff in colour with a creamy grey wash (put
on after baking) on which are painted red and black geometric designs and swans pluming themselves (Fig. 29). The
wash is sometimes omitted entirely, and sometimes replaced
by a true slip; there are a good many variations in form of vase
and selection of motifs. These craters were supplied with two
tilted horizontal loop-handles; their favourite decoration is a
series of metope-like panels, in each of which a highly stylized
swan is shown with upraised wing in the act of pluming itself.
Frequently, especially in relatively late pieces, the artist has
depicted the swan with its bill thrust forward, in which case
the wing generally looks something like a shop-worn
thunderbolt. The jugs are usually provided with a strainer
spout, obviously intended for the same purpose for which
the highland peoples of antiquity used reeds or pipes in
drinking beer – in order to strain out the beer without
swallowing barley husks. It is not difficult to infer from the
ubiquity of these wine craters and beer jugs that the Philistines were mighty carousers. In this respect again, archaeology is in full agreement with biblical tradition, as we see
from the story of Samson, where drinking bouts are mentioned several times in connexion with the Philistines,
though it is said emphatically of Samson that he drank
neither wine nor beer.

Just before the Philistines invaded Palestine the Canaanites
had begun to adopt the Egyptian practice of burying the
dead in anthropoid clay coffins, on the upper part of which
were moulded human features and occasionally some other

details. An example from the thirteenth century, with a very peculiar locally made hieroglyphic inscription, has been found at Lachish. During the twelfth and eleventh centuries

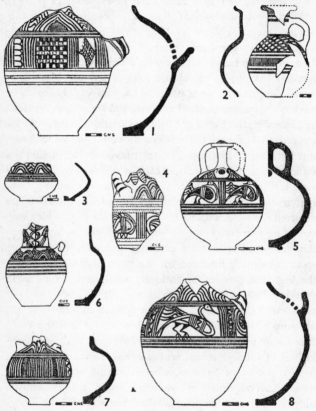

Fig. 29. Philistine pottery in Palestine Museum (1150–1000 B.C.).

we find these clay coffins in tombs with Philistine pottery at Tell el-Far'ah in the Negeb and in contemporary Iron Age tombs at Beth-shan. They occur also in various places in the

Delta of Egypt, often with foreign pottery and weapons. One has turned up south-east of 'Amman at the edge of the Syrian Desert; it must be dated rather later than the others. It seems probable that the popularity of this type of burial in this period was due partly, at least, to Philistine influence.

Through the dovetailing between archaeological and literary evidence which now becomes much more frequent in Palestinian archaeology, it is possible to fix dates much more closely. For example, the battle between Barak and Sisera, vividly described in the triumphal paean of Deborah, was fought 'at Taanach by Megiddo's waters' (Judg. v, 19). A comparison of the periods during which Megiddo and Taanach (only five miles to the south-east) were occupied, shows that the occupation of the two towns tended to be complementary, not simultaneous, just as at Ai and Bethel, which were too close to flourish at the same time except very briefly. For instance, Taanach was a flourishing town in Early Bronze III and IV, when Megiddo was unoccupied; again it was the capital of a large city-state in the middle of the fifteenth century, while Megiddo was occupied by a small Egyptian garrison. This total omission of any reference to Megiddo itself, while Taanach becomes the capital of the district, makes it practically certain that Megiddo was then in ruins. Now the excavation of the site has shown that after the destruction of Megiddo VII about the third quarter of the twelfth century, the site lay in ruins until it was occupied by the people of Stratum VI. The latter abandoned, for the first time in centuries, any attempt to adhere to the old fortifications and palace area and struck out along entirely new constitutional lines. The pottery points in a similar direction, since the ware of Megiddo VI is virtually identical with that of the Israelite hill-country. In Stratum V we find the building tradition of VI continued and new types of pottery employed, oriented rather towards the coast than towards the hill-country. It follows that the Song of Deborah may be dated archaeologically about 1125 B.C., a date which agrees exceedingly well with the literary and political requirements of its contents.

Another illustration of the way in which ceramic chronology and literary history complement one another may be seen in the vogue of different types of store-jar rims in the central hill-country of Palestine during the eleventh century. In the first three phases of Iron-Age Bethel the dominant vase was a large store-jar (pithos) with a very characteristic collared rim and equally characteristic coarse texture of clay. This same vase is found in abundance in contemporary Ai and Tell en-Nasbeh, as well as in the first Israelite occupation of Gibeah (Tell el-Ful); it is abundant in Beth-zur in the south and in Shechem in the north. At Tell Beit Mirsim and Beth-shemesh in the Shephelah it appears, but is not common. It appears occasionally in Megiddo VII and is excessively common in Megiddo VI (as the writer noted on the spot), but does not appear in V. Now, this type of pottery, which first appeared during the first half of the twelfth century, lasted until after the Philistine destruction of Shiloh, c. 1050 B.C., since the store-jars found by Schmidt and Kjaer in deposits preceding the conflagration exhibit the same shape and collared rims. In the period of Saul at Gibeah a new type of rim displaced the collared rim, which accordingly went out of use there well before 1000 (the minimal date for Saul's death). This same new rim appears at Bethel, Tell en-Nasbeh, and other sites in the following phase, so it was widely distributed and drove out the collared rim between 1050 and 1000, presumably in the third quarter of the eleventh century. It follows that the change of style of pithos rims is a valuable criterion for dating in a critical period of Israelite history. As our knowledge progresses we shall discover many similar criteria, which will ultimately enable the scholar to offer surprisingly precise dates for the contents of houses or homogeneous burials. Of course, nothing is likely to enable us to date the ordinary sherd more closely than within two or three centuries, and some sherds will doubtless always defy attempts to give them dates.

If we survey the archaeology of the period of the Judges, we cannot help but be struck by the extraordinary simplicity and lack of cultural sophistication which we find in the twelfth and early eleventh centuries. The contrast between the well-constructed Canaanite foundations and drainage systems of the thirteenth century and the crude piles of stone, without benefit of drainage, which replace them in the twelfth century, especially at Bethel, can scarcely be exaggerated. For this decline in the material arts of life there were two reasons. In the first place, the incoming Israelite tribesmen were a wild, semi-nomadic horde, who differed mainly from similar invading desert hordes in the speed with which they settled down. The archaeologist with no knowledge of biblical tradition would have to acknowledge some binding and driving force in Israel which differentiated it from ordinary nomadic invaders, like the tribes which overran Transjordan periodically and lived there in tents for centuries without settling down. In the second place, the Israelites were in a quasi-democratic, patriarchal stage of clan life and the old difference between patrician and half-free peasant had been largely erased by their conquest of Canaan. When they occupied a Canaanite patrician house, as happened at Bethel and Tell Beit Mirsim, they kept the old ground plan with little change, but the mode of construction and details of the resulting plan were as different as the inventory of the house. For one thing, it is clear that the Israelite family which occupied the ruined mansion actually lived in the ground floor as a rule instead of using the ground floor for storerooms and slaves, while living in the upper storey. The massive old fortress wall was allowed to stand, but few repairs were made; the Israelites were free men and could not be forced to work in the corvée. As the editor of Judges observed, at that time 'every man did what was right in his own eyes'.

No Israelite sanctuaries and very few amulets of this period have been discovered; the most interesting of the amulets are clay plaques, impressed from moulds, showing a naked woman with distended abdomen, to which both hands are convulsively pressed – obviously she is about to give birth to a child. It is very curious to note that she wears none of the insignia of a goddess, as in earlier and contemporary Canaanite plaques and figurines; we cannot yet say whether this fact is accidental or whether it has anything to do with Israelite hostility to idol worship. On the other hand, Strata VI and V of non-Israelite Beth-shan, dating from the twelfth and eleventh centuries B.C., exhibit a very rich and varied cultic furniture of clay and stone, and we learn even more about this material from contemporary non-Israelite Megiddo (VII–V) (Pl. 19). In the Canaanite sanctuaries of the Iron Age at Beth-shan were a great many whole and broken incense-stands or flower-pots (both explanations seem to be correct in principle), often with a serpent or serpents moulded in relief. A number of broken shrine-houses in several stories were discovered; one of them exhibited the *dramatis personae* of some Canaanite myth, including a naked goddess with doves, two male figures engaged in a fight, a serpent, and a lion. It is easy to imagine what a lewd and sanguinary myth may have been portrayed after the discovery and interpretation of a considerable fraction of early Canaanite mythology at Ugarit (cf. Chapter 8).

The oldest datable Israelite fortification of Iron I is the citadel of Saul on the summit of Tell el-Ful, three miles north of Jerusalem (Fig. 30). The remains of this fortress were cleared by the author in 1922 and 1933; little survived subsequent destruction and rebuilding except a corner tower and part of the adjacent casemate wall, dated by the pottery found in it to the age of Saul (*c.* 1020–1000 B.C.). The casemate wall

is an excellent example of a type which enjoyed great vogue in
Palestine in the eleventh and tenth centuries, and continued
in sporadic use into the latter part of Iron II. This type of
wall originated in Late Bronze Asia Minor, and was brought
to Syria by the Hittites; from Syria it spread southward
during the transition from Bronze to Iron. The fortress wall
of Saul consisted of two shells, each solidly constructed of

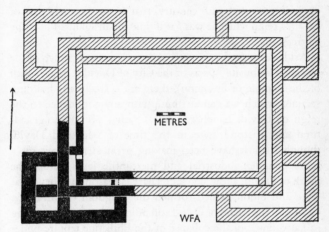

Fig. 30. Citadel of Saul of Tell el-Ful (c. 1000 B.C.), restored.

hammer-dressed masonry, laid in rough courses. The outer
shell was about 1·5 metres (three cubits) thick; the inner one
was about 1·20 metres wide. Between the two shells was a
narrow space divided by transverse partitions into a series of
long, narrow chambers. Some of these chambers were filled
with stones and earth; others were left empty for use as
store-rooms and were connected by doors with the interior
of the fortress. The total width of the wall could thus be as
much as 4·50 metres (about 14·75 feet) or as little as 1·50
metres. This casemate device was a clever way in which to

provide great real (and greater apparent) strength with the least possible expenditure of effort. It was even cleverer in the way it utilized all possible storage space inside the city wall. Other walls of the same character and nearly the same measurements are the casemate wall of Shechem, which may go back to the middle of the eleventh century (time of Abimelech, Judg. ix), and the casemate walls of Tell Beit Mirsim and Beth-shemesh, which belong to about the beginning of the tenth century, that is, to the early part of David's reign when he was fortifying Judah against Philistine aggression.

Aside from these casemate walls and probably much of the so-called 'Jebusite' glacis of the City of David (Ophel, south of the Temple of Solomon), there are scarcely any building remains which we can attribute with any confidence to the reign of David. Israel was still a rather primitive agricultural and pastoral state in the time of Saul and David, though it must have been making great strides towards a more complex industrial and mercantile level before the death of David, about 960 B.C. There is reason to believe that Tyre and Sidon, which formed the kingdom of Hiram (c. 969–936), the friend of David and Solomon, were then taking full advantage of the collapse of the Philistine empire under the blows of David to extend their trading empire into the western Mediterranean.

Recent finds have made it increasingly probable that the expansion of the Sidonian merchant empire came suddenly, in the half-century after David's great victories over the Philistines (between 990 and 980 B.C.). Among these finds may be mentioned the publication by A. M. Honeyman (1939) of a Phoenician tomb inscription from Cyprus, which must be dated in the ninth century B.C., at least a century before the Baal-Lebanon inscription, which had been the oldest Phoenician document from that island. This publication made it possible to explain and date the Nora stone from

Sardinia, which had always been an enigma; it turns out to have formed part of a decree inscribed on the stones of a wall, like the decree of Gortyn in Crete (sixth century B.C.). The Nora stone and two other fragments from Bosa are shown by their script to date from the ninth century, thus proving that Phoenician exploitation of Sardinia was already well developed by then, contrary to the views of Beloch and his followers. The oldest painted pottery from the site of the Tanit cemetery at Carthage almost certainly antedates the era of the city (814 B.C.), since it is closely related to painted pottery from Megiddo IV B (*c.* 975–925 B.C.); it thus seems to belong to the Kambe stage of Carthaginian history. Finally, the earlier Phoenician ivories from Carmona in the valley of the Guadalquivir in south-western Spain are in some respects more closely related to the ivories of Megiddo from the twelfth century than to the ninth- and eighth-century ivories of Samaria and Arslan Tash. This suggests that they may go back in part to the tenth century (Figs. 31, 32).

The age of Solomon was certainly one of the most flourishing periods of material civilization in the history of Palestine. Archaeology, after a

Fig. 31. Scene from ivory inlay, Megiddo, early twelfth century B.C.

long silence, has finally corroborated biblical tradition in no uncertain way. First came the sensational discovery by P. L. O. Guy (1928) at Megiddo of the stables of Stratum IV, which covered a considerable portion of the site and provided room for at least 450 horses at the same time. After a good deal of discussion, the relation between buildings of Strata V, IV B, and IV A has been pretty well

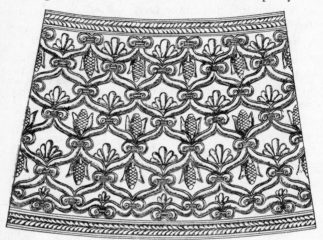

Fig. 32. Interlaced ornament on Megiddo ivory,
early twelfth century B.C.

cleared up. It seems certain that the stables go back to Solomon, in accordance with I Kings ix, 15, 19, etc.; it is equally certain that they continued in use, with extensive repairs, after Shishak's invasion, down through most of the ninth century, after which they were destroyed and abandoned. The stables were exceedingly well built – horses were better cared for than human beings in those days. The stables (except where the animals stood, where a cobbled floor was laid in order to prevent them from slipping) and the adjacent courtyard were paved with hydraulic lime plaster (made of crushed, unslaked lime). Each unit of stabling consisted of a central passage about 3 metres wide, flanked by two rows of stone pillars which served simultaneously as tie-posts and as supports for the roof. Beyond were two aisles for the horses, each 3 metres wide. Each unit accommodated about thirty horses.

Other buildings of Stratum IV B, the Solomonic phase, were also discovered at Megiddo, among them the residence of the governor, surrounded with a nearly square wall about 200 feet (60 metres) on a side.

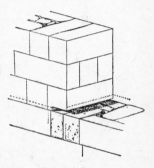

Fig. 33. Israelite masonry at Samaria, showing arrangement of blocks.

Solomonic masonry shows clear indications of having been borrowed from the Phoenicians; characteristic of it is the use of long, narrow blocks of well-hewn stone laid alternately in groups of two or three headers or stretchers (Fig. 33). Another characteristic of this masonry, dominant in the relatively inferior work of Megiddo, was the extensive employment of quoin construction, that is, of corners and piers of well-hewn ashlar blocks between stretches of rubble; like the casemate walls this was another clever device to obtain the maximum of strength with the minimum of outlay (Fig. 34). Exactly similar construction was found by Macalister at Gezer and attributed by him to Solomon, after he had compared notes with Schumacher, who was then working at Megiddo. The stables at Megiddo closely resemble similar constructions at Tell el-Hesi (Stratum V, about the tenth century B.C.), Hazor, and Taanach, all from the same general age.

Among the most interesting finds in Stratum IV at Megiddo were a number of proto-Ionic (better, perhaps, proto-

Aeolic) pilaster capitals of limestone. These pilaster capitals belonged to engaged columns which had originally lined the walls of a large room or corridor. Similar ones have been found at a number of other sites in Palestine, and all date between the tenth and the seventh centuries B.C. (Fig. 35). The oldest hitherto found is a painted miniature capital from Megiddo V, which cannot be later than the early tenth cen-

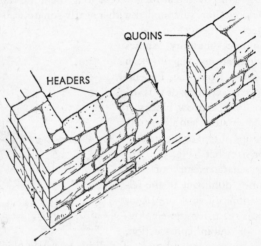

Fig. 34. Typical section of Iron Age wall, showing masonry elements.

tury. Curiously enough, none has yet been reported from Phoenicia itself, where published monuments from the Early Iron Age are still few and far between. But the Greeks of Cyprus and Ionia borrowed them from the Phoenicians about the eighth century B.C., and examples become frequent from the seventh century on.

The older Megiddo gateway of the Iron Age was almost certainly Solomonic; it contained three pairs of long narrow piers, separated by two pairs of deep bays. This plan also came from the north, where it appears at Zencirli and Car-

chemish in northern Syria in the late eleventh or the tenth
century. Originally this type of gate, with six long piers and
four long bays between the piers, arose from the typical
Middle Bronze gateway (Chapter 5), in which we have the
same number of piers and bays, but all shorter and more
symmetrically arranged. The same type of gateway appears

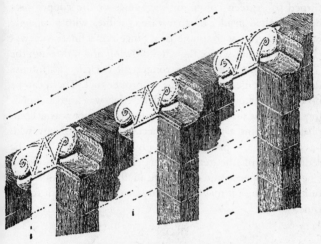

Fig. 35. Proto-Aeolic pilaster capitals from Samaria
(in restored architectural context).

also at Lachish and at Ezion-geber on the Gulf of 'Aqabah,
where it is almost certainly Solomonic in date.

No less unexpected than Guy's discovery of the Megiddo
stables were Nelson Glueck's excavation of the refineries of
Ezion-geber (Tell el-Kheleifeh) at the northern end of the
Gulf of 'Aqabah, in 1938. Much smaller installations of
similar type for smelting iron had been discovered by Petrie
at Jemmeh, but nothing remotely comparable to the copper
refineries of Ezion-geber has yet been found anywhere else in
the ancient world. The best-built of these refineries belong to
Stratum I, the oldest of the five main periods of occupation

in this site. The walls of the furnace-rooms were pierced with two rows of large flues, about 4 feet above the hearth bottom. The upper flues communicated with an air-channel which ran at the same height lengthwise inside the wall; the lower flues pierced through the wall. The heat of the furnace fires had baked the mud-brick surface of the wall, which had been turned to a green colour by the fumes of the copper ores being smelted inside. Earthenware crucibles with a capacity of 14 cubic feet were numerous. Since the refinery site was chosen at a point where the wind blowing down through the 'Arabah from the north is strongest, it is clear that intense heat could be generated by use of proper fuel. There can be no doubt whatever that Tell el-Kheleifeh was a great smelting plant, but just how the reduction of copper was accomplished remains a mystery to specialists in metallurgy who have studied the problem. It is highly improbable that the rediscovery of the tenth-century Phoenician methods of smelting copper would contribute anything to the industry of our day, though it may have been remarkably efficient for its time.

IRON II
Ninth-early Sixth Centuries

The chronology of Iron II is now clear in detail to archaeologists who have been working in stratified sites from that age. It is, however, true that even some recent publications require much correction in detail before we can accept the picture which they offer. One of the most important sites for this period is Samaria, where Reisner, Crowfoot, and their aids did an exceedingly good job of digging. Since Samaria was founded by Omri, Ahab's father, about 870 B.C., virtually all pottery found in it must be later than that date. The distinctive ware of the first occupation, with its continuous wheel-burnished red slip over a light buff clay, belongs entirely to the period between the second quarter of the ninth

Plate 1. Edward Robinson,
1794–1863.

Plate 2. Sir W. M. Flinders Petrie,
1853–1942.

Plate 3. James L. Starkey, 1895–1938.

Plate 4. The Mound of Megiddo.

Plate 5. Superimposed stratification of walls at Tell Beit Mirsim
(periods G-B).

Plate 6. The Mound of Beth-shan (from the north).

Plate 7. The Prehistoric Caves of Wadi el-Magharah (Garrod).

Plate 8. Flexed burial of Natufian Period.

Plate 9. Plastic Marl Statue from pre-pottery Neolithic of Jericho.

Plate 10. Carved fawn on end of bone implement from the Natufian Age.

Plate 11. Early Bronze stele from Shihan.

Plate 12. Re-used Early Bronze stele from Balu'ah.

0   5CMS

Plate 13. Hall of house from Tell Beit Mirsim G, with F foundation running across it (c. 1750 B.C.).

Plate 14. Battered wall of Middle Bronze Jericho (c. 1600 B.C.).

Plate 15. Scarabs of Middle Bronze II from Tell Beit Mirsim
(*c.* 1700–1550 B.C.).

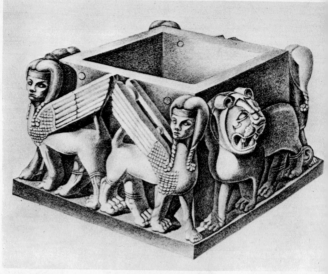

Plate 16. Ivory box with lions and cherubs from Megiddo
(*c.* 13th century B.C.).

Plate 17. Libation tray with lion in relief from Tell Beit Mirsim
(*c.* 1250 B.C.).

Plate 18. Ivory carving of cherub, Megiddo,
early twelfth century B.C.

Plate 19. House altars with horns from Megiddo
(tenth-ninth centuries B.C.).

Plate 20. Israelite stables at Megiddo (tenth-ninth centuries B.C.).

Plate 21. Foundation of city-wall of ninth-century Samaria.

Plate 22. A dye-plant of the seventh century at Tell Beit Mirsim.

Plate 23. Round tower of early Hellenistic Age at Samaria.

Plate 24. Ivories of Samaria.
Above: Harpocrates on a lotus. *Below:* A cherub.

Plate 25. Reverse of Lachish Ostracon, No. III (*c.* 589 B.C.).

Plate 26. Aramaic plaque mentioning King Uzziah of Judah.

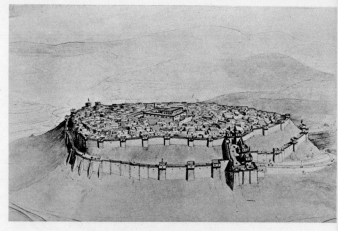

Plate 27. Preëxilic Lachish (restored view).

Plate 28. Interior of preëxilic house at Tell Beit Mirsim
showing four stone pillars.

Plate 29. Gezer Calendar (*c.* 925 B.C.). (The Palestine Exploration Fund.)

Plate 30. Ossuary mentioning an Elizabeth in Aramaic and Greek.

and the end of the third quarter of the eighth century B.C. When Kathleen Kenyon publishes her long-awaited study of the stratification and pottery of private houses from Iron II, we shall have a solid basis for subsequent chronological progress. Meanwhile the Crowfoot expedition was able to demonstrate that Reisner's chronology was wrong in some very important respects (cf. Chapter 2). The latter had distinguished three main Israelite building periods and had dated certain round towers in the wall of the acropolis to the age of Jeroboam II, in the eighth century B.C., whereas I. Ben-Dor discovered typical Hellenistic sherds in the constructional material which filled them. From this discovery, which confirmed other observations of Crowfoot, it follows that there were only two main phases of the royal Israelite palace, one in the time of the Omrides, the other under the dynasty of Jehu, almost certainly in the reign of its greatest king, Jeroboam II. The inscribed potsherds (ostraca) discovered by Reisner thus belong to the reign of Jeroboam II instead of dating from the time of Ahab, nearly a century earlier. This correction has removed a very serious obstacle to clarification of the chronology of Israelite inscriptions.

For the chronology of the second half of Iron II we have valuable evidence from Megiddo and especially from Tell Beit Mirsim. The dating of Strata III and II at Megiddo was perhaps unavoidably confused by the excavators, as they dealt with bewildering complexes of walls and repairs, whose intricate combinations made it difficult to attribute given loci and their contents to a given stratum. They made the further mistake of disregarding the clear-cut evidence of documentary sources, according to which Megiddo was in the territory devastated by the Assyrian troops of Tiglath-pileser III in 733 and was then made the capital of a new Assyrian province, two governors of which are mentioned by name in the Assyrian inscriptions. This means that Megiddo was almost certainly destroyed in 733 and rebuilt shortly afterwards. The contents of Stratum III are thus Israelite, not Assyrian. On the other hand, Stratum II was Assyrian, not Israelite; it was probably destroyed in 609, after the defeat of Josiah by Necho at the Battle of Megiddo. Tell Beit Mirsim is one of scores of large and small Jewish towns which were destroyed by the Chaldaeans in 597 and 587 B.C., after which the land lay fallow, with little or no sedentary population, until the late sixth century. The top stratum at Tell Beit Mirsim is fortunately very well preserved; the houses of the last decades before the Chaldaean conquest were found full of pottery and other objects, little of which had been removed before the town was given over to the flames by the victors. Since a great deal of lime was calcined in the process and the site was never again occupied, it is not surprising that 2500 years of winter rains, drenching every object left exposed, had covered almost every vase and potsherd with a tenacious crust of lime. This made it virtually impossible to recover any ostraca which may have been left at Tell Beit Mirsim by the contemporaries of Jeremiah. However, the great abundance of exactly dated pottery from the last decade or two of the First Temple, fully published in photographs and drawings (Fig. 36), fixes ceramic chronology precisely for this period. Between the fall of Israelite Samaria and the last phase of Tell Beit Mirsim there is a time of some uncertainty at the end of the eighth and the beginning of the seventh century, but finds in different places are gradually stabilizing our chronology of its pottery, too.

Our knowledge of the material culture of Iron II is also vastly greater than it was two decades ago. Here again our information comes chiefly from Samaria, Megiddo, Lachish, Tell Beit Mirsim, and Tell en-Nasbeh, though valuable finds and corroboratory evidence have come from a score of other large and small sites containing Iron Age remains (Figs. 37, 38).

The most exciting finds from Iron II are probably inscrip-

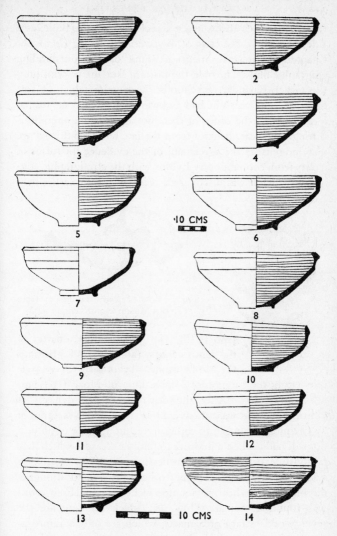

FIG. 36. Wheel-burnished bowls of seventh–sixth century B.C. from Tell Beit Mirsim.

tions, since they throw more direct light on the Bible, as a rule, than any other class of discoveries. Leaving details for Chapter 8, we may mention some of the outstanding epigraphic finds. The oldest important Israelite inscription is the Gezer Calendar, a schoolboy's exercise tablet of soft limestone, on which he had awkwardly scratched the text of a ditty giving the order of the chief agricultural operations through the year. It dates from the late tenth century, if we may judge from the agreement of the evidence for forms of letters from contemporary Byblus with the stratigraphic context in which it was discovered; it is thus a little earlier than

Fig. 37. Bowl of steatite incense pipe from Tell Beit Mirsim (eighth century B.C.).

Iron II (Pl. 29). To the third quarter of the ninth century (about 825 B.C.) belongs the Mesha Stone, a beautifully carved stele celebrating the triumph of Mesha, king of Moab (II Kings iii, 4), over Israel after the downfall of the dynasty of Omri. This stele was discovered in 1868 and was brought by Clermont-Ganneau to the Louvre, though not until local nomads had broken it in order to find the treasure which they fatuously expected to find inside the stone (Fig. 39). Not a single Israelite stele has hitherto been discovered, though a fragment of one bearing a single well-carved Hebrew word was found at Samaria (Fig. 40). Next in date are the seventy-odd ostraca of Samaria, which are only administrative dockets, but which throw a great deal of unexpected light on the history of Israel in the early eighth century B.C.

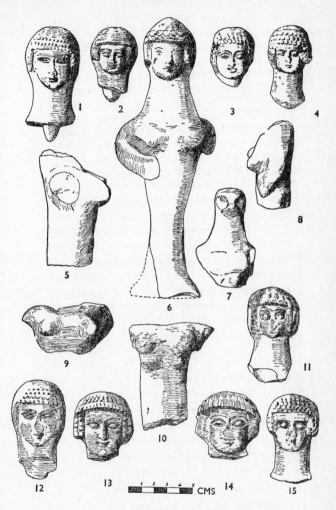

Fig. 38. Amulet figurines of the *dea nutrix* from Tell Beit Mirsim
(mostly from the seventh century B.C.).

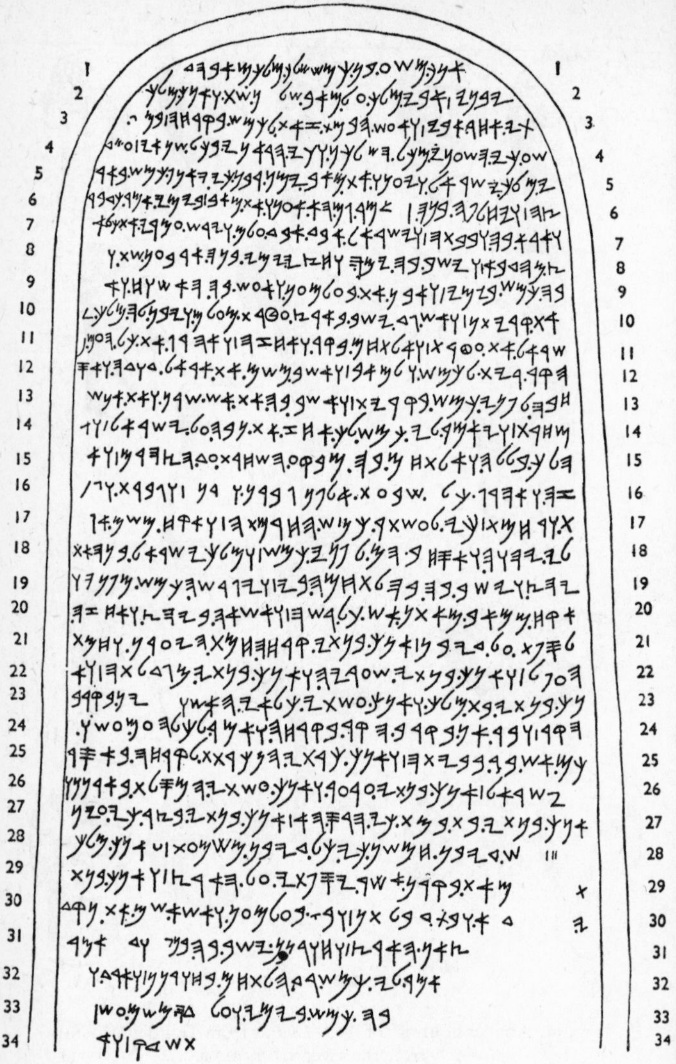

Fig. 39. Stele of Mesha, King of Moab (*c*. 835 B.C.).

(see above). To the end of the eighth century belongs a
beautifully carved inscription in the rock at the entrance to

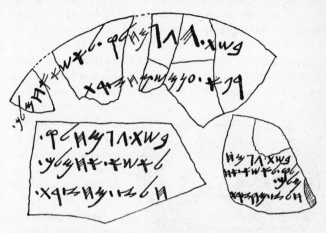

Fig. 40. Hebrew ostraca from Samaria (early eighth century B.C.).

the Siloam Tunnel, cut by Hezekiah through the hill under
the oldest city of Jerusalem (found in 1880); it is written in

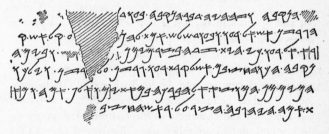

Fig. 41. Siloam Inscription (c. 700 B.C.).

elegant classical Hebrew and describes the successful com-
pletion of the work on the tunnel (Fig. 41).

But these finds, as well as hundreds of short inscriptions
on seals and other objects, pale into insignificance beside the

sensational discovery of the Lachish Ostraca in 1935 and 1938. These twenty-one documents, inscribed in ink on potsherds, belong mostly to the last few months before the capture of Lachish by the Chaldaeans in 589 or 588 B.C. Since language and contents are very closely related to the prose parts of Jeremiah, they are not only of intrinsic historical significance, but they also throw a great deal of light on the Bible. Nearly all the documents are letters, only a few being lists of names or business records. About six letters are almost entirely legible; the rest are virtually useless until they are attacked by someone with experience in microscopy as well as unlimited patience (Pls. 25, 27).

Fig. 42. Seal of Shema, officer of Jeroboam II (*c*. 775 B.C.).

Next in general interest to the inscriptions we may place the quantities of ivory inlay discovered at Samaria by Crowfoot and Sukenik in 1932–3. These ivories fit into a picture now well known from the finds at Megiddo (1937), which belong mostly to the first half of the twelfth century, as well as from similar finds at Nimrud (biblical Calah), mostly from the early ninth century, and Arslan Tash east of Carchemish, from the end of the same century. Fragments have also been found in Crete and elsewhere in the Eastern Mediterranean, while a considerable number were discovered over half a century ago at Carmona in south-western Spain (cf. above). In spite of the fact that virtually no examples have yet been discovered in Phoenicia itself, there can be no doubt that most of them came from Phoenician workshops; the Assyrian examples came largely from Damascus and northern Syria (Fig. 42).

Egyptian influence was dominant; it is easy to show that the Megiddo art arose under the influence of Canaanite imitations of Ramesside originals. The Samaria ivories belong to two groups, which may be provisionally dated to the eighth and ninth centuries respectively, though there is some evidence pointing to the contemporaneity of the groups. The first group consists of ivories carved in extremely low relief, with lavish use of gold foil and insets of lapis lazuli, coloured glass, and coloured paste (powdered glass frit), etc. Motifs are exclusively Egyptian in inspiration, including such mythological figures as Harpocrates on the lotus, Isis and Nephthys adoring the *djed* pillar, Horus holding Truth, etc. (Pl. 24). This group was certainly manufactured in Phoenicia, perhaps in the eighth century. The second group, which closely resembles the ivories from Arslan Tash (late ninth century), has higher relief and little or no inset work; it consists particularly of sphinxes, the lady at the window, lion and bull plaques, etc. This group may have come partly from the region of Damascus, like the Arslan Tash examples. The individual pieces found at Arslan Tash had been used as inlay for a ceremonial bed; one piece bore an inscription mentioning the name of Hazael, king of Damascus in the time of Jehu of Israel. In general the ivories were used as inlay to decorate expensive wooden furniture.

There are a good many excavated remains of fortifications from Iron II, but for lack of space we must limit ourselves to a few examples. The fortifications of Samaria reflect two main periods, that of the Omride Dynasty between *c.* 870 and 842, and that of the Dynasty of Jehu, *c.* 842–744 (Pl. 21). The constructions of the first period, both fortifications and buildings, are definitely superior in execution to those of the second. The acropolis wall from the time of Ahab was a casemate structure; on the north the casemates were long and narrow, with their axes at right angles to the wall, while on the south and west they were of the usual early Iron Age type. The thickness of the former section of the acropolis wall was about 10 metres, of the latter about 5 metres (Fig. 43). The masonry of this period was similar to that of Solomonic Megiddo, but uniformly excellent in quality. Rustic bosses appear in some of the foundations, but they were probably hidden from sight under the surface of the ground.

Remains of a gateway at what must have been the eastern end of Israelite Samaria differ radically from earlier gateways; they seem to reflect an early stage of the indirect-access type of city gate which we find at Tell Beit Mirsim in the seventh and early sixth centuries (Fig. 44). The latest

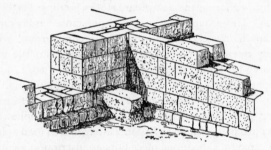

Fig. 43. Israelite masonry at Samaria (ninth century B.C.).

gateway of Lachish shows a similar idea. If this is the case also at Samaria, we have here, perhaps in the eighth century, the first known Palestinian example of this type of gateway, still familiar from the Damascus Gate in Jerusalem. Intermediate in date are the gates of Tell en-Nasbeh and Megiddo III. The former, which appears to date from the ninth century B.C., is a beautiful example of its type, with two pairs of flanking piers instead of the three pairs usually found in gateways of about the tenth century (Fig. 45). The Megiddo gateway, from the eighth century, also has two pairs of flanking piers. The older East Gate of Tell Beit Mirsim resembled the Tell en-Nasbeh gateway closely in plan, and probably dated also from the ninth century B.C. The type in question was common at about the same time in northern Syria; we cannot yet say which region preceded the other in introducing it. A very interesting feature of the Tell en-Nasbeh gateway is the presence of long stone benches in the partly enclosed area just outside the gate, where we may easily imagine

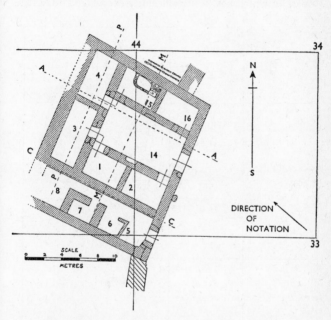

Fig. 44. West Gate-tower of Tell Beit Mirsim (early sixth century B.C.).

the elders of the town sitting and transacting business on cool summer evenings. At the West Gate of Tell Beit Mirsim we discovered that the northern part of the gate tower contained a rectangular court, entered through a wide doorway from the interior of the town. This open, lime-paved court gave access to six paved rooms, each provided with a stout door which could be barred to protect the person occupying it at night. Wall cupboards, a built-in basin for washing, and other conveniences suggested at once that this was the official guest-house of the pre-exilic Jewish town; the discovery of standard weights in it seems to prove that among the guests were merchants or tax-collectors, or both.

Tell Beit Mirsim is still the only town of the late Divided Monarchy which has been sufficiently excavated to lay bare

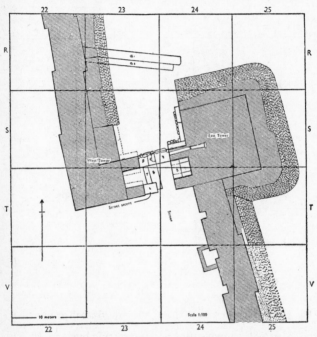

Fig. 45. City gate of Tell en-Nasbeh (ninth century B.C.).

extensive areas of private houses in a good state of preservation (Pl. 28). This makes it possible to draw an accurate picture of the way in which people lived in a small town of the time of Jeremiah (Pl. 22; Fig. 46).

It has often been assumed by radical critics of biblical history that there was no drastic break in the continuity of life in Judah as a result of the Chaldaean invasion. C. C. Torrey, in particular, has denied the historicity of the account of the Captivity in Kings, Ezekiel, and Ezra. After the shock of the Babylonian invasion the natives are supposed to have returned from their temporary hiding-places to their old homes, which were rebuilt if they had been destroyed. If these scholars are right only a few of the nobles were taken into exile, and even Jerusalem was quickly reoccupied and reconstructed. The account of the Restoration in Ezra is, according to Torrey, quite apocryphal. Here we shall not

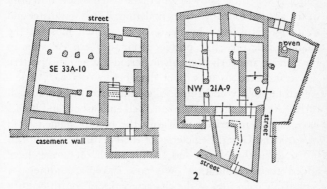

Fig. 46. Typical private houses from pre-exilic Tell Beit Mirsim.

attempt to go into details; it is enough in this connexion to say that a fair number of towns and fortresses of Judah have now been excavated in whole or in part; many other sites have been carefully examined to determine the approximate date of their last destruction. The results are uniform and conclusive: many towns were destroyed at the beginning of the sixth century B.C. and never again occupied; others were destroyed at that time and partly reoccupied at some later date; still others were destroyed and reoccupied after a long period of abandonment, marked by a sharp change of stratum and by intervening indications of use for non-urban purposes. There is not a single known case where a town of Judah proper was continuously occupied through the exilic period. Just to point the contrast, Bethel, which lay just outside the northern boundary of Judah in pre-exilic times, was not destroyed at that time, but was continuously occupied down into the latter part of the sixth century.

IRON III
c. 550–330 B.C.

Until recently the pottery of Iron III (Babylonian and Persian periods) was little known, and the archaeological obscurity of the age led to many errors in dating. Thus Macalister and Watzinger, followed by many others, dated most of the characteristic pre-exilic pottery from southern Palestine in the Persian and early Hellenistic periods. When this pottery was transferred to its proper date before 587 B.C., it left something of a void behind. Since then excavations at such early post-exilic sites as Beth-zur, Tell en-Nasbeh, and Bethel have helped materially to clarify the picture gained from Samaria and Gezer. Cemeteries of the Persian period at Tell el-Far'ah in the Negeb and 'Athlit south of Carmel have added their clarification. We now have, accordingly, a reasonably clear idea of the characteristics of fourth-century pottery. However, it is still uncertain just where the gap between the Iron III pottery of sixth-century Bethel and typical Persian pottery lay. The importance of this question lies mainly in the chronology of occupation, not so much in fixing the date of buildings or of art objects, which can as a rule be established by other criteria. Moreover, coins began to appear in the fifth century, and by the third century B.C. they had become abundant in excavated sites.

To judge from the results of excavations, the resettlement of Judah was a slow process, and it was not until the third century B.C. that the country recovered anything like its old density of population. The Persian authorities allowed the people of Palestine a good deal of autonomy. For example, the high priests of Judah, like the contemporary high priests of Atargatis at Hierapolis in northern Syria, received permission to strike their own coinage and levy their own temple taxes. Silver coins, struck in imitation of Attic drachmas, but with the Hebrew or Aramaic inscription *Yehud*, 'Judah', are being found in increasing numbers. Jar-stamps of the Persian and early Hellenistic periods bear the words *Yehud* or *Yerushalem*; others bear the enigmatic inscription *M-ts-h*, which has not yet been explained and may be some kind of abbreviated formula.

Greek influence increased steadily throughout this period. In the sixth century B.C. numerous Greek trading posts were established on the coasts of Egypt, Palestine, and Syria; excavations at these sites have brought quantities of Ionian and Attic black-figured pottery to light. At Tell en-Nasbeh a fine example of Clazomenian ware, unhappily broken, from the late sixth century was discovered. After the beginning of the fifth century Attic red-figured ware replaced Ionian and black-figured ware and soon became one of the most popular imports into the country; vases and sherds turn up in every excavated site of this period. We have hinted above at the importance of the Attic currency, which became the standard medium of exchange in Palestine more than a century and a quarter before the Macedonian conquest. Attic coins were locally imitated in the second half of the fifth century, and in the following century we find all sorts of barbaric modifications of the figures on the drachma, the owl of Athena being kept until it became unrecognizable.

The growth of Greek commercial relations with Palestine is paralleled and supplemented by a corresponding development of South Arabian trade. Relations with South Arabia are best illustrated by finds in such places as Jemmeh in the Negeb and Gezer in the coastal plain of Sharon. At all these places a characteristic class of objects, during the Babylonian and Persian periods, is formed by cuboid limestone altars of incense, standing on four short legs and with a shallow trough on top. The sides are elaborately decorated with incised geometrical patterns and rude drawings of desert flora and fauna, including especially palm trees, camels, wild goats, antelopes, and wild asses. At Hureidha in Hadhramaut, at the extreme southern end of Arabia, Miss Caton Thompson

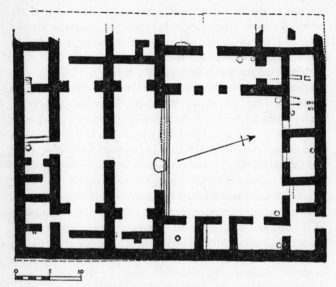

Fig. 47. Persian palace at Lachish (*c.* 400 B.C.).

has lately excavated a temple of the moon-god from the Persian period. In it she found a series of these altars, closely resembling the examples from Jemmeh. Any doubt about their function has been removed by her discovery of remains of a fragrant resinous substance in one of them. Slightly later altars of incense of the same general form, previously found, bear inscriptions in South Arabic listing the different kinds of incense (including balsam and spikenard) which were to be used. By this time Arab nomads had taken over most of southern Transjordan and the Negeb of Palestine; Minaean commerce was at its height, and Minaean caravan stations dotted the 1500-mile route from the spice country to Palestine and Egypt. The name of the dominant Arab chieftain in southern Palestine in the age of Nehemiah, Gashmu the Arab (Neh. vi, 1, 6, etc.), has recently been discovered in Lihyanite and Aramaic inscriptions, where he is called 'King of Kedar'.

A few buildings from this period have been excavated; the only one which merits special mention is the Persian villa on the summit of the mound of Lachish (Fig. 47). This structure, from the late fifth or early fourth century B.C., is strongly reminiscent in plan and detail of such early Parthian buildings as the small palace at Nippur in Babylonia, where we have a similar use of courts and columns. Of course, there are differences as well, which are evidently to be explained in part by the discrepancy in time. A good many tombs of the Persian period are now known; they vary greatly in character, but their date is fixed by the contents of the burials in question, which are often very rich. For instance, at Tell el-Far'ah in the Negeb, Petrie discovered a tomb containing a bronze bed and stool in a remarkable state of preservation, together with a beautiful fluted silver bowl and dipper, the handle of which is a slender nude maiden. It was, as usual, dated much too high by Sir Flinders, for when the pieces belonging to the bed were cleaned several incised Aramaic letters of the Persian period were found. J. H. Iliffe's comparative study has proved this date conclusively, and at the same time has established a contemporary date in the Persian period for some cist-graves at Gezer, which Macalister had called 'Philistine'. Such typological comparisons, when systematically and accurately made, yield just as sound results as any stratigraphy.

CHAPTER 7

Palestine in Graeco-Roman Times

—

In this chapter we shall sketch the present state of our knowledge of Palestinian archaeology from Alexander's conquest
in 332 B.C. to the victory of Christianity, early in the fourth
century A.D. Here we have to do with a history which has
never been quite forgotten. Hundreds of extant volumes in
Greek, Latin, Hebrew, and Aramaic describe the history and
culture of those six centuries, which Palestine fully shared
in its capacity as a minor province of the Macedonian and
Roman empires. Thanks to Josephus, the Apocrypha, and
the New Testament, as well as to the Mishnah, the Palestinian
Gemara, and other Jewish works in Hebrew and Aramaic,
we have ample literary information about conditions in
Palestine. However, there remain many obscure areas of this
history to be filled out. Greek papyri have brought us much
information about the state of Palestine under the Lagides
(Ptolemies) of the third century B.C. Nabataean inscriptions
have illuminated the political vicissitudes and the culture of
Transjordan before and after the turn of our era. Jewish
inscriptions in Aramaic and Greek have thrown light on
Jewish history. Greek and Latin inscriptions on coins and
buildings have made it possible to date a great many constructions and to follow the course of public life in otherwise
forgotten details.

Since many of the constructions with which we shall deal
in this chapter have always remained standing, it is sometimes naïvely thought that no further research on them is
necessary. This is not true at all; most of them require extensive clearing before yielding their secrets to the archaeologist.
Moreover, many buildings have been and some still are

erroneously dated; it is only within the past half century that competent scholars have learned to distinguish clearly between Herodian and older (or later) construction, and every new excavation in a Graeco-Roman site makes some readjustment of architectural chronology necessary. While inscriptions and especially coins generally replace pottery in this period, there are many cases in every dig where the humble potsherd yields decisive information bearing on the date of a Graeco-Roman structure (Fig. 48).

When one contrasts the poverty of architectural monuments known to belong to the successors of Alexander in Palestine and Syria with the wealth of such monuments in Egypt and Asia Minor, one is tempted to despair of an adequate archaeological picture of the Hellenistic Age. The situation is, however, by no means desperate. Owing to the continuous intercourse between all parts of the Hellenistic world and especially to the particularly close political and cultural relations between Palestine and Egypt, on the one hand, and Syria and Asia Minor, on the other, a very few architectural monuments from Palestine and Syria assume disproportionate significance. These few provide the concrete evidence from which we can reconstruct the entire picture by analogy, on the well-known principle *ex ungue leonem*, reconstructing something from a fragment by comparing it with another complete object of the same type.

While we have evidence from coins and pottery that many excavated sites were occupied during the time when the Lagides of Egypt ruled Palestine (*c.* 323–200), the only important monuments of the period in Palestine are the painted tombs of Marisa (Sandahanna), from the second half of the third century B.C. These tombs, which were discovered about 1902 and subsequently published by J. P. Peters and H. Thiersch, were excavated from soft limestone rock and decorated for the heads of a Sidonian colony, established here by one Apollophanes about the middle of the third century B.C. The walls were elaborately ornamented with painted designs and scenes; free spaces were occupied by inscriptions and graffiti in Greek. When the tombs were first

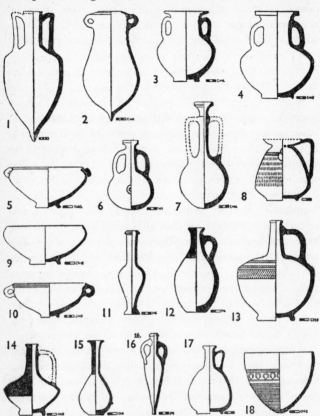

Fig. 48. Hellenistic Pottery in Palestine Museum.

opened the colours were extraordinarily bright; they have now faded away or have been destroyed to such an extent that little remains visible. The contents of frescoes and inscriptions are of considerable historical value; they enable us to describe one phase of the process of Hellenization in some detail. Since Marisa lay in Idumaea, the inscriptions also help us to reconstruct the life and religion of the Edomite settlement in southern Judah. The most interesting painting is a frieze representing a long procession of wild animals, probably based on some book of illustrations of wild life sketched from the famous zoological gardens of Alexandria. Not all of the beasts had, however, been known to the original artist from direct observation, since several of them are quite imaginary. The wealth of material in these tombs was so great that the authors of the official publication failed to discover or to record some of the most important items, including a fairly long Aramaic inscription and two candelabra which throw striking light on the two pillars which stood in front of the Temple of Solomon.

The following Seleucid period is better illustrated by monuments, and the Maccabaean period, which partly overlaps it (165–37 B.C.), is still better represented. The most interesting monument from the period of Seleucid domination is the mausoleum of the Tobiad family (founded by Tobiah the Ammonite, Neh. ii, 19, etc.) at 'Araq el-Emir in central Transjordan. We find there some rock-cut tombs, one of which bears the name 'Tobiah' deeply cut on the rock in Aramaic characters of the third century B.C. This Tobiah was a descendant of Nehemiah's foe and is probably to be identified with the Tubias of the Zeno Papyri from Gerza in the Egyptian Faiyum; Tubias was governor of Ammon just as his ancestor had been two hundred years earlier. Some distance away from this tomb there is a free-standing edifice, built of huge drafted stones in a vigorous early Hellenistic style (Fig. 49). Below the cornice two well-carved lions advance from the left to meet two others coming from the right. The details of the Corinthian capitals seem to preclude a date in the third century and to connect this building with Hyrcanus, the last Tobiad, whose building operations are described by Josephus; the structure would then date from about 175 B.C., just before the beginning of the Maccabaean Age.

The excavations at Samaria have brought to light Hellenistic fortifications which have been rather precisely dated by the most recent work of Crowfoot. The oldest are a series of round towers which were built along the line of the casemate wall of Israelite times (Pl. 23). These towers had been extremely well constructed; they were believed by Reisner to

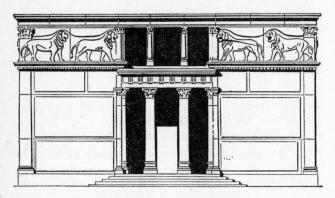

Fig. 49. Façade of Mausoleum at 'Araq el-Emir (c. 175 B.C.).

go back to the eighth century B.C., but Crowfoot and Ben-Dor have successfully established their early Hellenistic date, possibly between 323 and 321 B.C., when Perdiccas is said by Eusebius to have rebuilt Samaria. Perhaps a century and a half later, during the wars between the Seleucids and the Maccabees, was constructed a massive fortress with walls about 4 metres thick, dated by Reisner erroneously in the sixth century B.C.

The most interesting Maccabaean remains hitherto found in Palestine are at Beth-zur, commanding the north–south road from Jerusalem to Hebron at the boundary between

Judaea and Idumaea. Excavated by O. R. Sellers with the
writer's assistance (1931), it has yielded very extensive ruins
from this period. On the summit were the foundations of a

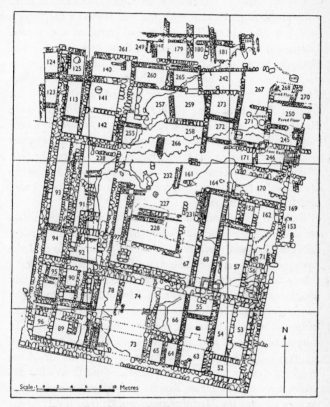

Fig. 50. Foundations of Hellenistic citadel at Beth-zur.

large fortress, showing three different periods of construction, all of which had unfortunately been destroyed to below
floor-level, a fact which made precise dating difficult (Fig. 50).
Fortunately, nearly 300 coins were discovered during the ex-

cavation; some 126 of them bear the names of Antiochus Epi-
phanes (175–164 B.C.) and his son Antiochus Eupator (164–
162). The evidence of the coins strikingly parallels that from
the First Book of Maccabees, in which Beth-zur is often
mentioned in connexion with the war between the Syrians
and the Maccabees. The excavators referred the second
fortress to the Macedonian general, Bacchides, who fortified
Beth-zur about 161 B.C. (I Macc. ix, 52), but Watzinger has
called attention to the Oriental character of its plan, differing sharply from the Hellenistic plan of the third and last
fortress. He is probably right in referring the third fortress to
Bacchides, in which case the second fortress must have been
built by Judas Maccabaeus between 165 and 163, as expressly
stated several times by First Maccabees. The first fortress,
which was preserved only in fragments, would then go
back to the Persian period, when relations between Judah
and Idumaea were tense.

Beth-zur, Gezer, and Marisa all exhibit interesting remains
of this period. At Beth-zur were found houses and shops,
fortifications and reservoirs; at Gezer were discovered the
ruins of a fortress of Simon Maccabaeus; Marisa yielded a
whole town of the period, with streets and houses built
according to Hellenistic principles (with streets running as
nearly as practicable at right angles, forming regular blocks
of houses) (Fig. 51). Among the most interesting small finds,
outside of coins, at Beth-zur were scores of stamped Rhodian
jar-handles, each bearing the name of the potter or of the
magistrate of the year. These jar-handles come from wine-jars
which were exported from Rhodes and other Aegean vintage
centres all over the Mediterranean world; they testify to the
presence of a Greek garrison in the Maccabaean Age. Some
two thousand Rhodian and other stamped Greek jar-handles
have been found at Samaria, which was, of course, a Hellenistic city. Miss Virginia Grace is at present engaged in preparing a corpus of the scores of thousands of jar-handle

stamps so far recovered from ancient sites all over the ancient world; if she can fix their dates with sufficient accuracy, these handles may become as important as coins for dating purposes. In this connexion it is important to realize that coins may throw light on many phases of ancient history.

Fig. 51. Plan of Hellenistic town of Marisa (second century B.C.).

For instance, at the three towns mentioned at the beginning of this paragraph the series of Jewish coins comes to an end about 100 B.C. This fact proves that the three towns were abandoned soon after Alexander Jannaeus * had conquered all Palestine and it became unnecessary to maintain strong

* Jannaeus (reigned 104-78 B.C.) was the most aggressive of the Jewish kings of the Maccabaean dynasty.

garrisons at these points; pottery evidence confirms the evidence of coins. The fact that not a single example of the bronze coins attributed to Simon Maccabaeus (143–135 B.C.) was found in any of the three towns is thus decisive confirmation of the views of scholars who had referred them to the end of the First Revolt.

In 37 B.C. the Maccabees were replaced by the Herodian Dynasty, whose first king, Herod the Great (37–4 B.C.), was a great builder and a lover of Greek culture. Under Herod we find the fullest flowering of Hellenistic architecture in Palestine, at the beginning of the last century of the Second Temple. His capital was Jerusalem, which he fortified and where he carried out his most imposing building operations. So completely did his constructions efface all signs of earlier building that no certain traces of the Temple of Solomon or of any older fortifications (except on the Ophel Hill) have so far been recovered by archaeologists. Thanks to the work of the Palestine Exploration Fund (see Chapter 2), continued on a much more scientific basis by C. N. Johns and other officials of the Palestine Department of Antiquities, it is now possible to combine the detailed descriptions of Josephus with the actual finds. Almost the whole length of the Herodian First Wall of Jerusalem can be traced and remains of the Herodian masonry identified. The finest example of Herodian masonry with marginal draft outside of the retaining wall of the Temple enclosure appears in the so-called Tower of David at the Jaffa Gate. The substructure of this tower represents either Hippicus or Phasael, probably the latter. The problem of the Second Wall of Herod, which protected the exposed northern side of the city, is still unsettled; most scholars identify this line of wall with Herodian traces which would seem to enclose an area between David Street and the Holy Sepulchre, leaving the latter outside the wall. However, it is still possible that Herodian stones built into the Hadrianic line of wall, now represented by the northern wall of Turkish Jerusalem, belong to a system of fortifications which ran along the latter line and thus represents the Second Wall, leaving the Holy Sepulchre inside the wall.

The splendid masonry of the great retaining wall of the Temple esplanade was believed to be Solomonic when it was first partly cleared down to bed-rock by Sir Charles Warren. Even to-day some writers take this for granted, and there are still a few specialists who believe that Warren did uncover fragments of the Solomonic structure. In the author's opinion this is most improbable; the Herodian builders went down into the native rock for their foundations, which had to sustain a tremendous thrust from the weight of heavy construction and filling inside the retaining wall. Even if Solomon's architects could have planned and built so massive a structure, there would have been no object in such a grandiose enterprise at that time; the First Temple was certainly not designed to be a centre of religious pilgrimage for multitudes, as was the case in the time of Herod. It is a pity that scarcely a single fragment of the Temple of Herod itself has been preserved. Only two chance finds can be referred with confidence to it: a complete and a partial example of a Greek inscription warning Gentiles not to enter the precincts of the Temple. Even these presumably belong to the last decades of the Second Temple, not to the beginning of our era.

If the debris under modern Jerusalem could be completely removed we should doubtless learn a great deal about the buildings of Herod which were standing in the time of Christ. The elusive problem of the location of Pilate's Praetorium has already been settled in favour of the Tower of Antonia, which Père Vincent has recently reconstructed from remains in various excavations in the vicinity of the north-western corner of the Temple Enclosure, against the alternative site near the Jaffa Gate and the adjacent Palace of Herod under the Armenian Garden (which has not yet been excavated). But after the meagre results obtained by the ex-

cavations of Captain Raymond Weill and R. A. S. Macalister
on Ophel and the much more extensive clearances of Père
Germer-Durand on the Western Hill (the traditional Zion),
it does not seem probable that excavations in Jerusalem
would bring many results of great historical importance.
Scientifically directed soundings and clearances like those of
C. N. Johns and R. W. Hamilton, along the lines of ancient
walls and inside building complexes, offer by far the most
promise, since the objectives are well defined and quite
attainable with modern archaeological technique.

Though a Jew by religion, Herod the Great was of Idu-
maean (Edomite) stock. When John Hyrcanus compelled the
Idumaeans to accept circumcision and adopt the Jewish
faith, three generations earlier, he was dealing with a people
which already considered itself as sharing the Patriarchs
Abraham and Isaac with Israel as common ancestors of both;
the Idumaeans rapidly became the most fanatical of all Jewish
groups. It is not surprising, therefore, that Herod was interested in such holy places as Hebron (Machpelah) and
Mamre (Abraham's Oak), which had long been sacred to
both peoples. The evidence of the unmistakably Herodian
drafted masonry of the great Haram at Hebron, as well as
the presence of numerous Herodian stones in Roman walls
at Haram Ramet el-Khalil, two miles north of Hebron, is
sufficient to establish their Herodian origin, in spite of the
absence of direct literary corroboration. Moreover, there are
definite stratigraphic indications of a Herodian phase of
construction at the latter place.

Josephus tells us at some length about Herod's building
operations at Samaria. The investigations of Crowfoot have
greatly reduced the amount of standing masonry which can
be attributed to the time of Herod, but what is left is very
respectable in quantity as well as superior in quality. However, most of the Herodian work at Samaria falls below the
high standards which we find in Jerusalem and Hebron. To

Herod belongs much of the Roman city wall of Sebaste, the podium (platform) on which the Augusteum (temple of Augustus) was erected, and probably the Doric stadium (which may be a few decades older). Most of the early building remains now standing above ground belong to the period between A.D. 120 and 230; see below.

Several of the finest tombs outside the wall of Jerusalem belong to the time of Herod the Great. An Aramaic inscription on the so-called Tomb of St James mentions several members of the priestly order of Bene Hezir (I Chron. xxiv, 15), three of whom seem to have been high priests in the reign of Herod. The adjacent 'Pyramid of Zacharias' would then be their monument, just as the Tomb of Absalom is the funerary monument belonging to the 'Tomb of Jehoshaphat'. Both the architectural decoration and the epigraphy of the inscription point to the reign of Herod.

In 1950–51 J. L. Kelso and J. B. Pritchard excavated Herodian building remains overlooking the Wadi Qelt, south of modern Jericho. Here Kelso cleared elaborate constructions belonging to the winter palace of Herod, which proved to be similar in masonry and art to Augustan work in Italy.

Herodian fortresses and constructions are scattered over Palestine, often in the most inaccessible places, such as his palace on the summit of Masada, overlooking the Dead Sea from the west. Little easier of access were also the castle of Machaerus, on the eastern side of the Dead Sea, and Alexandrium on the summit of Qarn Sartabeh in the central Jordan Valley. Best known to the public is the isolated summit of Frank Mountain, south-east of Bethlehem. None of these fortresses has been excavated, and the cost of excavation might well be quite out of proportion to the meagreness of the results. The ruins of the palace on Masada were surveyed by Adolf Schulten in 1932. One wonders, in less objective mood, whether it was Herod's conscience which drove him to seek refuge in ever more inaccessible strongholds from the ghosts of those he had so brutally murdered as well as from the living avengers of the dead.

After the death of the tyrant seventy-three years were to pass before the final catastrophe. To this period belong in particular the Third Wall of Jerusalem and the later tombs. The Third Wall was begun by Herod Agrippa and finished by the Jews during the First Revolt, A.D. 66–70. In 1838 Edward Robinson observed traces of a massive wall some distance north of the north wall of the Turkish City, and in 1841 he published his discovery of the Third Wall; in the same year Alderson made an independent and much more accurate plan of the same traces. For decades thereafter a debate raged with regard to the line of Robinson and Alderson, which was defended by such American scholars as Selah Merrill and Lewis B. Paton, but rejected by nearly all competent specialists, including such weighty names as G. A. Smith, Gustav Dalman, and especially L. H. Vincent. However, from 1925 to 1940 a series of accidental discoveries followed by systematic excavations under the direction of E. L. Sukenik and L. A. Mayer led to the recovery of almost the entire north line of this wall, leaving still only partly filled gaps at both ends. The masonry is exceedingly uneven, ranging all the way from superb drafted stones in the best Herodian tradition to great unfinished blocks packed with comparatively small stones. The location and course of the wall agree remarkably well with Josephus' detailed description. M. Solomiac has demonstrated that Robinson's description and Alderson's plan fit into the picture so perfectly that there can be little doubt that we now have almost the entire length of the Third Wall accounted for.

Around Jerusalem are a great many Jewish tombs of this period, and new ones come to light every little while. Some of these tombs are architectural monuments, like the Mausoleum of Queen Helena of Adiabene, cleared by F. de Saulcy in 1850 and 1863 (see Chapter 2), and the Tomb of the

Judges; both of these tombs date from the last few decades of the Second Temple. Many of them are comparatively uninteresting in themselves, but even they furnish elements in a whole chapter of architecture and art which remains to be written adequately. The most interesting objects found in unopened tombs are the caskets of limestone (ossuaries) in which the bones of a deceased person were collected after the flesh had decomposed. Many of these ossuaries bear short inscriptions in Greek and Aramaic naming the deceased and sometimes giving a few details about him (or her). E. L. Sukenik has made himself the leading authority on the Jewish tombs and ossuaries of Jerusalem, whose number he has doubled by his own excavations and researches. The ossuary inscriptions, now numbering in the hundreds, have considerable historical value for students of the New Testament in spite of their brevity.

The following anecdotal excerpt from the history of this branch of archaeological investigation will probably convey more about its nature and results than several paragraphs of description. In 1926 Dr L. A. Mayer (then on the staff of the Department of Antiquities) cleared a Jewish tomb southwest of Jerusalem and found a number of ossuaries with Aramaic inscriptions, which were published in 1928 by Dr Sukenik. On one ossuary the latter read and translated: 'Dositheus our father and for his widow'. However, in order to get the rendering 'and for his widow', which is itself illogical and strange in this context, he had to read the Hebrew word *almanah* instead of the Aramaic *armalta*. The mixture of languages would be very unusual. In December of the same year Père Savignac of the Dominican École Biblique in Jerusalem presented a paper at a meeting of the Palestine Oriental Society in which he discussed the script of this inscription and proposed another reading for the last word, reading two letters differently in order to obtain it. Though the reading was epigraphically better than Sukenik's and has turned out subsequently to be right, the proper name read by Savignac was otherwise unknown. Sukenik thereupon defended his own interpretation with vigour, pointing out how peculiar such a name would be. Immediately afterwards the late Avinoam Yellin arose and proposed that Père Savignac's reading be adopted and that the letters be read as an Aramaic phrase, *we-la le-miftah*, 'and do not open!' This solution was so obviously correct that it was accepted on the spot by nearly every philologian present. Sukenik took somewhat longer to convince; since then several examples of the same expression have been discovered in tomb inscriptions, two of them by Sukenik himself. In 1931, while studying the collections made many years before in the Russian archaeological museum on the Mount of Olives, Sukenik discovered a beautifully carved marble slab with an Aramaic inscription; the object had probably been in the museum since before 1894, when the scholar who collected most of the objects died. The inscription was translated, with assistance from I. N. Epstein (one of the foremost Aramaic philologians of our day): 'Hither were brought the bones of Uzziah, king of Judah–do not open!' (Pl. 26). One of the most distinguished authorities objected to the inscription on various grounds, but none of the arguments is valid. Moreover, how could a forger have foreseen the complicated process by which the reading of the final phrase would be established, many years later?

Aside from the remains in Western Palestine belonging to the Herodian and sub-Herodian periods, the most important monuments of greater Palestine come from the Nabataean kingdom in Transjordan, especially from its capital, Petra. Ever since the discovery of Petra by Burckhardt in 1812 it has attracted wide attention, not only from scholars but also from tourists generally. Until after the First World War its inaccessibility limited the number of visitors, at the same time that it enhanced its romantic appeal. The advent of the motor car made it incomparably easier to visit it, and there have been a number of excavations there since 1929 under the direction of George Horsfield, Agnes Conway (later Mrs Horsfield), and Margaret Murray.

Strabo correctly described Petra, towards the end of the first century B.C., as 'a city situated in a valley ... bounded on all sides by cliffs'. Access to it is obtained by a circuitous passage between lofty cliffs, called the Siq. The Siq is 2 kilometres in length and seldom more than 10 metres wide; the cliffs which line it reach a maximum height of 100 metres. The red and brown sandstone cliffs, between which Petra nestles, are lined with tombs, many of them monumental in the fullest sense of the term. Among these magnificent mausolea two stand out by their splendour: el-Khazneh and Qasr Far'on. Both may be dated in or immediately after the reign of the greatest Nabataean king, Aretas IV Philodemus (c. 9 B.C.–A.D. 40), who played much the same role in the modernization and adornment of Petra that his older contemporary, Herod the Great, had played with respect to Jerusalem. The research of such eminent historians of architecture as Wiegand, Wulzinger, and Horsfield has conclusively proved that the principal rock-hewn monuments with architectural façades were mausolea devoted to the memory and the cult of the dead. There is no solid basis for the common explanation of these structures as temples, though some of them naturally contained chapels where the gods were worshipped.

Horsfield's excavations have proved that there were three stages of pre-Byzantine occupation at Petra: an early Nabataean occupation from the fourth century B.C. to the first century B.C.; a classical Nabataean stage from the first century B.C. to the Roman occupation in A.D. 106; a Roman stage in the second and third centuries A.D. Characteristic of the second and early third stages, from about 50 B.C. to about A.D. 200, is the presence of thin, delicately painted

Nabataean ware, which is found in all settlements of this period in southern Transjordan. To the first stage belong many crenellated pylon tombs (with façades like Egyptian pylons surmounted by crowsteps) of mixed Egyptian and

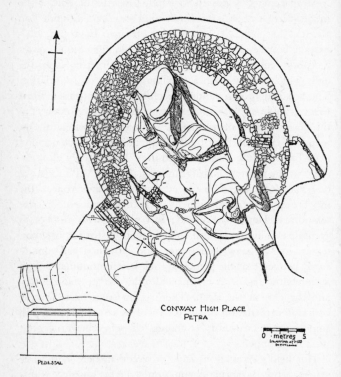

CONWAY HIGH PLACE
PETRA

0 . metres . 5

PEDESTAL

Fig. 52. The Conway High Place at Petra.

Perso-Mesopotamian form; in the second stage the simple pylons are decorated with Hellenistic gables, mouldings, and cornices. Besides these tombs and mausolea, private houses and shrines, including at least one major temple (ed-Deir), were hewn from the soft sandstone. One painted house in Siq el-Barid has been shown by the style of its frescoed walls to belong to the middle of the first century B.C. or a little later.

A unique feature of Petra is constituted by a number of 'high places', open-air sanctuaries of the gods, all going back to the early period of Petra's history. The oldest datable high place was excavated by the present writer in 1934 and named the Conway High Place after its discoverer; it is essentially a circular processional way around a sacred rock. This high place stood on the highest point inside the walled city of Petra; the evidence of pottery and coins shows that it was in use from the first century B.C. or earlier down to Christian times, when it was destroyed (Fig. 52). Since the Nabataeans were an Arab tribe, it is scarcely surprising to find numerous North- and South-Arabic parallels for processional ways around sacred objects. Another class of high places is much more ancient in origin and probably carries on the tradition of ancient Israelite high places more closely than any other extant installations. The first example of this class was discovered by George L. Robinson in 1900; a number of others have been subsequently discovered. The so-called Great High Place of Robinson stands on the highest point of the Zibb 'Atuf ridge, west of the Khazneh and south of the Roman Theatre. The main feature of the high place is a rectangular court sunk about $\frac{1}{2}$ metre into the rock platform and nearly 15 metres long. Just west of the court are two altars, one square and the other round; each is hewn from the solid rock. Two flights of rock-hewn steps lead up to the installation from below (Fig. 53). As with the high places of the Bible, these installations served particularly as places where feasts in honour of the gods could be held on specified occasions, particularly in summer. Near the Great High Place are two obelisks carefully hewn out of the surrounding rock, which was then used for building purposes by the Nabataean inhabitants of Petra. Since at least 6 metres of rock had to be removed over a considerable area in order to expose

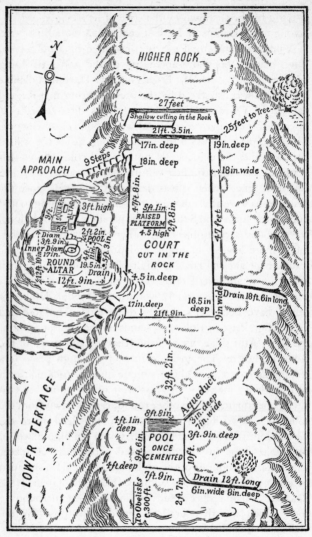

Fig. 53. The Great High Place at Petra.

these free-standing obelisks, it is obvious that they cannot be older than the first century B.C., when the great period of building began. However, the type of sacred pillar which we have at Zibb 'Atuf reflects a much more ancient tradition in Transjordan, going back at least to the last centuries of the third millennium (cf. Chapter 4).

The explorations of Nelson Glueck have shown how thickly the Nabataeans settled in the lands once occupied by Edomites and Moabites, and how intensively they cultivated the soil. He has also excavated a Nabataean sanctuary on the summit of the lofty isolated hill of Jebel et-Tannur, south-east of the southern end of the Dead Sea (1937). Glueck has pointed out several similarities between this complex and the Great High Place at Petra which suggest that the shrine was originally an open-air place like the latter. Just as we found at the Conway High Place at Petra, successive builders were careful to cover up or enlarge, not to destroy, previous installations. The earliest shrine at Tannur is correctly dated by Glueck about the turn of our era; the evidence of pottery and the indirect evidence of a Nabataean inscription seem to be decisive. The second and third sanctuaries were much more elaborate; they were decorated with a wealth of carved figures and designs, many of them of great importance for the history of pagan Syrian iconography in the second and especially the third century A.D., to which they must be dated. As Glueck has correctly seen (despite his dating the second and third shrines too early), the deities worshipped here were the Syrian Zeus-Hadad and Atargatis, not the Nabataean Dusares and his consort Allat, though the two pairs of divinities may well have been identified in actual practice.

The oldest surviving Roman construction in Palestine, after the end of Jewish independence in A.D. 70, are the Roman camp and circumvallation (siege wall) at Masada on the western shore of the Dead Sea, where a group of intransigeant Jewish patriots held out until A.D. 73. These installations were carefully explored in 1932 by a German expedition interested in remains of Roman military works. A similar circumvallation had previously been discovered by Albrecht Alt at Bittir, the site of the last stand of Bar Kokhba, leader of the Second Jewish Revolt about A.D. 135. In this connexion it may be observed that the identification of this site was long disputed, in spite of the identity of the name, chiefly because of the small size of the ruin of Bar Kokhba's fortress, Khirbet el-Yehud. However, the fact that most of the coins of the Second Revolt, where provenience is known, may be traced to Bittir, in conjunction with the existence of the Roman circumvallation, removes all possible doubt about this identification.

The Roman emperor Hadrian determined to do away with political Judaism completely; one of his first steps was to rebuild Jerusalem as a Roman colony, under the name Aelia Capitolina. No Jews were allowed to settle in Aelia, which remained the name of the city down to Arab times. This fact assures the archaeologist that all ancient Jewish tombs at Jerusalem antedate the fall of the Second Temple in A.D. 70. Since the plan of Aelia remained virtually unchanged for centuries, except for the addition of buildings and quarters outside the walls, it has been found quite possible to reconstruct it. It has been supposed that Aelia was unwalled; this was *a priori* improbable, in view of the insecurity of the times, and has been disproved by the latest soundings of R. W. Hamilton. Aelia was not only walled, but there has been little change in the line of city wall since Roman times; the Turkish wall of the early sixteenth century remains substantially a restoration of preceding walls on or beside the old wall of Aelia. This does not mean that there were no modifications of the system of fortifications. For instance, the Byzantine empress Eudocia is said to have constructed a wall to protect the holy places; Bliss thought he had identified the line of the Eudocian wall above the foundations of

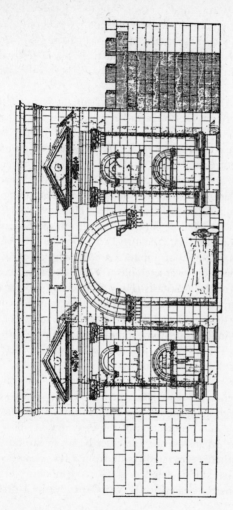

5 metres

Fig. 54. The North Gate of Gerasa, south elevation.

the wall of Herod the Great south of the Ophel and 'Zion' hills. Whether he was correct or not we cannot yet say; Hamilton's soundings at the north wall of the old city of Jerusalem have convinced him that there was a restoration of this wall in the early fourth century A.D., before the time of Eudocia.

Thanks to descriptions and excavations it is possible to reconstruct Aelia Capitolina rather more accurately than is true of Herodian Jerusalem, in spite of the full (though often confusing) accounts of Josephus. There were two principal colonnaded streets at right angles to each other; the most important of them was the present Damascus Road, leading from the Damascus Gate to the Temple Area, along the north–south axis, or *cardo*, of the city. This street is clearly portrayed in the plan of Jerusalem given on the Mosaic of Madeba, from the sixth century A.D. On the site of the Temple was a temple of Jupiter Capitolinus, patron of the city; north-west of it was a temple of Venus, later replaced by the Basilica of the Anastasis (Holy Sepulchre). No trace of these two temples has been discovered; they must have been thoroughly destroyed by the Christians. In most of the excavations in Jerusalem are found tiles stamped with the name of the Tenth Legion (*legio decima Fretensis*), which was long stationed here as a garrison.

While the Hellenistic cities of the Decapolis,* east of Jordan, had been in existence since the first century or two after Alexander's conquest, it was not until Trajan's annexation of the Nabatene and his creation of the Provincia Arabia (A.D. 106) that the expansion of these cities began in earnest. The only city hitherto excavated (aside from a few clearances at 'Amman, Greek Philadelphia) is Gerasa (modern Jerash), which was partly cleared in the years 1925–34 by Horsfield

---

* The Decapolis was a confederation of (theoretically) ten Greek cities, among which were Damascus, Gadara, Gerasa, Philadelphia, as well as one city, Scythopolis (Beth-shan), west of the Jordan.

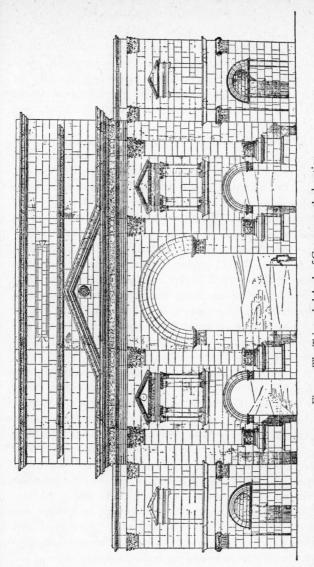

o̶—̶—̶—̶—̶—̶—̶ 5 metres

Fig. 55. The Triumphal Arch of Gerasa, south elevation.

and the members of the Anglo-American excavation successively directed by Crowfoot, Fisher, and McCown. The city
was bisected, from north to south, by a colonnaded street
along the cardo, the well-preserved pavement of which has
been cleared for almost the entire length of the street. At the
northern end was the monumental North Gate (Fig. 54),
built by Trajan in A.D. 115. At the extreme south end, beyond the South Gate, Hadrian built a Triumphal Arch (Fig.
55) in A.D. 130; however, the expected incorporation of this
structure into a new line of wall, enclosing a new quarter,
failed to materialize. The principal building of the city was
the majestic temple of Artemis (Fig. 56), in honour of the
patron-goddess of Gerasa; work on it must have lasted for
decades before and after A.D. 150, when the massive Pro-
pylaea of the temple were dedicated. Second to the temple of
Artemis was the impressive temple of Zeus, erected about
A.D. 163 (Fig. 57). The Antonine period, in which these
splendid temples were built, was in many respects the most
flourishing age of pagan Syria and Palestine. For lack of
space we must pass over the hippodrome and theatres, as well
as other buildings in Gerasa from the second and third centuries A.D.

The remaining cities of the Decapolis contain many Roman
structures, but few of those still above ground approach the
size of those at Gerasa. Outside of the Decapolis in Samaria,
we find a series of elaborate building projects from the late
Antonine and the Severan period, c. A.D. 180–230, according
to Crowfoot. To this period belong the east–west colonnaded
street (formerly thought to be Herodian), the forum colon-
nades, and the Roman basilica, as well as the Corinthian
Stadium. All are built of the same material and in the same
architectural style, proved by details of the Corinthian capitals to belong to the age in question. Coins show that
Samaria became Sebaste under Severus, a fact which explains
this sudden activity in construction; the change in status was

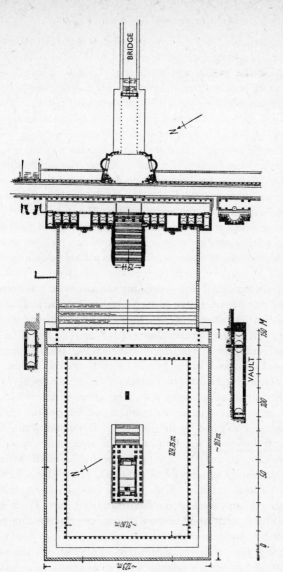

Fig. 56. The Artemis Temple complex at Gerasa.

evidently favoured by the Roman emperor, and the cost was defrayed from the imperial treasury.

During the second and third centuries A.D. a period of synagogue building began, after the general destruction of synagogues in connexion with the two Jewish revolts. Until the work of Kohl and Watzinger, followed more recently by Sukenik, who is now *facile princeps* in this field, it was believed by many scholars that some of the ruined synagogues of Galilee went back to the time of Christ, before the First Revolt. There can no longer be any doubt that this view was wrong and that no standing ruins can be dated before the Antonine period, at the very earliest. The synagogues of Palestine which have hitherto been discovered and cleared belong to two principal phases, the second of which began in the first half of the fourth century, when Rabbi Abun gave official permission to have mosaics representing living creatures introduced into synagogue construction. It is noteworthy that this statement of the Jerusalem Talmud had been lost until 1931, when I. N. Epstein published an early manuscript from Leningrad containing it.

The institution of synagogues may be traced back through archaeological finds in Egypt and Delos to the third century B.C.; we may rest assured that there were synagogues in Palestine at an even earlier date. The oldest archaeological trace of a synagogue in Palestine is an inscription from Jerusalem, published by its discoverer, Raymond Weill, in 1920; it mentions the building of a synagogue by one 'Theodotus, son of Vettenus, priest and chief of the synagogue'. Since Theodotus had obviously received his name from the Roman family of the Vetteni (*gens Vettena*), he or an ancestor must have been a freedman from Italy. There is, accordingly, very good reason to connect this synagogue with the Synagogue of the Freedmen, mentioned in Acts vi, 9 among the strongest supporters of Jewish orthodoxy against St Stephen. Synagogues began as rooms in private

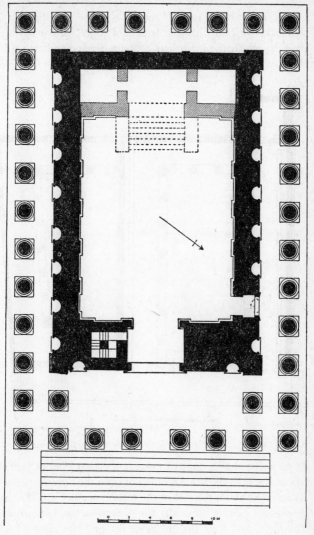

Fig. 57. The Temple of Zeus at Gerasa.

houses, as we know from Dura and elsewhere; in Palestine, however, we find only the later and more formal basilica style, in which the main hall contains a nave and two side aisles, separated by two rows of columns.

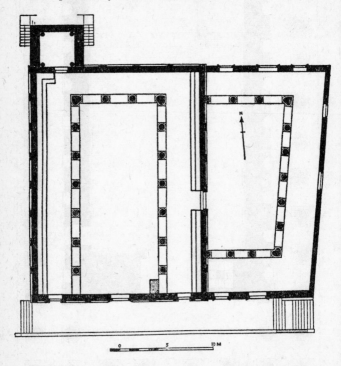

Fig. 58. The Synagogue of the third century A.D. at Capernaum.

As noted above, none of the extant synagogues of Galilee are earlier than the late Antonine or even the Severan period, somewhere about the end of the second century A.D. To this first phase belong especially the synagogues at Capernaum, Chorazin, and Kefr Bir'im. Since the first two towns both figure prominently in the Gospels, it is a pity that no earlier

remains have yet been discovered. It is by no means unlikely
that there are foundations of an older synagogue under the
ruins of the third-century synagogue of Capernaum, but no
one is likely to pull down this splendid structure on the
chance of finding inferior remains beneath it. The excavation
of the synagogue at Capernaum was begun by two German
archaeologists, Kohl and Watzinger, in 1905, and was completed in 1926 by the Franciscan fathers who own the site;
it has been partly restored and is one of the most satisfying

Fig. 59. The Kefr Bir'im Synagogue, restored.

places to visit in all Palestine (Figs. 58, 59). The synagogue
was well built of white limestone, contrasting vividly with
the black lava of which the surrounding houses were constructed. The main hall is rectangular, nearly 25 metres in
length and three-fourths as wide; east of it is a colonnaded
court. The building was elaborately decorated with carved-
stone ornament; its walls may have been covered originally
with painted frescoes like the walls of the nearly contemporary
Dura synagogue. The latter, constructed in A.D. 244, was
found almost intact by the Franco-American expedition which
excavated it in 1932; its richly painted walls have yielded a

wealth of material for historians of art. The Dura Synagogue, with the aid of data from the tombs of the Catacombs in Rome and the third–fourth century necropolis at Beth-shearim (Sheikh Abreik) in Palestine, has already demonstrated the previously unsuspected extent of early Christian dependence on Jewish art of the Roman period. Here again archaeology proves the correctness of the old philosophical adage, *natura non facit saltum*; there is a continuity in all the apparent discontinuity of history. It is a far cry from the art of the Ghassulian to the art of the Jewish synagogues of Galilee, but a clue of Ariadne runs through the labyrinth; the archaeologist's task is to find this clue!

CHAPTER 8

Peoples and Languages, Writing and Literature
in Ancient Palestine

—

SINCE Palestine is a bridge between continents, its population has always been mixed; it is improbable that there has ever been a period since the early Palaeolithic in which different physical types and languages were not represented. It is, therefore, even more difficult to determine national and cultural ties by physical criteria in Palestine than elsewhere in the world. This is still true of modern Palestine, where Arab and Jew, though differing radically in culture and national identity, are in part almost identical in physical type and are in general subject to much the same physical variations, while their languages are little farther apart than French and Italian. To be sure, we find certain physical types dominant in one period and certain others dominant in the next. Thus, for example, the long-headed (dolichocephalic) type which had been in the ascendancy in Early Bronze Megiddo was displaced in the Middle Bronze by prevailing broad-headedness (brachycephaly). In other parts of the country, however, there may have been a different situation, so it is scarcely safe to speak of any one type as representative.

The linguistic situation is much simpler, since language has always been a primary indication of belonging to a given national culture, while shape of skull and colour of hair are usually meaningless in this respect. Our evidence for the language of any period is derived from different sources. The actual speech of a people is not necessarily the same as the language of its formal written documents, so one cannot always assume that the spoken language was the same as that of the inscriptions which are found in any special region or period. For example, about 1400 B.C. Babylonian cuneiform was the language of official documents in Palestine. Yet it is certain (see below) that the people did not speak Babylonian. In the Nabatene about the time of Christ all inscriptions are in standard Aramaic, but since the personal and tribal names found in them are Arabic, it is certain that the Nabataeans spoke Arabic. Virtually no Aramaic inscriptions are found in Palestine and Syria in the third and second centuries B.C. (see below), yet we know from many clear indications that the people spoke Aramaic, several dialects of which emerged triumphant over Greek at the end of the age of Greek ascendancy.

The evidence of place-names and personal names is of primary importance in determining what languages were spoken in different periods. Palestine contains a stratified succession of place-names; every phase of linguistic domination down to Modern Hebrew is represented. Since place-names are exceedingly tenacious, as Edward Robinson discovered more than a century ago (Chapter 2), each period of settlement is likely to leave a deposit of place-names. The oldest names are those of rivers and mountains, as a rule; in Palestine the names which they bore in the earliest historical tradition are all demonstrably or probably Semitic – but of archaic types which do not always lend themselves to obvious linguistic interpretation. Semitic are the names of Lebanon (*Labnan*) and Antilibanus (*Sharyan*), of Carmel and probably of Tabor, of Gilboa and Gilead. Equally Semitic are the names of Jordan and Yarmuk, Jabbok and Arnon. It is true that the name of Tabor has been combined with that of Mount Atabyrion on Rhodes, while the name of the Jordan sounds like that of the supposed streams called *Iardanos* in the Iliad and Odyssey. However, the passages in question are very obscure and the alleged *streams* have never been identified, while a mythical *prince* by that name is well attested.

Moreover, the name 'Jordan' has a perfectly good Semitic form and etymology.

If we turn to names of towns, we find that all the preserved names of Palestinian places inhabited in the fourth and third millennia B.C. are Semitic, or at least have that appearance; the difference between early Semitic and non-Semitic place-names is easy to recognize when one moves into northern Syria. Then come Canaanite and Amorite names from the second millennium, mostly old tribal names of transparently Semitic origin; to this stage belong, for example, the names ending in 'ammu, 'people', such as 'Ibleam' and 'Jokneam'. Both millennia share names of towns derived from shrines which stood there; examples are 'Beth-shemesh' (House of the Sun), 'Beth-yerah' (House of the Moon), 'Beth-dagon, Beth-anath, Beth-horon, Bethlehem, Bethel'. In Israelite times we find place-names emerging from names of clans and families, while other place-names were derived from local peculiarities such as trees or springs; in the latter case it is often impossible to say when the name first came into use. Aramaic followed Hebrew as the standard tongue of Palestine and for more than a thousand years the people of Palestine spoke the language of Jesus. Then came Arabic, which gradually displaced Aramaic, until the last speakers of the latter in northern Galilee died, probably less than five hundred years ago. Sometimes a name is preserved for thousands of years, changing its form to suit new linguistic requirements in pronunciation, grammatical form, and meaning. Thus the name of Bethlehem, though scarcely changed in pronunciation for at least 3500 years, meant successively 'Temple of the God Lakhmu' in Canaanite, 'House of Bread' in Hebrew and Aramaic, 'House of Flesh' in Arabic.

As we have already pointed out in Chapter 3, the dominant bony structure and skull form of the purest known Hamitic and Semitic tribes of to-day already appear in the Mesolithic of Palestine, nearly 10,000 years ago. Without denying that there were many movements of non-Semitic peoples across Palestinian soil between that date and the third millennium B.C., it seems only reasonable to suppose that the Semitic element has remained primary in the ethnic make-up of Palestine ever since. The Semites are shown by their language to have been an offshoot of the Semito-Hamitic stock. The chief Semitic languages of antiquity were Accadian (Assyro-Babylonian), West Semitic, and South Semitic, the last of which may be subdivided into North Arabic and South Arabic (Minaean, Sabaean, Ethiopic, and various other ancient and modern dialects). Any such sub-division is merely a matter of convenience, and has far less genetic significance than the corresponding divisions of Indo-European which have been made during the past century and a half of linguistic research. The ancient Semitic tongues, outside of Accadian, were so closely related to one another in grammar and pronunciation (phonetics) that each dialect had much in common with all its neighbours, and the shift from one dialect to another would often be as gradual as such dialectal shifts are to-day in France or Germany. At the beginning of the Patriarchal Age in the early second millennium, the differences between the different Semitic dialects were scarcely greater than the differences between the principal Arabic dialects of to-day. Even Accadian was no more distinct from West Semitic than Maltese is from Iraqi Arabic. The differences between them at that time were con-siderably smaller than between the principal Romance languages to-day.

The Hamitic branch included Egyptian, the Libyan (Ber-ber) languages and dialects, and the Cushitic tongues of the upper basin of the Nile. Egyptian, being nearer Semitic geographically and chronologically, resembles Semitic more closely than do the other Hamitic languages. In the oldest Egyptian inscriptions, from the beginning of the third mil-lennium, we already have a language widely divergent from

Semitic. Professional linguists can relate this language to Semitic almost (but not quite) as closely as they can relate Hittite to the previously known Indo-European tongues; but a Western Semite could not have understood Egyptian without learning the language, and this would not have been any easier than Russian is for an Englishman. Whole declensions of pronouns and conjugations of verbs, long lists of words, basic elements in pronunciation and syntax were common to both, but the languages were very different and must have sounded even further apart to their speakers.

In the middle of the second millennium B.C. the northern Semitic tongues all lost the ending of the indeterminate noun, which had been *m*. For instance, 'good dog' had been *kalbum tabum*; it now became *kalbu tabu*. However, they still kept the three case-endings of the noun (nominative *kalbu*, genitive *kalbi*, accusative *kalba*, just as in Classical Arabic). The loss of the 'mimation' was perhaps the most important difference between the Hebrew of the Patriarchs and that of Moses. Careful study of recently discovered texts of the fifteenth and fourteenth centuries B.C. proves that the case-endings were still carefully distinguished by the scribes who wrote the Amarna Tablets, by the author of the Ugaritic poems, and by the Canaanites whose names were recorded by the Egyptians. Egyptian transcriptions from the late thirteenth and twelfth centuries show that the Canaanites were already dropping their case-endings. Study of the oldest Hebrew poetry proves that this shift was under way in the thirteenth century and had been completed by the late twelfth (Song of Deborah). At the same time the standard Hebrew of the Old Testament was being formed; by the tenth century it was fully developed and with the help of inscriptions we are beginning to elucidate the steps of its subsequent progress. Classical Hebrew shared with Phoenician and Aramaic its own loss of case-endings, together with a shift of the accent towards the end of the word. All three dialects, as well as some other minor ones, such as Moabite, developed the demonstrative pronoun *ha* into an article, exactly as the Romance languages did with the older Latin pronoun *ille*. Hebrew and Phoenician prefixed the article to the noun, as is done by the western Romance tongues; Aramaic affixed it, as done by Roumanian. This divergence created an even greater difference in pronunciation; in Hebrew one said *hammélek*, 'the king', where Aramaic had *malká*, 'the king'. Again, whereas Hebrew word-order tended to be the same as that of other West Semitic tongues, such as Arabic, Aramaic followed the pattern of Assyro-Babylonian (itself influenced by its Sumerian substratum). These examples help to explain how such a slight basic difference could yield such a great superficial divergence in later Hebrew and Aramaic. Add to these grammatical differences the fact that Aramaic and Hebrew vocabularies naturally diverged increasingly, and it becomes easier to understand how the two sister tongues could grow so far apart in less than a thousand years.

In the course of historical times various non-Semitic peoples settled in Palestine. About the seventeenth century B.C., during the disturbed Hyksos Age (Chapter 5), hordes from the north and north-east poured over the land, establishing a new, largely non-Semitic, patrician caste which maintained its own old traditions and reduced the native population to serfdom. Thanks to the cuneiform tablets from Palestine (Chapter 6), we have a considerable number of personal names dating from the fifteenth and fourteenth centuries. Nearly two-thirds of the non-Egyptian names in them, belonging to persons native to Palestine, are Semitic; of the remaining names nearly all (easily a third of the total) can now be identified without hesitation as Indo-Aryan. These Indo-Aryans were part of the great southward migration which brought the Vedic Indians south-east into Punjab and the precursors of the Mitanni south-west into northern

Mesopotamia. Over a hundred personal names belonging to them have been found in cuneiform tablets from Mesopotamia, Asia Minor, Syria, and Palestine, all dating between the years 1600 and 1250 B.C. As P. E. Dumont has shown, perhaps a fourth of these names, like Indaruta (name of a prince of Achshaph in the Amarna Tablets), are identical with names in the Vedas and other early Sanskrit literature, or with good Sanskrit appellatives; most of the rest are formed from well-known Sanskrit words, according to well-established principles of name-formation.

These names provide evidence that such Indic deities as Indra (the storm-god), Yamin, and Surya (the sun-god) were once briefly worshipped in Palestine; evidence previously discovered in the Hittite capital of Boghazköy proves that the same Indo-Aryans also revered the well-known Sanskrit divinities Mitra (Mithra), Varuna, and the two Açvin. Araunah the Jebusite, from whom David is said to have purchased the site of the Temple, seems to have the same name as Arawana or Ariwana, a prince of the Damascene in the early fourteenth century B.C.

A few Hurrian names appear in the cuneiform tablets of the Late Bronze Age from Palestine, though the main mass of the Hurrian migration seems to have halted in central Syria. That there are no more Hurrian names in Palestine is partly to be explained by the fact that the Amarna Tablets very seldom mention any but chieftains; the chieftains of the Hurrians were nearly all Indo-Aryans. The Hurrians were wholly unknown to scholarship until the publication in 1889 of a large Amarna tablet containing a letter written in Hurrian by Tushratta, king of Mitanni. In 1915 the name 'Hurrian' was discovered in a tablet from Boghazköy, and since 1920 there has been rapid progress in the recovery of new Hurrian documents in various parts of the ancient world. In 1941 E. A. Speiser published a grammar of Hurrian which placed this subject on a solid scientific basis. The Hurrian language was a complex agglutinative tongue, resembling Sumerian or Turkish more closely in structure than either Semitic or Indo-European, but not related to any of them. The Hurrians seem to have been a broad-headed mountaineer people, which migrated into the plains of northern Mesopotamia in the third quarter of the third millennium, but which never lost contact with its mountain home. They now turn out to have been one of the principal intermediaries between the Sumero-Accadian culture of Mesopotamia and the West. For more than a thousand years (*c.* 2300–1200 B.C.) this people played a major role in southwestern Asia; it then gradually disappeared. In the Hebrew Bible the Horites appear in Edom, but in the Greek Bible they are also the dominant ethnic group in Shechem and Gibeon (the name is corrupted to 'Hivite' in the Hebrew Bible, because of the extremely close resemblance between *r* and *w* in the square Hebrew alphabet). A curious symbiotic relationship is known to have existed between the Hurrians and the Indo-Aryans, in which the former are the inferiors, the latter generally their superiors, wherever we have enough documents to judge. Since the Hittite inscriptions make no ethnic distinction between the two elements in the Hurrian partnership, we may safely suppose that the Israelites did not either. In other words, the term 'Horite' of the Greek Bible applied both to the Hurrian patricians and their Indo-Aryan chieftains. It is interesting to note that 'Abdu-Kheba, prince of Jerusalem in the Amarna Age, bore a name formed with that of the principal Hurrian goddess, Kheba.

In the early twelfth century (Chapter 6), new peoples from the islands and coasts of the northern Mediterranean settled on the coast of Palestine; the Philistines are the best known of these Sea Peoples, as the Egyptians called them. So little is definitely known of their language and their native culture that it is rather futile to speculate on either at present. No remains of the Philistine script or language are known, aside from a few personal names transcribed into Egyptian, Hebrew, and cuneiform. The proof brought by J. Bérard and V. Georgiev in 1950–1 that the name 'Philistine' is identical with 'Pelasgian' confirms the evidence of pottery that they came from the Aegean basin. The decipherment in 1953 of the Mycenaean Linear B script, which appears on some 2500 tablets found at Cnossus in Crete and at Pylus and Mycenae in Greece, should bring vital new evidence to bear on the Philistine problem. And the discovery of fragments of inscribed Carian and Cypriote tablets makes it not unreasonable to expect Philistine tablets in the lowest strata of their cities.

When we turn to the subject of scripts, Palestine provides a variety as striking as the rarity of inscribed objects in general. It now seems likely that there were pictographic experiments in Palestine and Syria towards the end of the fourth millennium, not long after the beginnings of pictographic writing in Mesopotamia and Egypt. This has been rendered probable by Dunand's discovery of about thirty seal impressions on the handles of jars from his late Chalcolithic (Aeneolithic) cemetery at Byblus (which must not be confused with the same number of later impressions of seal-cylinders on pottery, mentioned in Chapter 4). Some of the impressions contain a dozen or more separate 'pictographs' arranged in a regular order which reminds one superficially of the Mayan glyphs. Only the future can tell us whether we are really dealing here with a kind of writing or not.

In the latter part of the third millennium we appear to have a new script (or scripts) of syllabic character in Syria and Palestine. At Byblus, Dunand has discovered about a dozen inscriptions written in a previously unknown syllabic script, which he has named 'pseudo-hieroglyphic'. They appear on fragments of stone stelae, on tablets and spatulas of bronze, etc.; one appears on the base of a small Egyptianizing statue

dating about the eighteenth century B.C. Since most of
these documents were found in mixed debris or re-used in
later walls, their range is not yet certain; they seem to extend
from about the eighteenth century B.C. to about the fifteenth, but future discoveries may require modification
of these dates. The script was undoubtedly influenced somewhat in form by Egyptian hieroglyphs, while its syllabic
character suggests the influence of the cuneiform script.
Some 114 different characters have so far been distinguished,
and one may safely estimate the original number of signs to
have been somewhere between 125 and 150 – a very suitable
number for different possible combinations between twenty-
eight to thirty early Canaanite consonants and three vowels
(*a*, *i*, *u*), placed before and after each consonant: e.g., *ba*, *bi*,
bu, *ab*, *ib*, *ub*. Since some of the combinations would probably
never be used, it is safe to reckon the actual number of signs
well below the possible total. The distinguished French
philologian, Édouard Dhorme, has published a decipherment of these texts (1947), but since his efforts do not as yet
yield cogent results it will be well to withhold judgement
until more work has been done.

It is possible that one document in this script is already
known from Palestine. The upper part of the Balu'ah stele,
discovered in Moab (1930), exhibits several of the same
characters, though it is so badly weathered that the identification of the script is subject to caution. There are good
reasons for considering the carved scene which now occupies
most of the stele as much later than the inscription at the top,
which is carved in an entirely different technique and has been
weathered much more than the scene below. To the arguments for this view, which have convinced most scholars
who have examined the stone subsequently, must be added
the archaic shape of the stele itself, which cannot be paralleled
in the second millennium or later, but which has rather close
parallels in the Naram-Sin Stele of Victory, from about 2200

B.C., as well as in a very ancient stele from Rum Qaleh in northern Syria. The latter has been correctly dated by Przeworski in the late third millennium B.C. because of Mesopotamian analogies. Balu'ah itself and many other sites in Moab have been proved by exploration to have been occupied in the last centuries of the third millennium and the very beginning of the second (see Chapters 4 and 5).

Two other scripts are known to have been indigenous to Palestine and Syria: the cuneiform alphabet of Ugarit (Ras Shamrah) and the Phoenician linear alphabet. Nothing was known about the former until 1929, when C. F. A. Schaeffer discovered the first tablets and other objects inscribed in wedge-shaped characters at Ras Shamrah and Minet el-Beida on the northern coast of Syria. Since then hundreds of tablets bearing texts in this script have been found at Ugarit. In Palestine two short inscriptions in these characters have hitherto been found: one around the edge of a long, narrow clay tablet from the Late Bronze of Beth-shemesh, about the fourteenth century B.C.; the other on a copper knife from the neighbourhood of Mount Tabor, dating from about the same period or a little later. Curiously enough, both the Palestinian examples are written in a type of script which varies slightly in form from normal Ugaritic. Moreover, one tablet from Ugarit is written in the Palestinian form of the script – and like the two Palestinian examples it runs from right to left instead of from left to right like all normal Ugaritic inscriptions! There can thus be no doubt that this script had considerable vogue in place and time. All the datable texts from Ugarit belong to the first third of the fourteenth century, but the script must be older, since it had already been altered slightly to adapt it for use in writing Hurrian.

The inventor of this alphabet certainly knew a little about Accadian cuneiform, since he copied the use of the Mesopotamian tablet and stylus, writing from left to right in approved Accadian fashion. He was also more or less

familiar with Egyptian or some Semitic consonantal alphabet
based on Egyptian principles, since all his characters are consonantal with three exceptions: instead of having one sign
for the so-called glottal catch (Semitic *'aleph*, found in English
in such combinations as 'her ['] aunt') he devised three, one
for each of the vowels *a, i, u* with the glottal catch. It has been
thought that the inventor of the cuneiform alphabet imitated
the forms of the early West Semitic letters or of selected
cuneiform characters, but all the comparisons so far made are
intrinsically improbable. It is much more likely that the inventor selected all possible permutations of simple horizontal, vertical, or oblique wedges, combining them into
groups which he arbitrarily identified with phonemes (separate sounds actually used in forming words and their grammatical combinations). For example, one horizontal wedge is
t, two horizontal wedges in a line make *a*, three in a line make
n. Similarly one vertical wedge is *g*, two vertical wedges in a
line make *z*, three in a line *kh*. Two parallel wedges placed
horizontally make *p*, three make *h*; two placed vertically make
ts (written as dotted *s* by linguists), three make *l*. This looks
for all the world like intelligent invention, not like adaptation
or imitation.

The second Palestinian script invented in this general age
is the linear alphabet from which are derived Hebrew,
Syriac, Arabic, Amharic, and many other Oriental scripts,
besides Greek, Latin, and all the derived European scripts.
The date of the prototype of this script has gradually been
raised. In 1868 the discovery of the Mesha Stone pushed it
back to the middle of the ninth century, and subsequent finds
have carried the date of the earliest inscription in an orthodox
form of the same script, intelligible throughout, to about
1000 B.C. or a little earlier (the Ahiram Sarcophagus, discovered by Montet in 1923). Then, in 1906, Petrie reported
his discovery of several inscriptions in Sinai written in a
hitherto unknown script, which looked something like

Egyptian hieroglyphs, but had too few different characters to
be anything but alphabetic. Ten years later the Egyptologist,
Alan Gardiner, announced that he had partially deciphered
these texts which were, he believed, in a script which seemed
to be the source of our alphabet. His solution was based on a
very ingenious and plausible combination of four or five
characters occurring several times together in these inscriptions (shepherd's crook), house, eye, crook, cross,
reading each as the Hebrew character whose name has the
corresponding meaning. In other words, he accepted the
long-previously suggested view that the Hebrew letters had
developed from simple pictures of objects whose initial consonants were taken as the phonetic value of the pictures in
question. This is called the acrophonic principle, much used
in elementary primers for children (c as in 'cat', d as in 'dog',
etc.). The combination of five characters he thus read
l-B-ʽ-l-t, 'to the Lady (Baalath)', which seemed doubly
plausible because the local Semites were known to worship a
goddess called by the Egyptians 'Hathor', which was the
name they also gave to the contemporary Baalath of Byblus!
This brilliant discovery of Sir Alan's underlies all successful
later efforts at decipherment. The total number of proto-
Sinaitic inscriptions, mostly very short, has now been raised
to about 25 by subsequent expeditions to Serabit el-Khadem
in Sinai (including three sent out by Harvard University).
Owing to erroneous dating and archaeological interpretation
of the function of the inscriptions, little progress was made
until 1948, when a University of California expedition discovered clues which made successful decipherment possible.
The inscriptions prove to date from *c.* 1500 B.C. and to be
written in a good Canaanite dialect. Incidentally, Sir Alan
Gardiner's results were astonishingly correct as far as they
went.

Since 1930, at least three short inscriptions (of a few letters
each) from the Middle Bronze Age have been discovered in

Palestine. Happily a date between 1800 and 1500 is certain for all three (from Gezer, Shechem, and Lachish). Together they have only fourteen letters, and only one inscription is certainly complete, so decipherment is obviously out of the question until additional material is found. Of the nine or ten characters three ('hand', 'head', and 'house') are certainly identical with corresponding characters in the proto-Sinaitic alphabet and several others look very similar. Moreover, the two scripts agree in being written vertically, as a rule. The forms of some letters in these earlier inscriptions from Palestine are clearly older than those of the characters in the inscriptions from Sinai, which are in turn considerably more archaic than the thirteenth-century inscriptions from Palestine.

When we come to the thirteenth and twelfth centuries, our situation is much better. Lachish has yielded at least two alphabetic inscriptions which can be partly read, and roughly contemporary documents have been found at Beth-shemesh and elsewhere. One stone fragment, which was cleverly deciphered by Grimme, comes from Byblus. The script of these inscriptions stands just where we should expect if it is really intermediate between proto-Sinaitic and later Phoenician. For some twenty years many scholars dated a number of the early Byblian inscriptions of the Ahiram group about the thirteenth century, because of the finding of two fragments with part of the name and titles of Ramesses II of Egypt (about 1301–1234 B.C.) in the debris which filled the tomb of Ahiram and its entrance shaft. However, this was at best only the highest date (*terminus a quo*) which could be assigned to the tomb; its actual date might be considerably lower. The discovery of several other inscriptions in the same script, incised on statues of the Bubastite Pharaohs Shishak and Osorkon I (late tenth century), led an increasing number of scholars to date all documents in this particular type of Phoenician script between 1050 and 900 (Fig. 60). Recently

Dunand has discovered that the sherds from the debris of the tomb of Ahiram cannot precede the beginning of the tenth century, thus compelling us to lower the date of the tomb to

Ahiram (Byblus) before 975 B.C.	Gezer Calendar	Abibaal (Byblus) cir. 925 B.C.	Cyprus (Honeyman) 900–825 B.C.	Ben-hadad (Aram) cir. 850 B.C.	Mesha (Moab) cir. 840 B.C.	Ahiram (Byblus) before 975 B.C.	Gezer Calendar	Abibaal (Byblus) cir. 925 B.C.	Cyprus (Honeyman) 900–825 B.C.	Ben-hadad (Aram) cir. 850 B.C.	Mesha (Moab) cir. 840 B.C.

Fig. 60. Table of Hebrew-Phoenician scripts, showing comparative date of Gezer Calendar.

about 1000 B.C., or even a little later. So we have a gap between the Lachish and other inscriptions from before c. 1220 B.C. and the Byblian texts from the tenth century; it is partly filled by three twelfth-century arrowheads from el-Khadhr

SINAITIC SCRIPT	DESCRIPTION OF SIGN	CANAANITE SCRIPT OF 13th CENT. B.C.	CANAANITE SCRIPT OF c. 1000 B.C.	SOUTH ARAB SCRIPT OF IRON AGE	MODERN HEBREW SCRIPT	PHONETIC VALUE
	OX-HEAD				א	ʾ
	HOUSE				ב	b
?					ג	g
	FISH				ד	d
	MAN PRAYING				ה	h
?					ו	w
?					ז	z
	?		"		ד̄	ḏ
	FENCE ?				ח	ḥ
	DOUBLE LOOP		"		ח̄	ḫ
?					ט	ṭ
?					י	y
	PALM OF HAND				כ	k
	"OX-GOAD"				ל	l
	WATER				מ	m
	SERPENT				נ	n
?					ס	s
	EYE	O	O	o	ע	ʿ
?			"		ע̄	ġ
	THROW STICK				פ	p
?					צ	ṣ
	BLOSSOM		"		צ̄	ḍ ẓ
	?				ק	q
	HUMAN HEAD				ר	r
	BOW		W		ש	ṯ ś
	?		"		ש	š
+	MARK OF CROSS	+	+	X	ת	t

HEBREW NAME	PHOENICIAN SCRIPT OF 8th CENT. B.C. BAAL LEBANON KARATEPE		OLD GREEK SCRIPT OF 8th CEN. B.C.	HEBREW CURSIVE OF c. 600 B.C.	GREEK NAME	MODERN GREEK SCRIPT	MODERN ROMAN SCRIPT
ALEPH	𐤀	𐤀	𐤀	𐤀	ALPHA	A	A
BETH	9	9	ß	9	BETA	B	B
GIMEL		∧	Γ	1	GAMMA	Γ	G
DALETH	⊿	⊿	Δ	𝛼	DELTA	Δ	D
HE		∃	∃	∃	EPSILON	E	E
WAW		Y	F	𝑓			∨
ZAYIN	I	I	I	⊐	ZETA	Z	Z
HETH	目	目	目	ㅂ	ETA	H	H
TETH			⊗	⊗	THETA	Θ	
YODH	⊋	⊋	𝑆	𝑇	IOTA	I	I
KAPH	𝑌	𝑌	K	𝑢	KAPPA	K	K
LAMEDH	∟	∟	∧	∟	LAMDA	Λ	L
MEM	ᛗ	4	ᛰ	𝟰	MU	M	M
NUN	𝑏	𝑏	N	𝟹	NU	N	N
SAMEKH	𝐓		𝐓	𝑏	XI	Ξ	
AYIN	O	O	O	O	OMICRON	O	O
PE		⊃	⊏	⊃	PI	Π	P
SADE		ᛗ	M	ᛯ			
QOPH	ℙ	Φ	Φ	φ			Q
RESH	⊿	𝐪	⊳	𝐪	RHO	P	R
SHIN	W	W	ξ	W	SIGMA	Σ	S
TAW	†	✗	T	✗	TAU	T	T

near Bethlehem, published in 1954 by J. T. Milik and F. M. Cross, as well as by miscellaneous items.

In recent years, the discovery of many new inscriptions in Palestine and Syria, together with the correction of some erroneous older dates, has greatly stabilized epigraphic chronology. Just as experts in handwriting can date English documents within a few decades by the character of the writing, and exactly as palaeographers and papyrologists can date mediaeval texts or Greek papyri within narrow limits by careful analysis of forms of letters and peculiarities of spelling, etc., so epigraphers who specialize in Hebrew and Phoenician script are learning to date their material by use of analogous methods. Of course, the specialist must reckon with local variations and with different kinds of script – lapidary (carved on stone) and cursive (written with a quill or reed pen in ink) – but the principles remain the same.

A most interesting problem, which is being brought close to solution by the steady improvement of our chronology of writing, is the long-debated question of the time at which the Greeks borrowed their alphabet from the Phoenicians. That they actually did borrow the alphabet was contested for a time, but it is now quite certain. Not only are the Greek letters without any prehistory, but the affiliated Hebrew–Phoenician letters have a prehistory going back centuries before the earliest possible date of the borrowing. The discovery of the Ahiram Sarcophagus induced the eminent French savant, René Dussaud, who had been one of the most vigorous supporters of the Aegean theory of the origin of the Phoenician alphabet, to reverse his stand completely. Moreover, the names of the Greek letters, which are meaningless in Greek, are nearly all obviously derived from the meaningful Hebrew names, and – even more important – the letters follow the same order. The antiquity of these names of the letters is further attested by the fact that many of the Ethiopic letters have the same names, though the order is different and the ancestral alphabets must have diverged from each other before the thirteenth century B.C. at the very latest.

The chief protagonists of the debate about the time at which the Greeks took over the alphabet are Berthold Ullman and Rhys Carpenter. The former compares isolated letters, looking for parallels wherever he can find them; he dates the borrowing of the Phoenician alphabet by the Greeks somewhere about the twelfth century B.C., or even earlier. The latter insists on comparing whole alphabets (that is, on taking all forms of letters from single inscriptions, which are thus guarantees of a common date for every character in them) rather than heterogeneous characters; he decides on a date towards the end of the eighth century B.C. as the most reasonable. Ullman's date is rendered virtually impossible by the fact that archaic forms of such letters as *m* and *k*, which cannot possibly have formed the prototypes of the earliest Greek forms, persist in all inscriptions in the Semitic alphabet hitherto discovered down into the ninth century, during which later forms replace them in Palestine as well as in Syria and Phoenicia. The Greek alphabet cannot, therefore, have been introduced before the ninth century. This conclusion agrees with negative evidence from Greek sources; not a single Greek inscription antedating the eighth century has yet been discovered, in spite of all the excavations of the past century. Rhys Carpenter, on the other hand, forces his case by arbitrarily depressing the date of the earliest Greek inscriptions to the seventh century, in which he insists that the latest Dipylon ware and the latest forms of geometric pottery must be dated. Moreover, he insists that the Greeks must have borrowed their script from a lapidary Phoenician prototype, instead of from a graffito cursive, that is, from a stiff ('block') handwriting of the type commonly used by merchants for scratching a record of some transaction on a potsherd or a sliver of stone. As is well known, lapidary writing is more conventional and more conservative than cursive; it would not lend itself so well to practical use. In the author's long-held opinion, based on the comparison of alphabets found in single inscriptions, not on scattered forms, the Greek alphabet was borrowed from the Phoenician either in the late ninth century or more probably in the early eighth century B.C.

Turning from systems of writing to the contents of written records, we enter the field of philology, the study of written documents and literary works. This field of research was developed to a high degree of excellence by Greek and Latin scholars in the seventeenth and eighteenth centuries A.D.; Semitic scholars imitated their methods closely in dealing with the known Semitic languages, such as Hebrew, Aramaic, Arabic, and Ethiopic. A century ago, when the archaeology of the Near and Middle East was still in its swaddling clothes, there were already good dictionaries and grammars of these languages, and considerable progress had been made towards the goal of putting the study of Semitic literatures on the same level of accuracy and sound method which had been attained by classical philology (if we except such vagaries as reckless emendation of obscure passages). As the languages of the newly discovered inscriptions, many of them completely extinct, were deciphered, philologians – mostly German – began employing the methods which had been perfected by classical scholars to work out the grammars and dictionaries of the new tongues: Egyptian and Accadian, Sumerian and Hittite, Phoenician and South Arabian, Elamite and Hurrian. To-day the languages for which there are most documents, such as Egyptian, Accadian, and Sumerian, are well understood by competent scholars, and their interpretation follows methods similar to those employed by Greek and Latin scholars. Hittite is not far behind; Hurrian lags behind mainly because there are not sufficient texts. Phoenician and Ugaritic are almost as well understood as archaic Biblical Hebrew.

Most of the inscriptions deal with business transactions or are formal documents of religious or political nature. We have Egyptian and Sumero-Accadian religious literature and *belles lettres*; enough has survived to make it certain that there was once an extensive written literature in the strictest sense of the word in Hittite and Hurrian. For a long time it seemed that there was no hope of our discovering any of the long-lost Canaanite literature which may once have flourished in Palestine and Phoenicia. Then came a stunning – though delightful – surprise when C. F. A. Schaeffer discovered clay tablets at Ugarit containing extensive fragments of Canaanite mythological and religious literature from the beginning of the fourteenth century B.C. Parts of at least four epic cycles have been published by Charles Virolleaud and are now being studied by scores of older and younger Semitists. Three of these epics, which are concerned with the deeds of the storm-god Baal and his sister Anath, with the exploits and sufferings of King Keret, and with the death and revival of Daniel's son, Aqhat, must have been very long; we possess several tablets of each. For a number of years it was believed by some scholars that these epics originated in southern Palestine, but this view is now generally rejected. Allusions in them show that they originated in Phoenicia proper, the region of Tyre, Sidon, and Byblus, with Lebanon and Sirion (Antilibanus) in the hinterland. The deities of these epics are the gods of the Canaanites in Palestine as well as in Phoenicia; the later Phoenician inscriptions, formal as they are, contain many literary reminiscences of Ugaritic literature. Moreover, we now know that the poetry of the Hebrew Bible, especially its older portions, swarms with allusions to the Canaanite verse of which the Ugaritic epics are merely samples. As we shall see in Chapter 10, the discovery of Ugaritic literature is already compelling scholars to revise some of their theories with respect to the date of biblical Hebrew literature rather drastically. At the same time, it clarifies the meaning of many obscure words and passages in the poetry of the Old Testament. Up to now, no Canaanite literary tablets have been found in Palestine, though we have two short inscriptions in the alphabetic cuneiform of the epics. At any moment, however, this silence may be broken as unexpectedly as it was at Ugarit. Since Palestine was generally a poor and culturally backward part of Canaan, we have no guarantee that any such find will be made. It is even possible that literary texts were copied out on cuneiform tablets only at Ugarit in the early fourteenth century B.C. As this seems hardly plausible, we may continue to hope for new finds of the same nature.

Owing to the limitations of space, we shall give only one other illustration of the kind of light shed by archaeology on ancient literature, although it requires some rather detailed explanation. In 1897 the discovery by Grenfell and Hunt at Behnesa (Oxyrhynchus) in the Egyptian Faiyum of a quantity of Greek papyri, including many literary texts, focused the attention of scholars on the question of the language of the New Testament. During the past half-century papyrologists have been very active, and a great many previously obscure words and grammatical usages in the Greek New Testament have proved to be excellent *Koine*, that is, Greek as employed by ordinary men all over the Greek-speaking world of that day. At first the enthusiasm of scholars like Adolf Deissmann, who became the leader in this new branch of research, carried the day; it became common belief that New Testament Greek was the ordinary vernacular of the first century A.D. and that the striking divergences between it and the Greek of authors like Diodorus or Plutarch, or like Philo and Josephus, were due simply to the fact that the writers of the New Testament were unlettered men. But this was simply not true; there remained a big difference between the Greek of the New Testament and the language of the letters and business documents of unlettered Greeks in Egypt. Arthur Darby Nock, one of the foremost living authorities on the period, wrote recently:

'Any man who knows his classical Greek authors and reads the New Testament and then looks into the papyri is astonished at the similarities which he finds. Any man who knows the papyri first and then turns to Paul is astonished at the differences. There has been much exaggeration of the *Koine* element in the New Testament.'

In view of this situation it is scarcely surprising that scholars began reacting to it. As long as the Greek of the New Testament remained unparalleled because of the lack of any writings except sophisticated literary works like Philo and Plutarch from the period of Jesus and the Apostles, it was hard to arrive at any objective conclusion. Now it became evident that there must really have been strong Hebrew and Aramaic influence on New Testament Greek in order to explain the apparent Semitisms in the New Testament as contrasted with *Koine*. After all, the writers of the New Testament (including almost certainly Luke) were Jews, and Aramaic was their mother-tongue. It had commonly been supposed that it was the lack of a native command of Greek and of a Hellenic education which prevented the writers of the New Testament from writing good Greek. Now it was increasingly suggested that this strange Greek, which was neither literary nor *Koine*, was really translated Aramaic. Such scholars as C. F. Burney and C. C. Torrey, following occasional hints by earlier students, maintained that much of the Gospels and the Acts had been translated from written Aramaic sources. In other words, they held that the Semitic colouring was not due to lack of education on the part of the ancient writers, but was rather the outcome of too great fidelity to the Aramaic original which they were translating. From 1912 to 1941 Torrey published an impressive series of books and papers, in which he undertook to establish his contention by proving mistranslations of written Aramaic original texts. In *The Four Gospels, a New Translation* (1933) Torrey retranslated part of the New Testament, replacing what he considered to be misunderstandings of the supposed Aramaic originals by his own interpretations of the Aramaic as reconstructed by himself. Needless to say, the book created a sensation, since Torrey was a first-class authority on Aramaic and a very well-trained philologian – not a quasi-charlatan like so many *soi-disant* scholars who create sensations in the daily Press.

The basic method was sound. Torrey began with the analysis of types of translation Greek which are admitted by all scholars, such as the Septuagint (the Greek translation of the Old Testament, made in the third and second centuries B.C.) and certain books of the Apocrypha and Pseudepigrapha. Comparing such samples of translation Greek with literary Greek and *Koine*, he had no trouble in showing that parts of the New Testament exhibit the same Semitic background, traceable in syntax, word-order, use of words, etc. Moreover, these translated works show many cases of mistranslation, where the scribe misunderstood the Hebrew or Aramaic original, either misreading a word or selecting the wrong sense where there were different possible meanings. We are all familiar with this kind of thing. I remember seeing in two independent English translations of German books the curious statement that ancient Egyptian barbers spent much of their time making the rounds in order to search for news. This attribution of the functions of a modern journalist to the ancient barber is based solely on confusion of German *Kunden*, 'customers', with the same word in the sense of 'news'! Almost every modern translation offers amusing examples of this kind of thing. A careful reader who knows the two languages well has no trouble in spotting such mistakes.

One real difficulty is, however, that we are still not fully informed about the possibilities of late Hellenistic Greek in the provinces. There are no literary works written in any contemporary Greek except the elaborate rhetorical style of

Alexandria and the atticizing style characteristic of Athens and its imitators. The *Koine* seems to have been used only for conversation or for everyday writing on the part of semi-literate persons. A much more serious difficulty is the almost complete absence of contemporary Aramaic literature. Biblical Aramaic, the Aramaic of the Elephantine Papyri (mostly discovered in 1903–7 at the southern end of Egypt proper), and the language of the Nabataean and Palmyrene inscriptions (first century B.C. to the third century A.D.) all reflect various stages of the standard literary Aramaic of the Persian Empire, as has been demonstrated by E. Sachau, H. H. Schaeder, and others. Jewish Aramaic, as found in the Palestinian Talmud and the oldest translations of the Bible (Targums), reflects the speech of the third century A.D. and later. If there were any doubt about the date of the extant Jewish Aramaic of Palestine, it would be dispelled by the finding of many synagogue inscriptions from the fourth–sixth centuries A.D., all in this language. The Samaritan dialect of Aramaic, though badly preserved in mediaeval and modern copies, goes back at least to the time of Marqa, in the fourth century A.D. The Aramaic of the Babylonian Talmud was at home in Babylonia during the same centuries; Mandaean was practically the same dialect in a still later form; Syriac was the speech of northern Mesopotamia, especially Edessa, in the second and third centuries A.D. and later. Finally there is Christian Palestinian Aramaic, our knowledge of which we owe chiefly to the manuscript discoveries of two English ladies, Agnes Smith Lewis and Margaret Dunlop Gibson, at Sinai; it seems to have been spoken in Palestine between the sixth and the ninth or tenth centuries A.D.

Against Torrey's views stand two additional difficulties which are hard to overcome: (1) none of the dialects of Aramaic which we have sketched above was spoken in Palestine in the time of Christ; (2) there are no Aramaic literary works extant from the period between the third or second century B.C. and the second or third A.D., a period of over three hundred years. There can be little doubt that there was a real eclipse of Aramaic during the period of the Seleucid Empire (312 B.C. to the early first century B.C.), since scarcely a single Aramaic inscription from this period has been discovered, except in Transjordan and the adjacent parts of Arabia, which were relatively freer from Greek influence than Western Palestine and Syria proper. After this epigraphic hiatus, Palmyrene inscriptions began to appear in the second half of the first century B.C.; recent excavations have brought to light an inscription dating from the year 44 B.C. Inscriptions in Jewish Aramaic first appeared about the middle of the first century B.C., and became more abundant during the reign of Herod the Great, just before the Christian era (see above). They thus help to clarify the actual Aramaic of Jewish Palestine in the time of Jesus and the Apostles. If the Megillath Ta'anith, or 'Scroll of Fastings', a list of official Jewish fasts with accompanying historical notations, really precedes the year A.D. 70, as held by some scholars, it belongs to our period, but it is safer to date it in the second century A.D., in accordance with its present chronological content.

It is surprising how little evidence there is of a pagan Aramaic background in Christian Syriac literature, which began in the late second century A.D. with Bardaisan. Of course, there were pagan Syriac documents, an example of which from the year A.D. 243 turned up recently at Dura. Formal Syriac inscriptions may be traced back to about the Christian era. But the one literary work which was certainly taken over by the Christians from pagan sources was the Proverbs of Ahiqar, and the Syriac Ahiqar may now be compared in considerable detail with extensive Aramaic fragments from the late fifth century B.C., discovered at Elephantine in Upper Egypt. These two ancient editions diverge so widely from one another that we can speak only of a common oral tradition, not of a derivation of the Syriac from the

Aramaic Ahiqar through written channels. It seems, therefore, that there is actually more evidence against the continuity of Aramaic written literature through Hellenistic
times than there was before recent archaeological discoveries.
It is not at all improbable that the Seleucid monarchs, in their
zeal for Hellenism, ordered that all Aramaic books be burned.
The Dead Sea Scrolls, discovered since 1947, are almost all
written in Hebrew, and the few Aramaic documents such as
the Book of Lamech are written in a late hand, probably dating after the Christian era. It is most important to note that
the vast majority of non-biblical fragments hitherto found
are in Hebrew.

Archaeological evidence, as we see, does not support the
view that the Gospels were written in Aramaic. Moreover,
when such a relatively long inscription as the epigraph referring to the alleged bones of Uzziah is discovered, the
language contains such unexpected elements as the Samaritan
form of the word for 'bones' instead of the normal older and
younger Aramaic form, and as the archaic form of the verb
'it is (they are) brought', previously known only from the
Book of Daniel. The danger of making mistakes in trying to
reconstruct the original Aramaic of Jesus is thus greater
than ever. Other evidence makes it increasingly probable
that the Aramaic element in the Gospels comes from the
translation of orally transmitted documents, that is, of oral
Aramaic records of the words and doings of Jesus. When we
recall the extent to which oral transmission of the words of
the rabbis was emphasized in contemporary and later Jewish
schools, such handing down by word of mouth seems only
reasonable. As just pointed out, the new archaeological light
on the oral transmission of the Proverbs of Ahiqar strengthens
our case. Christians may thus continue to read the Greek
Gospels without apprehending serious errors in translation
(though there were, of course, many slight changes of meaning in the shift from Aramaic to Greek).

CHAPTER 9

Daily Life in Ancient Palestine

—

SINCE the available space makes it impossible to go into detail, we shall limit ourselves to contrasting simple environmental conditions of life in three different periods: the time of Jacob (which we shall fix somewhat arbitrarily about 1750 B.C. in Middle Bronze II); the time of Elijah (about 850 B.C.); New Testament times (last century of the Second Temple, from Herod the Great's reign to the fall of Jerusalem in A.D. 70).

THE TIME OF JACOB
Middle Bronze II

In all probability we may date the patriarchal generation to which Jacob belonged somewhere in the eighteenth or seventeenth century B.C.; for convenience we shall date it about 1750 B.C. This was a period in which the nomadic Western Semites were settling down rapidly (see Chapter 5) and Palestine was growing apace in population and wealth. Trade relations had reached a level higher than any known in preceding centuries. People were accustomed to move about freely from country to country, as we know from the Cappadocian tablets (between 1850 and 1750 B.C.), the documents from Larsa and Babylon, and especially the Mari texts (after about 1750 B.C.).* There was no serious language barrier anywhere in the Fertile Crescent, since West Semitic was understood everywhere and the related Accadian of Babylonia was the *lingua franca*, the tongue of diplomacy and business. Moreover, political and cultural ties between

* The author's Mesopotamian dates average 64 years lower than those of Sidney Smith of the British Museum.

Egypt and Palestine continued to be close, and Egyptian was understood in all important Palestinian centres, while West Semitic was spoken in many parts of northern Egypt.

The Indo-Aryan movement from the north-east had not yet reached Mesopotamia, and horse-drawn chariots were still very rare and probably rather slow, compared to their speed two or three centuries later. There was, accordingly, no feudalism of the type which became dominant in the latter part of the Middle Bronze Age. In Palestine there was as yet no clear distinction between fully settled and nomadic populations. The recurrent process of settling down had begun again a century or more earlier and had by now dotted Western Palestine with fortresses in which tribal chieftains lived, while most of their subjects must have lived in surrounding hamlets made up of small clusters of huts or tents. In times of peril they moved into the fortress or fortresses of their chief. During the winter the population of the fortress was doubtless considerably greater than it was in summer, when people could live in improvised shelters of stones and boughs without fear of rain. The custom of living in such improvised huts in summer, especially during the grape harvest, survived into Israelite times as a feature of the Feast of Tabernacles (literally, 'Huts'); it is found to-day among the more recently settled Arab peasants.

The traditional stories of the Patriarchs, as preserved in Genesis, picture them as semi-nomads, dividing their time between care of flocks and herds on the one hand and agricultural activity on the other. In this respect they were very much like the semi-nomadic Arabs ('*Arab*) of Palestine until very recently. The principal difference in exterior mode of life was that the modern Arabs (who are half-way between the true nomads, *bedu*, and the fully settled peasants, *fellahin*) used to tent in the Negeb (South Country), the Coastal Plain, Esdraelon, the Jordan Valley, the eastern desert of Judah, and the wilder parts of Galilee, whereas the Hebrew

Patriarchs are pictured as roaming through the hills of central and southern Palestine and as moving only occasionally down into the Negeb. The view of radical critics of the nineteenth century that the life of the Hebrew Patriarchs was a fiction invented by writers of the Israelite Monarchy, who took their cue from the life of contemporary Bedouin, is wholly misleading, though certain details were doubtless added by tradition to suit the inherited picture to the facts of later periods. Nearly three centuries after the time of Jacob (as here stated) the Amarna Tablets give us a picture which is in some respects like that of the Patriarchal Age in Genesis. In these documents the semi-nomadic 'Apiru ('Khabiru') appear as groups roving about the hill-country, just as the Patriarchs are represented as doing in Genesis. Whether the 'Apiru are to be identified with the 'Ibrim (Hebrews) of Genesis is an elusive problem into which we need not enter here. Quite independent of this possible identification is the light shed by inscriptional allusions to the 'Apiru on the historical role of the Patriarchs.

In the eighteenth century B.C. the ass was the chief beast of burden. In the Cappadocian and the Mari tablets we hear of caravans of asses, but never of caravans of camels; the oldest published reference to the camel dates from the eleventh century B.C. Moreover, the great mass of archaeological evidence now available yields only two or three doubtful representations of the camel during the entire period from the beginning of the third to the end of the second millennium B.C. Efforts to attribute more representations of the camel to this long period have so far been unsuccessful. Of course, there can be no doubt that wild camels were common in North Africa and south-western Asia in neolithic and chalcolithic times; representations of them are found on the cliffs which line the Nile Valley and at Kilwa in Transjordan, while camel figurines were not uncommon in late predynastic Egypt. It would appear that the early wild camel was

nearly exterminated in the regions bordering on the Fertile
Crescent in the course of the third millennium, and that it
was slowly domesticated in more remote parts of Arabia
during the second millennium, appearing rather suddenly in
larger herds towards the end of that millennium. Our oldest
certain evidence for the domestication of the camel cannot
antedate the end of the twelfth century B.C. These facts do
not necessarily prove that earlier references to the camel in
Genesis and Exodus are anachronistic, but they certainly
suggest such an explanation. Of course, such anachronisms
in local colour no more disprove the historicity of the underlying tradition than Tissot's painted scenes of Bible life
falsify the biblical story by depicting its heroes as modern
Palestinian Arabs.

The famous tableau of Beni-Hasan, dated in the year 1892
B.C., paints an unforgettable picture of a small clan of semi-
nomadic tribesmen from Palestine in the early Patriarchal
Age (Fig. 61). Under the guidance of their chief, who bears
the good abbreviated Semitic name Absha, thirty-seven of
them, men, women, and children, are said to have brought
stibium (black pigment) from Shutu in central Transjordan
to the court of the nomarch of the district (in Middle Egypt,
just north of Amarna). Both men and women wear woollen
tunics made by sewing together strips of cloth woven in
brightly coloured patterns; these tunics are draped over one
shoulder, leaving the other bare. The only difference between men's and women's tunics indicated by the artist is
that the women's reach half-way between ankle and knee,
while the men's stop at the knee. However, some of the men
wear long white (linen?) tunics, and some of them wear
short tunics reaching only from the waist to the knee. The
men generally wear sandals, but the women are shown wearing low leather boots. For weapons they carry a composite
bow, throw-sticks, and darts. The least-expected items of
luggage are a lyre carried by one of the men and two bellows

carried (with other things) by the asses. Obviously we are dealing here with travelling metal-workers, something like the tinkers of later times, who were still a sufficient oddity in Egypt to be represented for posterity by the local prince. As a whole this group perfectly illustrates the very ancient story in Gen. iv, 19–22, where the family of Lamech is described as including specialists in pastoral life, in playing the lyre, and in copper and iron working! Since it is unlikely that the dress of the Palestinian semi-nomad changed appreciably in the following century or two, we can scarcely go far wrong if we picture Jacob and his family as clad in much the same way. However, before the end of the Middle Bronze Age Canaanite dress had changed drastically, following the importation of Mesopotamian and North Syrian fashions.

THE TIME OF ELIJAH
Iron IIa

Nearly a thousand years elapsed; the Bronze Age reached its climax and declined, giving place to the Iron Age; the Western Semites were largely displaced by the irruption of non-Semitic peoples, whom they absorbed – but only in time to be displaced or absorbed in their turn by the Israelites and the Philistines. The heroic days of the Israelite Conquest were followed by a long and painful period of adaptation to the country and of suffering under the onslaughts of belligerent neighbours. Then came the glorious days of the United Monarchy, followed again by disruption. Two generations after the Division of the Monarchy (about 922 B.C.) appeared the solitary figure of the great prophet Elijah, coming from the rural simplicity of Gilead into the cosmopolitan sophistication of Samaria. Life had become much more complex in the middle of the ninth century B.C. than it had been a thousand years earlier. The caravans of asses which characterized the Patriarchal Age had been replaced by

Fig. 61. Representation of Asiatic visitors at Beni-Hasan (c. 1892 B.C.).

caravans of camels which brought the spices of South Arabia and the products of the northern oases to Mediterranean ports. Horse-drawn chariotry had largely replaced infantry, and was rapidly being replaced in its turn by cavalry. The little fleets of timid sea-going barks, which had plied the waters of the Mediterranean as far as Cyprus and Crete, had been replaced by larger fleets of stately Phoenician galleys bound for the copper refineries of Sardinia and the mineral wealth of Spain. New arts and crafts had sprung up in every direction.

No longer did Israelite women have to depend exclusively on water from the nearest stream or spring; almost every house of the ninth century had its own cistern, where winter rain was stored for use throughout the year. Much greater attention was now paid to cleanliness and sanitation. Quite aside from the Mosaic Law itself, with its emphasis on personal hygiene and on avoidance of practices or foods which foster the spread of disease, is the evidence of archaeology. Cisterns were not only numerous, but they were generally provided with settling basins to keep out as much mud and extraneous matter as possible; these cisterns caught relatively pure water from roof-tops rather than muddy water from the streets and courts of the houses. The members of the most ordinary household actually lived in the upper story of their home, not on the ground level as common folk had in earlier times; the ground floor was used for storage and for working quarters. Subterranean drains were employed increasingly as time went on in order to keep the interior of towns as dry as possible.

The Israelite peasant and craftsman of the age of Elijah was far better off than his precursors in the tools at his disposal. Instead of the wooden sickles lined with flint sickle-edges which the sons of Jacob had to use when they reaped grain, there were sharp iron sickles, with which at least twice as much grain could be reaped in a given time. It is true that these sickles were short and that the reaper had to grasp the ears of grain with one hand while he lopped them off with the other (just as we see in Egyptian relief paintings); the day of the long scythe was far in the future. The carpenter had iron tools of every kind, which immensely facilitated his work: large iron axes and adzes with which to cut down his trees and trim his beams or boards; thin iron saws in frames (our bucksaws) with which wood could be sawed much more cheaply than was possible with copper saws; great sledge hammers and little chisels and gouges.

The wealth, which poured into the Canaanite (Phoenician) cities on the coast of northern Palestine from all parts of the ancient world, made it possible to develop a kind of mass production which was almost as great an improvement over older handicraft as modern conveyor-belt manufacture is over older machine production. Comparison of Israelite pottery of Iron II with Middle Bronze ware is very instructive in this respect. For all the care and artistic skill devoted to making individual pieces in the Middle Bronze Age, the rapidly fabricated ware of the ninth–seventh centuries was much better suited to its functional purposes than was the earlier pottery. It is interesting to scan the inventory of articles designed for use by women of the people in a typical Israelite site and to contrast it with objects from a site of the early second millennium. In the latter we generally find rough, locally made jewellery; in the former we find corresponding articles made of cheap materials, but by skilled craftsmen. Thus we find little round palettes of hard limestone for use in preparing face paint and cosmetics; the margins are covered with accurate geometric designs far superior in skill of execution to the awkward hand-carved designs on cheap wares of earlier times. There are many cheap bone pendants, but they were gracefully turned and were obviously available in large quantities at low price.

The Assyrian reliefs show us how the Israelites dressed at

that time. In the Black Obelisk of Shalmaneser III, carved only a few years after the death of Elijah, we see the Israelite envoys of Jehu, king of Israel, bringing tribute to the Assyrian monarch. The Israelites are represented as wearing the same clothing as the men from northern Syria and southern Armenia, but since this clothing is entirely different from that worn by men from the south and east of the Assyrian Empire, we may safely trust the Assyrian artist with a certain amount of accuracy (though not as much as displayed by Egyptian artists). The men of Israel wear long fringed tunics, over which are fringed mantles, both presumably of wool; on their heads they wear short stocking caps, which are bound in place like turbans, while on their feet they wear high boots turned up at the toes in Hittite fashion. A century and a half later, Sennacherib's capture of Lachish in Judah was celebrated by Assyrian artists; here the men of Judah appear with their tunics drawn up to their knees and fastened in place by their girdles, while the women are shown with long tunics and mantles.

New Testament Times

Again some nine centuries rolled around, bringing with them many changes in the way of living and many improvements in material culture. The Assyrian and Babylonian Empires gave way to the vaster Persian Empire, which was then conquered by Alexander of Macedon. The Hellenistic Age saw several shifts of political power, and in 63 B.C. Palestine was incorporated by Pompey into the Roman Empire, whose extent had already dwarfed that of the Persian Empire. The world of the Mediterranean was now one, and the fashions of Athens and Alexandria were copied in the Western Mediterranean, while Roman public life was imitated in the eastern provinces. The results of archaeological excavation in Palestine itself tell us extremely little with regard to the life of the common people in the time of Christ.

On the other hand, we have the remarkably preserved ruins of Pompeii (destroyed by an eruption of Vesuvius in A.D. 79) to guide us, elucidated by a mass of contemporary literary evidence. The New Testament, Josephus, and especially the Mishnah contribute their quota of valuable direct information from the Jewish point of view. Of course, all this must be critically used; Pompeii was in Italy, not in Galilee, and the Mishnah was compiled a century after our period.

The most profound transformation was intellectual, though there were also many striking changes in material civilization. Six centuries of philosophical discussion had accustomed intelligent persons, barbarians as well as Greeks, to think along superficially logical lines and to employ abstract concepts in any discussion. The straightforward empirical wisdom of Elijah's time had too often, in fact, been displaced by the rotund phrases of the dialectician. It had now become easy to use education to conceal wisdom and easier still to cover up one's real designs by specious rhetoric. In material civilization, deductive mathematics and science had now entered the field. The results of the work of geometers and astronomers were evident in greatly improved methods of measuring time and space. Relatively accurate maps gave the man in the street a far clearer idea of the world in which he lived than was possible in Elijah's time. Medicine and surgery, though still primitive from our point of view, had improved greatly; the use of minerals and organic substances in the arts and crafts had been so greatly extended that there would be little further progress in these directions until the late Middle Ages.

Metallurgy had continued to develop, and steel was just coming into use in the first century A.D. The Romans had discovered during the first century B.C. how to make true concrete, an invention which was already revolutionizing the arts of construction and engineering. Such figures as Archimedes of Syracuse (second century B.C.) and Hero of

Alexandria (first century A.D.) were applying mathematical knowledge to the invention of clever mechanical devices. The water-wheel made irrigation cheaper; the rotating stone mill, turned by asses, relieved women of the arduous task of grinding flour with a saddle quern such as was still used in the days of Elijah.

Thanks to the discoveries at Pompeii and other less important Roman sites, we can form an excellent idea of how people of means lived in that period. It made little difference in general to men of substance where they lived, since they would always endeavour to keep up with prevailing fashion in the way their houses were planned and decorated, in the clothes they wore and in their amusements and avocations. The Roman house (*domus*) was merely a later stage of the typical Hellenistic house which preceded it; characteristic of it were the semi-public part around the outer court, or *atrium*, and the more private part, centring around a colonnaded court, which was called by its Greek name, 'peristyle'. The *atrium* (several of which were found in a large mansion) might be 'Tuscan', in which case it was nearly covered by extensions of the adjoining roofs, except for an open space in the middle through which came light and under which was the basin known as the *impluvium*, where the rain-water from the roof was collected and fed into a cistern. The *atrium* might also be tetrastyle, in which case it was surrounded by a colonnade supported by a pillar at each corner of the little court; it might again be a peristyle atrium, like the peristyle around which were grouped the more intimate chambers of the house.

Of course, we must not expect to find much similarity between the houses of the poor in different parts of the Roman Empire; the only common features were their small size and their simplicity. In Palestine, stone and mud-brick remained the chief building materials, just as in earlier times. It is, however, a serious error to assume that the houses of common folk in ancient Palestine were roofed with vaults of stone and plaster or of mud-brick, as is true to-day (after many centuries of progressive destruction of forests). The extensive use of vaults came to Palestine from Iran and Iraq in mediaeval times; earlier houses were commonly covered with flat roofs consisting of wooden joists, on which were laid planks supporting smaller branches and sticks, over which again was a thick layer of lime marl (*hawarah*). The marl roof had to be rolled after each heavy rain in order to keep it water-tight; the cylindrical stone roof-rollers which were used for this purpose had come into use in Iron II, and have continued in use with little modification until to-day. Houses with wooden roofs caught fire with comparative ease compared to the extraordinary difficulty – if not absolute impossibility – of destroying a modern Arab village by fire.

The inventory of these houses also differed considerably from the contents of an ordinary Arab house of a generation or two ago. Where the Arab slept on a thin mattress or pile of mattresses placed on a rush mat stretched on the floor, the Israelites and the Jews of the New Testament period generally slept in beds – high beds if the owner of the house was rich, low cots if he was poor. In Israelite times people sat on chairs or stools and often ate sitting at a table. By New Testament times the Greek custom of reclining at meals had gained the day, and guests always reclined at formal dinners. Another point to be remembered is that the common people of an ancient Jewish village were much cleaner than the inhabitants of a native village a generation ago. Then people washed their hands before eating, instead of waiting until afterwards if they washed them at all. Then the practice of taking frequent baths, or at least of partial bathing, was imposed by their law on all Jews, while Greek habits of bathing the entire body must have penetrated far down through the social strata of the day. These are only illustrations of the relatively high level of public and private cleanliness which then existed, contrasting strikingly with the habits of the population of Palestine, both Christian and Moslem, a few decades ago. Much was gained by giving up the suffocating detail into which the Mosaic law had developed; much was also lost by surrendering the ancient sanitary taboos and the empirical refinements suggested by centuries of practical experience in applying these rules.

Clothing and jewellery, hairdressing and other aids to beauty were all assimilated to the fashions of the day. The dress of the Jew consisted essentially of the same garments, including tunic and mantle, shoes or sandals, and a hat or cap of some kind to protect the head, that were worn by contemporary Greeks. It is entirely erroneous to portray the men of that day as clad in the modern Arab *qamis* and *'abayeh*, with a *keffiyeh* and *'uqal* covering the head; the Arab turban and the Turkish fez were equally unknown, though high conical tiaras were often worn by pagan priests of the time.

The food of the common people of Palestine had been extended and diversified in the nine centuries which separated Elijah from Jesus and his disciples. Among cereals, rice was now grown in wet terrain, though it had not yet replaced the other grains for food to the extent that it did in late Arab times. We do not yet hear of the succulent pilau, in which mounds of tender rice, flavoured by pouring melted butter and gravy over it, are surmounted by piles of roasted mutton, broken into convenient pieces for individual consumption and crested with dainty white morsels from the fat tails of sheep (already well known in Israelite times). Instead of rice, wheat or barley groats were cooked together with tender morsels of mutton, as well as with vegetables of various kinds. Among the vegetables many familiar modern kinds were still unknown. Instead of the familiar beans and peas of to-day there were coarse horse-beans and tasty lentils; chickpeas took the place of popcorn and peanuts. Various kinds of

cucumber and vegetable marrows served instead of the unknown squashes and pumpkins of to-day. Tomatoes were
entirely unknown. On the other hand, onions, leeks, and
garlic played just as great a part in the food of the ancient
Mediterranean as they do to-day; their unrivalled dietary
importance is only now being realized by Western scientists.

If we turn to fruit and nuts, we also find almost as many
differences as similarities between New Testament times and
to-day. Bananas and citrus fruits (except the citron itself)
were still unknown in Palestine. Peaches and apricots were
still unknown; prickly pears had certainly not yet been introduced. On the other hand, olive trees grew everywhere in
much greater abundance than to-day, after centuries in which
every olive tree was taxed by a rapacious treasury. The Arabs
still call unusually large and old olive trees *zeitun er-Rum*,
'olive trees of the Romans'. Vineyards were far more
numerous than they are to-day, and wine-presses hewn from
the solid rock are among the commonest indications of
antiquity, for during the past thirteen centuries the majority
of Palestinians have not allowed wine to touch their lips,
grapes being used only as fruit. Raisins and figs, honey and
dates took the place of the sugar cane, which was not to be
introduced until the Middle Ages. However, many kinds of
fruit which are less popular to-day were then relished for
lack of anything better. Almonds, walnuts (introduced in the
Persian period), apples and pears of inferior quality, pome-
granates, and sycamore figs (now eaten only by the poorest,
but then punctured and grown much larger than to-day)
were among the staples of the age.

One important change in diet between the time of Elijah
and that of the New Testament was the introduction of
domestic fowls and eggs into everyday life. The earliest
certain representation of a cock is on a seal from Tell en-
Nasbeh discovered by the late W. F. Badè and dating from
the beginning of the sixth century B.C. (Fig. 62). In the Per-

sian period the domestic fowl became known also to the Greeks. The introduction of barn-yard fowls and their useful product to household economy was a matter of the utmost practical importance. Geese were already known, and ducks were coming into more general popularity in this period. Turkeys were, of course, not to be introduced for a millennium and a half.

As the reader will have noted, there were very many changes in everyday life during the long period spanned by the history of the Bible, from the beginning of Israel in the Patriarchal Age to the Fall of the Second Temple and the end of the New Testament age. Multifarious as were these changes, they were insignificant when compared to the transformation in the world of the spirit, both intellectual and aesthetic. We are entirely safe in saying that the intellectual gap between Jacob and St Paul was wider than that between the latter and our own day, though the material change of the past few centuries undoubtedly dwarfs that between Jacob and Paul.

Fig. 62. Seal of Jaazaniah from Tell en-Nasbeh, showing fighting cock (c. 600 B.C.).

CHAPTER 10

The Old Testament and Archaeology

—

IN one's enthusiasm for archaeological research, one is sometimes tempted to disregard the enduring reason for any special interest in Palestine – nearly all the Hebrew Old Testament is a product of Palestinian soil and Israelite writers, while most of the events which underlie the Greek New Testament took place in the same sacred terrain. Though the Old Testament contains a synthesis of the best that had been contributed by the ancient East, it was transmuted by Hebrew religious insight into a work which rises mountain-high above even the highest hills of Egypt and Mesopotamia, and which is permeated through and through with the elusive fragrance of Palestine. Similarly the New Testament, though its contents reflect a synthesis of Jewish faith and thought with Greek logic and beauty, has to do mainly with things that happened in Palestine and with the words of a Teacher who spent virtually His entire life there.

It is frequently said that the scientific quality of Palestinian archaeology has been seriously impaired by the religious preconceptions of scholars who have excavated in the Holy Land. It is true that some archaeologists have been drawn to Palestine by their interest in the Bible, and that some of them had received their previous training mainly as biblical scholars. The writer has known many such scholars, but he recalls scarcely a single case where their religious views seriously influenced their results. Some of these scholars were radical critics; still others were more conservative critics, like Ernst Sellin; others again were thorough-going conservatives. But their archaeological conclusions were almost uniformly independent of their critical views. There have been a few cases like that of Sir Charles Marston, whose untrained enthusiasm led him to misinterpret certain discoveries by Garstang and Starkey. The violence done to scholarly objectivity by some of these Palestinian excavators is slight indeed when compared to the damage to Egyptology which resulted from the wholesale brigandage of Belzoni and Passalacqua, or the airtight monopoly of the field by Mariette and the ruthless spoliation of royal tombs by Amélineau. Nor should we forget that some of the foremost scientific excavators, such as Petrie and Reisner, won some of their fairest laurels in Palestine. As an illustration of the caution practised by leading Palestinian archaeologists it is interesting to recall that Petrie and Bliss, Macalister and Watzinger, followed by virtually all others, nearly always set their dates far too low, while in Egypt dates were generally placed far too high. Here we have the curious spectacle of an archaeological chronology being progressively raised in Palestine, while in Egypt it has had to be progressively lowered.

While not a single piece of papyrus or ostracon containing a biblical fragment from pre-Maccabaean days has yet been found in Palestine, the inscriptions to which we referred particularly in Chapter 8 have given us a very clear idea of the physical appearance of the original writings of the Old Testament. Thus the forms of letters and the spelling of the Gezer Calendar from the late tenth century give us information with regard to the external characteristics of such early biblical prose compositions as the account of the events preceding the death of David and the coronation of Solomon in II Samuel. The spelling of the Gezer Calendar and contemporary Phoenician inscriptions helps us to fix a date in that same century for such early poems as II Samuel xxii (Psalm xviii) and enables us to prove that earlier poems like the Oracles of Balaam could not have been written down appreciably later. The Ostraca of Samaria, from the early eighth century, give us a very exact idea of the script and orthography employed in the time of the Prophet Hosea. The Siloam inscription, from about 700 B.C., is an excellent illustration of Isaiah's writing and spelling (though he may have used a somewhat more cursive script in writing his own compositions). Most striking of all is the light thrown by the Lachish Ostraca on the script, spelling, and language of Jeremiah's time.

The foregoing inscriptions were all in Hebrew; after the Exile all Jewish inscriptions, aside from a few very short ones on seals and coins, were written in Aramaic. Palestine itself has yielded a number of Aramaic ostraca from Samaria, Tell el-Far'ah, and elsewhere, written in exactly the script and language of Jewish papyri and ostraca of the fifth century B.C. which have been found in Egypt. As we shall see below, these texts are in the same language as the Aramaic of Ezra (aside from slightly revised spelling, such as we have in the Hebrew of Jeremiah); the Aramaic of Daniel is substantially the same, but shows its later date in grammatical details and Greek loan words.

Until the year 1947 Egypt had been kinder to students of the Hebrew biblical text than Palestine. Before papyrus fragments in Hebrew began turning up in Egypt a few years ago, the oldest dated Hebrew manuscript of any part of the Old Testament was the Codex Petropolitanus from the year A.D. 916. Several undated manuscripts have been placed a little earlier by Paul Kahle, but the palaeographic criteria are insufficient to establish their dating beyond doubt. At Oxyrhynchus in the Egyptian Faiyum some Hebrew biblical fragments from the Byzantine period have been found, but none seems to be earlier than the fourth century A.D. In 1902 the Nash fragment containing the Ten Commandments and the Shema ('Hear, O Israel ... ') was discovered in the Faiyum; it was at first dated in the second or possibly first century A.D., but the great recent increase in our knowledge of contemporary Hebrew–Aramaic script now proves that it antedated the Herodian Age and must be attributed to the preceding late Maccabaean period. To the same period belongs the Fuad fragment of the Greek Deuteronomy, in which the scribe left blank spaces wherever later Greek texts have *Kyrios*, 'the Lord'; in these spaces a Jewish scribe then inserted the four Aramaic (square Hebrew) letters of the divine name YHWH, which was no longer pronounced, but simply written and replaced in reading by *adonai*, 'my Lord'. The Hebrew–Aramaic letters used in writing the Tetragrammaton are exactly the same as those employed for the same purpose in the Nash Papyrus, a fact which furnishes weighty additional proof for the early date of the latter.

But these finds, promising as they were, are dwarfed into insignificance by the epoch-making manuscript discovery made in the summer of 1947. At that time some Bedouins discovered an ancient cave in the cliffs above the north end of the Dead Sea. In it they found a number of large broken jars, in which some precious scrolls had been put for safety, wrapped in linen cloth and well sealed. Nearly a dozen rolls of leather and parchment were recovered and sold to the monks of the Syrian Orthodox Convent of St Mark in Jerusalem and the Hebrew University in Jerusalem. Four scrolls which were brought to the United States by the Syrian archbishop, were subsequently sold to Israel, so all the scrolls of the original find are now in Israeli Jerusalem. All but one of the original lot of scrolls were published between 1950 and 1954; they are revolutionizing our knowledge of the textual criticism of the Hebrew Old Testament, of the Essene sect, and of the background of the New Testament (see p. 249). Early opposition to the antiquity and authenticity of the new Qumran material has rapidly faded away before the mass of corroborative evidence, and there can no longer be any doubt that it dates before the Roman occupation of this region in A.D. 69. Nearly all the Qumran scrolls antedate the Christian era.

In the excavation of the first Qumran cave G. L. Harding and R. de Vaux found sherds from over forty jars in which the scrolls had been stored, as well as quantities of linen in which the scrolls had been wrapped. The pottery is Hellenistic-Roman, from the last century of the Second Temple (*c.* 30 B.C.–A.D. 70), and the linen has been dated by radiocarbon to the time of Christ, with a considerable margin of statistical uncertainty. Additional discoveries of the greatest importance have been made in a cave directly below the Essene settlement of the same period (dated by coins), near the first cave. Excavations in this new cave in 1952 have yielded masses of scroll fragments, containing parts of nearly every book in the Hebrew Bible, besides original Essene books and fragments of apocryphal and pseudepigraphical works. Apart from the intrinsic value of these finds, they provide conclusive palaeographic evidence for the antiquity of the Scrolls. A number of documents and fragments in later script found in 1952 further south, at Murabba'at, dating from the time of Bar Cochba (*c.* A.D. 130–5), further confirm the early date of the Qumran Scrolls.

By far the most important of the new scrolls is a complete roll of the Book of Isaiah, intact except where it has been damaged by the vicissitudes of time. This roll was written, according to its script – which is much more archaic in a number of respects than that of the Nash fragment – somewhere in the latter part of the second or the early part of the first century B.C. – about 100 B.C. in round numbers. It is thus about a thousand years older than the Codex Petropolitanus and nearly as much earlier than the very oldest rolls of the Hebrew Bible which were previously known to be extant.

Besides the Fuad fragment of the Greek (Septuagint) of Deuteronomy there is the recently discovered Rylands fragment, which dates from the second century B.C. and is thus probably the oldest biblical manuscript fragment yet discovered. Next in age are some of the Chester Beatty papyri, which may be dated as early as the second and third centuries A.D., one or two hundred years older than the oldest parchment codices of the Greek Bible, widely known as the Vaticanus and the Sinaiticus. Recent discoveries have thus nearly filled the former gap between the original translation of the Hebrew Bible into Greek during the third and second centuries B.C. and the earliest manuscript attestation of the Septuagint translation. We are thus in a position to reconstruct the script and spelling used in virtually every phase of the history of the Hebrew Bible and its Greek translation. In the light of such evidence it is a far cry from the time, half a century ago, when adventurous European savants could seriously date the composition of a considerable part of the Hebrew Bible in early Roman times! Lest this idea seems unduly grotesque, it may be added that there were outstanding scholars at that time who dated parts of chapters and even whole chapters of the Hebrew Bible in the first century B.C. In the next chapter we shall note equal absurdities in dating parts of the New Testament.

Turning now to the question of the way in which the Old Testament assumed its present form, we enter into a field where literary criticism based on internal evidence held the field undisputed until recently. Now we see extrinsic evidence pouring in from archaeological discoveries in all the countries around Palestine, especially Egypt, Syria, Mesopotamia, and Asia Minor. Combining this evidence with other finds, including the indications of cultural relationships which have been recovered from Palestinian mounds, as frequently noted in our earlier chapters, we are now able to paint a fairly satisfactory picture of the actual situation. The Hebrews brought with them from their original Mesopotamian home the hallowed cosmogonic stories which they had learned there. To these ancient stories, handed down for uncounted centuries by word of mouth, were added the poetic narratives of the Patriarchs, which were subsequently adapted to the form of prose saga in which they have survived in the Hebrew Bible. Then came the soul-shaking events of the Exodus and the Wanderings, which were handed down in poetry and prose, together with the teachings and institutions of Moses. Gathered together in various compilations, the documents of the Mosaic Age were gradually formed into a single collection, which was completed in approximately its present form before the Restoration at the end of the sixth century B.C. The contents of our Pentateuch are, in general, very much older than the date at which they were finally edited; new discoveries continue to confirm the historical accuracy or the literary antiquity of detail after detail in it. Even when it is necessary to assume later additions to the original nucleus of Mosaic tradition, these additions reflect the normal growth of ancient institutions and practices, or the effort made by later scribes to save as much as possible of extant traditions about Moses. It is, accordingly, sheer hypercriticism to deny the substantially Mosaic character of the Pentateuchal tradition.

As this ancient nucleus of Israelite *torah* grew into its present form, other parts were added. First came the great historical compilation made by the so-called Deuteronomist, a deeply religious scholar who probably flourished about the end of the seventh century B.C. This writer gathered a considerable body of material, beginning with the book of Deuteronomy (later removed from his collection and included in the Pentateuch, to which it belongs by virtue of its contents), and ending with II Kings. All these priceless documents were copied or abridged with the greatest care, and some of them were reproduced verbatim. Through most of the work of the Deuteronomist are interspersed additions and commentaries from his hand, written in a very characteristic style which resembles that of the prose parts of Jeremiah and the Lachish Letters in a number of important respects. This style is highly rhetorical, but nearly always very clear, in spite of its elaborate syntax. The content of the additions written by the Deuteronomist reflects the prophetic view of the close relation between sin and punishment, as well as the author's consciousness of overhanging doom.

Some two centuries after the historical work of the Deuteronomist came the compilation made by the Chronicler, consisting of I and II Chronicles (Paralipomena), Ezra, and Nehemiah. Here again, we find painstaking care and accurate reproduction of the compiler's material, in which he followed such sources as the books of Genesis, Samuel, and Kings, as well as the memoirs of Ezra and Nehemiah. The rest of the Chronicler's matter comes from older written documents and oral tradition; this added matter is strikingly uniform in style and language, showing strong Aramaic influence on a stilted Hebrew which betrays its scholastic origin. Moreover, this supplementary matter is identical in style, language, and special interests with the memoirs of Ezra, written in the first person. From this fact, some scholars (e.g. C. C. Torrey) have deduced that the Ezra Memoirs are late and apocryphal, while others (including the present writer) have inferred that Ezra himself was the Chronicler. It is a fact that virtually all concrete objections to the latter view have been disproved or are in process of being refuted by recent archaeological discoveries.

The poetic literature of the Old Testament was distributed by older scholarly tradition among virtually all phases of Israelite history, while modern critical scholars have been disposed to date most of it (except for the nucleus of the older Prophetic books) after the Exile. Archaeological discoveries tend to modify both extreme positions, as we shall illustrate below with specific examples. In the light of the Ugaritic remains of Canaanite religious literature, many of the Psalms must be pushed back into early Israelite times, not later than the tenth century. There is thus no longer any reason to refuse a Davidic date for such Psalms. At the same time, it has become improbable that any of them descend below the fourth century B.C., and the assumption that there are Maccabean Psalms, dating from the second or early first century B.C., has become almost incredible. We find a similar situation in Proverbs, since the discovery of Egyptian and Sumerian collections of proverbs from the third millennium B.C. makes the antiquity of such collections certain, while resemblances to later Egyptian, Accadian, and Canaanite literature suggest that much of the biblical book dates from pre-exilic times. On the other hand, there is now less reason than ever to date Job and Ecclesiastes before the sixth–fifth and the third centuries B.C. respectively.

In the foregoing chapters we have had occasion to mention many examples where the facts brought to light by Palestinian archaeology agree with specific points in biblical history; we have also referred to the close general parallelism between archaeological and literary evidence. Since early Palestinian inscriptions are still few, we must concentrate our attention mainly on evidence of strictly archaeological character. One of the principal services of the archaeologist to the biblical scholar has been in the identification of modern sites with ancient towns mentioned in the Old Testament. Sometimes this has been made easy by the identity of ancient and modern names, confirmed by the parallelism found to exist between the archaeological and the literary history of given places. The parade example of convergent lines of evidence is the case of Gezer. Clermont-Ganneau (Chapter 2) identified biblical Gezer with modern Tell Djezer on the strength of the name (since Arabic *dj* regularly corresponds to Hebrew *g*), which he found still preserved to-day and already recorded in an Arabic work of the fifteenth century A.D. Not long afterwards he discovered several inscriptions, deeply carved in the rock outside the ancient town, bearing the Aramaic words 'boundary of Gezer' in

letters of the first century B.C. Macalister's subsequent excavations, the results of which can now be more accurately
dated than was possible at the time of the excavation, confirmed Clermont-Ganneau's discovery in the most complete
way. More recently, the identification of Lachish with Tell
ed-Duweir, proposed after confrontation of the biblical data
and the statements of Eusebius in the fourth century A.D.
with the results of surface examination of the site, has been
strikingly confirmed by Starkey's excavations. The ostraca
published by Torczyner mention the town in a context which
practically compels us to identify Lachish with Tell ed-
Duweir, but the identification would be certain even without
this epigraphic evidence.

Many other sites have been archaeologically fixed without
any evidence from inscriptions. For example, in 1928 Garstang discovered the ancient Galilaean town of Hazor at Tell
el-Qedah, south-west of Lake Semechonitis, after several
scholars, including the writer, had been hunting for it in vain
for years. The archaeological situation agrees perfectly with
the topographical indications from the Bible and other documentary sources, and there is no other possible site for
Hazor. It is, therefore, not surprising that every competent
student immediately hailed the identification as definitive.
Many previously identified sites have subsequently been excavated, with full confirmation of the identifications. Examples with which the writer was actively connected, are
Shiloh, Gibeah of Saul (Tell el-Ful), Bethel, and Beth-zur,
where the archaeological history of the sites has proved to be
in the fullest accord with the indications preserved in the
Bible and Josephus. Shiloh flourished in the period of the
Judges and was abandoned after a conflagration which
destroyed it not far from the middle of the eleventh century
B.C.; this destruction coincides with the events mentioned in
I Sam. iv. After the Philistine destruction Shiloh lay in ruins
for centuries, just as stated repeatedly by Jeremiah. Gibeah

had been occupied during the period of the Judges and was destroyed at least once by fire during this time, as related in Judges xx; it reached the climax of its prosperity in the period immediately following the destruction of Shiloh, when the summit of the hill was crowned by a strongly built fortress dating from the period of Saul, who resided there according to biblical tradition. Various scholars had expressed doubt about the identification of Bethel with modern Beitin, in spite of the perfect agreement of the modern site with all non-archaeological requirements, because there seemed to be no evidence of early occupation. However, excavation proved that the archaeological history of Beitin was identical with literary indications for Bethel throughout, from the time of Joshua to that of Vespasian. At Khirbet et-Tubeiqah north of Hebron, where several scholars had independently located Beth-zur, excavation brought to light perfect concordance with the data of First Maccabees. The writer was director or archaeological adviser of the expeditions which dug the last four towns which we have mentioned; the results of these excavations have naturally made an ineffaceable impression on his mind, an impression confirmed by innumerable finds of other archaeologists. Biblical historical data are accurate to an extent far surpassing the ideas of any modern critical students, who have consistently tended to err on the side of hypercriticism.

Thanks to archaeological determination of the site of most biblical places, it is also possible to establish the age and historical significance of many lists of towns in the Bible. A good case in point is the list of Levitic cities in Josh. xxi and I Chron. vi, which Wellhausen, followed by most subsequent critics, considered an artificial product of some post-exilic scribe's imagination. Careful examination of this list in the light of all known archaeological facts makes it quite certain that the list is much more ancient, and that the only time when all the towns mentioned in it were in Israelite possession was under David and Solomon. Not a single town in the list can be shown to have been founded at a period subsequent to the middle of the tenth century B.C., though several cannot be much earlier than this date. A date between about 975 and about 950 B.C. may thus be fixed for the extant form of the list, which seems to have had a prehistory going back to the Conquest.

Palestinian archaeology is much less helpful in throwing direct light on biblical personalities, mainly owing to the scarcity of inscriptions. Actually, more biblical personages are mentioned in inscriptions discovered outside of Palestine than in documents found in the country. Yet there is a great deal of indirect light. It is far easier to appraise the careers of the Patriarchs, of Joshua, Gideon and Samson, of Samuel, Saul, David, and Solomon, than it formerly was. The scanty light now shed on the building operations of Saul and David, and the rich new information bearing on the constructions of Solomon (Chapter 6), are most welcome aids to our understanding of the evolution of Israelite material culture under these rulers of United Israel, who thus become much more tangible figures than they were. The events of the Omride Dynasty and the period of Jeroboam II also become much more sharply focused now that we know what the culture of Samaria was like in their day. The same is true of the times of Uzziah and Hezekiah in Judah. The end of the monarchy of Judah has been so brightly illumined by the discoveries at Lachish, Tell Beit Mirsim, and other sites, that Jeremiah's life and times can no longer be drastically misinterpreted by competent scholars.

We have had occasion in Chapters 5 and 8 to mention the sensational discoveries of Canaanite literary texts at Ugarit (Ras Shamrah) on the coast of northern Syria. Ugarit lay at the northern end of Canaan, which included all western Palestine; its people spoke a Canaanite dialect, and their scribes copied out Canaanite epics, dealing with mythological exploits of the deities Baal and Ânath, and with legendary adventures of the heroes Keret and Aqhat (son of the Daniel mentioned in Ezek. xiv and xviii between Noah and Job as one of the wisest of ancient sages). All these epics can be shown from their contents to have originated in the heart of Canaanite culture, that is, in Phoenicia; they must have been just as well known in the Canaanite towns of Palestine about 1400 B.C. as they were at Ugarit. The Phoenician inscriptions from tenth-century Byblus swarm with literary reminiscences of this epic literature.

The religious texts of Ugarit were nearly all discovered by C. F. A. Schaeffer between 1929 and 1933; since then scarcely any tablets of a religious nature have been discovered. Numerous parallels between Ugaritic and Hebrew literary style and vocabulary were noticed immediately by the editor of these documents, Charles Virolleaud, but it was not until 1936 that H. L. Ginsberg made some far-reaching observations with regard to common structural elements. He pointed out that in Hebrew verse we sometimes find a very characteristic form which recurs in Ugaritic: a-b-c: a-b-d, in which each letter stands for a separate word or pair of short words, the first two of which are repeated in the second half of the poetic line. For convenience we may call each half line a colon and each line a bicolon; the terms hemistich and stich (or stich and distich) are used to denote the same verse units. Ginsberg showed also that this basic form was often expanded in both literatures to a tricolon, in which the repetitive formula varies somewhat. Canaanite poetry, like later Hebrew, was basically accentual, that is, it was composed of four, five, or six 'feet', each of which was accented. There is reason to believe that syllables were also originally counted, but the evidence is still indecisive, though we are quite certain that unaccented syllables were not counted in classical Hebrew poetry. A very good example of this particular stylistic form and at the same time one of the best illustrations of the survival of Canaanite literary elements in Hebrew literature is the following tricolon from a tablet of the Baal Epic, which describes the battle between the storm-god and the sea-dragon Yam (also appearing in Hebrew poetry):

> Behold, thine enemies, O Baal,
>> Behold, thine enemies shalt thou crush,
>> Behold, thou shalt smite thy foes!

In Psalm xcii, 9 this passage recurs with slight changes as follows:

> For behold, Thine enemies, O Lord,
>> For behold, Thine enemies shall perish,
>> All doers of evil shall be scattered!

The tricolon appears in the Aqhat (Daniel) Epic not infrequently; a good case is the following:

> Do thou ask for life, O lad Aqhat,
>> Do thou ask for life and I'll grant (it) thee,
>> Eternal life, and I'll accord (it) thee!

We find similar stylistic devices in the Song of Deborah, e.g., Judg. v, 30:

> A spoil of dyed stuffs for Sisera,
>> A spoil of dyed stuffs embroidered,
>>> Dyed and embroidered from the necks of the spoiled!

The range of stylistic variation in this type of verse-form is very considerable, but the theme of rhythmic repetition of words is common to all of them. We now know that it was most popular in Israelite literature during the thirteenth and twelfth centuries B.C., and that it rapidly lost ground thereafter, being abandoned entirely by the tenth century, except where older Canaanite poems were adapted to Israelite purposes and where single poetic passages or lines were re-used in archaizing verse. This repetitive or climactic parallelism is characteristic of the Song of Miriam (Ex. xv), celebrating the triumph of Israel over Egypt at the Exodus, and in the closely related Song of Deborah, describing the victory of Israel over Sisera towards the end of the twelfth century. In these two triumphal poems we have an accumulation of repetitive parallelism which exceeds anything so far found in

Ugaritic literature or in later Israelite poetry (aside from Psalm xxix and the archaizing Psalm of Habakkuk). This situation cannot be accidental, particularly as the literary genre of the triumphal poem, celebrating military victory, was then at the climax of its popularity in ancient times; non-Israelite examples from the period are the Egyptian poems describing the victories of Ramesses II over the Hittites, of his son Merneptah over the Libyans, and of Ramesses III over the Sea Peoples, as well as the great triumphal song of the Assyrian king Tukulti-Ninurta I in honour of his victory over the Babylonians. If we had original Canaanite triumphal poems from the same thirteenth and twelfth centuries, we may rest assured that we should find similar heaping up of repetitive parallelism.

In this connexion it is instructive to note that the Song of Deborah has in general been attributed by all critical scholars to the early part of the period of the Judges, while the Song of Miriam, in spite of its very close stylistic resemblance to the former, has been regarded as much later – even as in part post-exilic. This late dating is largely due to Ex. xv, 17, which mentions 'the mountain of Thine inheritance' as the site of the residence of Yahweh on earth. Not unnaturally this expression has been taken as referring to Mount Zion and the Temple of Solomon (or of Zerubbabel). Unfortunately for this plausible argument, the home of Baal in the Canaanite epic, which was composed not later than 1400 B.C., is also said to have been 'on the mountain of his inheritance'. It follows from this and other similar facts that there is no longer the slightest valid reason for dating the Song of Miriam after the thirteenth century B.C. Of course, this does not mean that every phrase or line is equally old, since these ancient poems were probably handed down for generations by word of mouth.

The wealth of new Canaanite evidence for rare and archaic words or phrases in biblical Hebrew is overwhelming; it is gradually enabling philologians to clear up many obscurities which have baffled translators since the time of the earliest Greek translators in the third and second centuries B.C. Following are some examples. In Psalm lxviii, 4 we have a curious expression which has been commonly rendered literally as 'rider on the evenings', or by a reasonable guess as 'rider on the heavens'; in Ugaritic the expression occurs frequently with only a very slight consonantal divergence from the transmitted Hebrew spelling as 'rider on the clouds', referring to the storm-god Baal. In Hebrew poetry this beautiful appellation has been transferred to Yahweh, without carrying with it any mythological connotation. In Psalm lxxxix, 19, where the Authorized Version renders 'I have laid help upon one that is mighty; I have exalted one chosen out of the people', Ugaritic evidence proves that we must translate 'I have placed a youth above the mighty man; I have raised a young man above the people'. The context shows that David is meant.

A good many new words must be included in future Hebrew dictionaries; among them is a word for 'glaze', first identified by H. L. Ginsberg and now combined with a word which appears in both Ugaritic and Hittite. Proverbs xxvi, 23 is rendered in the Authorized Version: 'Burning lips and a wicked heart are like a potsherd covered with silver dross', a figure which is archaeologically impossible to understand, quite aside from its semantic obscurity. We must now translate: 'Like glaze crusted over pottery are smooth lips and an evil heart'. Another hitherto misunderstood expression in Proverbs is *beth-heber* (Prov. xxi, 9; xxv, 24), rendered 'wide house' in the English Bible. Ugaritic and Assyrian both have this term, vocalized correctly as *bit khuburi*; the latter was first rendered 'store-house', but a text of the Old Assyrian king Erreshum, published by Landsberger, now establishes the sense of 'brewery, beer-house'. The biblical verses thus mean: 'It is better to live in the corner of a roof-terrace than with a brawling woman in a beer-house'. The implications are obvious.

Light has been thrown on hundreds of other words, including many whose meaning was inferred but not proved, as well as many whose meaning still remains somewhat doubtful. A very striking example is in Isa. xxvii, 1, where the Authorized Version reads: 'In that day the Lord with His sore and great and strong sword shall punish Leviathan the piercing serpent, even Leviathan that crooked serpent; and He shall slay the dragon that is in the sea'. The Baal Epic of Ugarit calls Leviathan (Lotan) a viper, employing exactly the same appellations which are translated above 'piercing' and 'crooked'. The new spelling and context in which these words are found go far towards explaining them. This verse also refers to the *tannin* (dragon) in the sea; the same monster is mentioned in the Ugaritic texts.

Sometimes the new evidence supports time-honoured interpretation against modern conjectural innovations. Thus in Gen. i, 2, the words 'And the Spirit of God moved upon the face of the waters' have been taken by some modern scholars to mean that a mighty wind (literally 'wind of God') blew over the water of the primordial ocean, while other scholars, taking their cue from Phoenician mythology, have rendered 'And the Spirit of God brooded (like a nesting fowl) on the water' (hatching life from chaos). Several passages in the Aqhat Epic neatly confirm the meaning suggested by Deut. xxxii, 11, 'to soar over like an eagle (vulture)'; it thus becomes certain that we must render Gen. i, 2 'And the Spirit of God was soaring over the surface of the water'.

As in the case of many other sensational archaeological finds, the historical bearing of this new material was at first exaggerated by some distinguished authorities who believed that Ugaritic literature threw direct light on the beginnings of Israelite history in the Patriarchal Age. The name of Terah, father of Abraham, as well as of other figures in Genesis, was erroneously discovered in the enigmatic new documents. It was thought that the beginnings of Canaanite history had somehow been interwoven with the early history of Israel, and that the patriarchal narratives of Genesis and the tales of Ugarit were in part divergent forms of the same original sagas. These premature ideas were accepted by many writers and found their way into widely used handbooks. Now they have been abandoned by virtually all students of Ugaritic literature, since they cannot be squared with our rapidly increasing knowledge of the grammar and vocabulary of this new Canaanite dialect. Yet it will be a long time before the last traces of such divagations are eliminated from modern handbooks dealing with biblical history.

On the other hand, the extraordinary discoveries of André Parrot at Mari on the Middle Euphrates (Chapter 5) since 1935 are in the process of yielding authentic information about the Patriarchal Age. Aided by finds of contemporary and somewhat later date made by Mallowan at Chagar Bazar in north-western Mesopotamia and by Chiera and others at Nuzu (Yaghlan Tepe) in north-eastern Mesopotamia, the tablets from Mari are illuminating all corners of the age in question. Dossin and Jean are editing the thousands of tablets from Mari; every new publication of theirs helps us better to understand the life and times of the Hebrew Patriarchs. Abraham, Isaac, and Jacob no longer seem isolated figures, much less reflections of later Israelite history; they now appear as true children of their age, bearing the same names, moving about over the same territory, visiting the same towns (especially Harran and Nahor), practising the same customs as their contemporaries. In other words, the patriarchal narratives have a historical nucleus throughout, though it is likely that long oral transmission of the original poems and later prose sagas which underlie the present text of Genesis has considerably refracted the original events. This process of handing down the ancient tradition by word of mouth from generation to generation led to the omission of many details which would have interested a modern historian, but it also brought about a recasting of tradition in more dramatic form, emphasizing its religious and pedagogical values. Our gain is thus far greater than any possible loss.

A very remarkable example seems to be the enigmatic fourteenth chapter of Genesis, which describes the triumph of Abram over the Mesopotamian kings headed by Chedorlaomer of Elam. A generation ago most critical scholars regarded this chapter as very late and as quite unhistorical. Now we cannot accept such an easy way out of the difficulties which the chapter presents, since some of its allusions are exceedingly early, carrying us directly back into the Middle Bronze Age. For instance, the strange word for 'retainers', used in verse 14, which occurs nowhere else in the Bible, is now known to be an Egyptian word employed in the Execration Texts of the late nineteenth century B.C. of the retainers of Palestinian chieftains, and used in the same sense four centuries later in one of the Taanach tablets. Several of the towns mentioned in this chapter are now proved to be very ancient, and the archaic words and poetic expressions with which the chapter abounds are clear indications of an old verse form underlying the present text.

Another example is the story of the Exodus, which was of such perennial interest that it circulated in different poetic and prose forms for centuries, being modernized and refracted in the process. Yet the biblical account remains substantially historical. For instance, the University of California expedition to Sinai in 1947–8, in which the writer took part, confirmed geographical details which had often been rejected. Similarly, the writer's study of the Hayes list of Asiatic slaves (1954) has proved that even such trivial points as the names of the midwives (Ex. i, 15) are true for the middle centuries of the second millennium, despite previous assertions to the contrary.

CHAPTER 11

The New Testament and Archaeology

—

It is much more difficult to apply the results of archaeological research in Palestine to the New Testament than to the Old. In the first place, the latter spans a period of over a millennium and a half, whereas the New Testament covers less than a century. From the time of Moses to that of Ezra nearly a thousand years had elapsed; from the beginning of Jesus' ministry as recorded in the Gospel of Mark to the end of Acts we reckon only about a third of a century. Moreover, while a high proportion of the contents of the historical books of the Old Testament are national in scope, the happenings recounted in the New were shared as a rule only by small groups of private individuals. The impact of archaeology on New Testament studies has also been much less obvious, because the Graeco-Roman period of Mediterranean history was incomparably better known than the preceding ancient Oriental phase before the beginning of modern excavation. Yet the importance of archaeology for this period of biblical history is already very great and is growing year by year.

No other work from Graeco-Roman antiquity is so well attested by manuscript tradition as the New Testament. There are many more early manuscripts of the New Testament than there are of any classical author, and the oldest extensive remains of it date only about two centuries after their original composition. The only manuscript of the Greek New Testament antedating the fifth or sixth centuries A.D. which was known to exist a century ago was the Codex Vaticanus, a vellum (parchment) text preserved in the library of the Vatican, but it was at that time virtually inaccessible to scholars and had scarcely been utilized at all by textual critics. In 1859 a German scholar, Constantin Tischendorf, discovered a parchment codex of equally old date in the monastery of St Catherine at Mount Sinai, and was able to acquire this precious text for the Tsar of Russia. In 1933 the Codex Sinaiticus, having been purchased from Russia by the British Government, became the chief treasure of the British Museum, which now houses two of the three most important Greek biblical manuscripts in the world (the other being the fifth-century Codex Alexandrinus). Dating from the first half of the fourth century A.D., the Vaticanus and the Sinaiticus now represent the most valuable extant authorities for the text of the New Testament.

Over seventy years after the discovery of the Codex Sinaiticus, an equally remarkable find was announced (1931): the papyrus leaves of the New Testament in the Chester Beatty collection. Some 126 imperfect leaves belonging to books of the New Testament are included in this collection; all are attributed by Sir Frederick Kenyon and his colleagues to different parts of the third century A.D. The fragments of the Gospels are believed to date back to the first half of the century. In 1935 C. H. Roberts published a papyrus fragment of the Gospel of John which he had found among the treasures of the John Rylands Library at Manchester; though only a scrap, it possesses exceptional importance because it is written in a hand attributed to the time of Trajan or more probably Hadrian (died A.D. 135). In the same year H. I. Bell and T. C. Skeat published a larger papyrus fragment of the British Museum containing a small part of an account of the life of Christ based on all four Gospels, including St John. The original author had treated his sources much more freely than was considered permissible by later harmonizers, like Tatian, who wrote in the late second century (a parchment fragment of his Harmony of the Gospels, from the early third century A.D., was discovered at Dura and published, also in 1935, by

C. H. Kraeling). The early date of the British Museum 'Harmony' is proved by its hand, which is attributed by competent specialists to the first half of the second century A.D.

These remarkable discoveries have dealt the *coup de grâce* to such extreme critical views of the New Testament as the speculations of the Tübingen School, founded by F. C. Baur, and the Dutch School, headed by Van Manen. According to the Tübingen School less than half a dozen books of the New Testament were written in the first century A.D., and the Gospel of St John was written as late as the second half of the second century. Van Manen, Loman, and their followers denied the authenticity of all the Pauline Epistles, which they also relegated to the second century. A date for John in the first half of the second century has remained popular in radical biblical circles until very recently. Under the impact of the new finds, a strong reaction has recently set in, materially aided by C. C. Torrey's view that John is a translation from an Aramaic text written down well before A.D. 70. Some radical scholars (e.g., Erwin Goodenough) now consider John as the earliest of the Gospels instead of the latest.

In Chapter 8 we discussed the theory of Aramaic *written* sources for the Gospels at some length, pointing out that the archaeological evidence does not favour this approach. On the other hand, we noted that the case for Aramaic *oral* sources has been greatly strengthened by recent investigation. In other words, the Gospel traditions were formed in Aramaic-speaking communities in Palestine; they were not put into Greek until the dispersion of the Jewish Christians of Palestine during the First Revolt of A.D. 66–70. It has been assumed by most recent New Testament scholars that there was comparatively little interruption in the life of Christian communities in Palestine as a result of the First Revolt. This attitude is almost as completely disproved by archaeology as we found to have been true of similar recent hypotheses about the effects of the Chaldaean invasions of Judah in the early sixth century B.C. (Chapter 6). Since this fact is not generally realized, some explanation is necessary.

After years of increasing restiveness on the part of the Jewish population of Palestine, marked by frequent riots and harsh repression, the First Revolt broke out in A.D. 66, and lasted for four years. During this time the Jews of Galilee and Jerusalem suffered most, since the two chief centres of rebellion were located there. Most of the Jewish population which escaped death was sold into slavery. The completeness of this catastrophe is illustrated by the fact that not a single synagogue of the early Roman period has yet been discovered in any part of Palestine. All known synagogue remains belong to the end of the second century A.D. or later (see above, in Chapter 7). The devastation spread by Roman armies was greatly increased by the native pagan population, which ruthlessly massacred the Jews and destroyed their homes and public buildings. After the suppression of the First Revolt the condition of the Jews remained exceedingly difficult, and the principal focus of Jewish life in Palestine shifted to the Coastal Plain around Joppa and Lydda. It has sometimes been supposed that the Jews returned to Jerusalem and continued to maintain some sort of communal life there. Archaeological evidence is wholly against this view. Not a single one of the many Jewish tombs which have been excavated in the region of Jerusalem can be dated to the period after A.D. 70; every inscribed ossuary hitherto discovered near Jerusalem belongs to the last century of the Second Temple (30 B.C.–A.D. 70).

The Christians suffered even more than the rest of the Jewish population, since they were treated as Jews by their pagan neighbours and were hated as pacifists and defeatists, as well as heretics, by their own people. In one of the bitter outbreaks of anti-Christian feeling which flared up during the years immediately preceding the First Revolt, James, brother of Jesus and head of the Christian community in Jerusalem, was killed. It is highly probable that most of the Christians in Jerusalem and the larger towns of Galilee, where nationalist feeling ran highest, escaped from their homes before the beginning of the First Revolt. Later Christian tradition recalled that the Christian remnant had fled from Jerusalem to Pella before the last Roman invasion of Judaea. The dispersion of the Jewish Christians broke the continuous chain of tradition which had connected Jesus with apostolic circles through eyewitness accounts of the deeds and words of the Master. Their oral traditions had already been schematized in various literary forms, which have been classified by form-critics of the school developed by M. Dibelius and R. Bultmann since 1919. These traditions probably faded away rapidly when they were put into Greek dress, but they were quickly replaced by written collections, particularly by the Synoptic Gospels which were compiled around a Petrine nucleus and by the Gospel of John, which transmitted the more intimate view of the Master which had been handed down by the Apostle John. It is regarded as probable by nearly all conservative critics that the oldest Gospel, Mark, was compiled before A.D. 70; John was regarded by early Christian tradition as the latest of the Gospels, and a date between A.D. 80 and 90 appears not unreasonable; Matthew and Luke may date from the intervening period, between A.D. 70 and 80.

Form-critics are no doubt correct in emphasizing the practical role which the Gospels played in the early Church, a role which may well account in part for the survival of certain traditions at the expense of others. This, however, is very different from the highly subjective and improbable view which form-critics usually hold, that much of the content of the Gospels was adapted or even invented to suit situations which arose in the life of the Church. In other words, most form-critics suppose that the Gospels reflect the life of the sub-apostolic Church as against the traditional view that the Gospels are original documents antedating the sub-apostolic Church. Archaeological data already speak with no uncertain voice against the vagaries of radical form-criticism according to Dibelius, and even more decisively against the extreme views of some of his followers. The Gospel of John is in a peculiarly vulnerable position, against which Bultmann, in particular, has carried on an unremitting campaign for decades. John is supposed by these scholars to contain virtually no original historical matter, but to reflect an early second-century Christian group tinged more than a little by gnosticism.

Against this position the ancient historian, A. T. Olmstead, reacted in 1942 by insisting that the narratives of John (which he separated arbitrarily from the speeches) were written down in Aramaic before A.D. 40 and were later put into Greek. He maintained, accordingly, that the narratives of John are the oldest and most authentic sources for the biographer of Jesus. Though this theory is drastically opposed to both early Christian tradition and modern critical analysis and is, moreover, arbitrary in its literary approach, one can still recognize the basically sound judgement of a trained historian. The Gospel of John is, of course, essentially different from the matter-of-fact collections of the synoptic tradition in reflecting the point of view of a single apostle rather than the combined tradition of the Apostolic Church. John had been forced like Peter to leave Palestine; he settled in Ephesus, where he is reputed to have lived to a great age before the publication of the Gospel in which his memories are imbedded. The combined tradition of the Synoptic Gospels was likely *a priori* to yield better sequence of events and more characteristic utterances of the Master, but it was bound on occasion to sacrifice vividness and local colour. In the following paragraphs we shall give some miscellaneous illustrations of the accuracy of local colouring in John, which clearly indicates that these traditions were put into substantially their extant form before A.D. 66–70.

In both the Synoptic Gospels and John, but much more often in the latter, we find the Aramaic term *rabbi*, rendered *didaskalos*, 'master, teacher', in Greek (e.g., John i, 38; xx, 16), applied to Jesus. Many rabbinic scholars have insisted that the use of this expression in the Gospels is an anachronism borrowed from the usage of the second century A.D., when it was commonly employed in the Mishnah and other written sources. However, in 1930 E. L. Sukenik excavated a tomb in the property of the Hebrew University on Mount Scopus, and discovered in it an ossuary (see Chapter 8) on which was the Greek name Theodotion in Aramaic characters, as well as the Greek word *didaskalos* as title of the man who bore this name. Henceforth it cannot be safely alleged that the Gospel of John is anachronistic in this particular respect. It was formerly asserted by some scholars that personal names employed in the Gospels, especially in John, were fictitious and had been chosen for specific purposes because of their meaning. The ossuary inscriptions disprove such speculations by preserving many of these very same names (Pl. 30). Thus we find commonly on them, not only Miriam (Mary), but also Martha, Elizabeth, Salome, Johanna, etc. The name Sapphira (Acts v, 1) also appears repeatedly. Jesus (Jeshua) and Joseph are, of course, among the commonest names of the period, and an ossuary containing the name of a 'Jesus son of Joseph', though exciting surprise at first, reflects one of the most ordinary combinations of the time. The name Lazarus, in the same abbreviated form *La'zar* (for *El'azar*, Eleazar) which we find in the Gospels, is quite common on the ossuaries.

Turning to topographic allusions, we will limit ourselves to a few illustrations from John, precisely because it has been more severely criticized for bad topography than the other

Gospels. We must first recall what was said above, that the Gospel of John was less interested in external environment and order of events than the Synoptic Gospels, a fact which greatly enhances the interest of the topographic allusions which actually occur in this book. In John xix, 13 we are told that Pilate had Jesus brought before him at a place called *Lithostroton* (the Stone Pavement, *par excellence*), or in 'Hebrew' (i.e., Aramaic) *Gabbatha* (literally, 'ridge, elevated terrain'). We are not told that this pavement was at the Praetorium, as taken by tradition for granted. For decades there has been a debate about the location of the Praetorium, with the evidence rather favouring a location near the Palace of Herod and the Jaffa Gate. But the location of the Lithostroton has been settled by the brilliant investigations of L. H. Vincent, utilizing both the outcroppings of rock in the region of the Tower of Antonia (at the north-western corner of the Temple Enclosure) and the excavations carried on quietly for many years by the Dames de Sion and the Franciscans of the Convent of the Flagellation (Fig. 63). Père Vincent has determined the extent of the magnificent early Roman pavement under the Ecce Homo Arch as not less than 2500 square metres. He has also been able to prove that this pavement was the court of the Tower of Antonia, standing on a rocky elevation rising above the surrounding terrain, to which the Aramaic name *Gabbetha* was very properly applied. The Ecce Homo Arch was built *over* the pavement, long after the latter had been buried under the ruins of Antonia, by the Roman builders of Aelia Capitolina; there is nothing to justify the frequently expressed opinion that the arch itself belongs with the pavement. A clear-cut tradition like this must go back to the period before the pavement had been buried under fallen constructions during the catastrophe of A.D. 70. This striking archaeological confirmation of the Greek and Aramaic names preserved in John cannot be accidental.

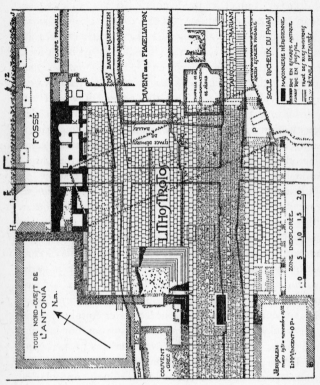

Fig. 63. Plan of archaeological remains, around the Lithostroton (after L. H. Vincent).

The same is true of other topographic allusions in the Gospel of John. In iii, 23 we hear that John the Baptist was conducting his work at 'Aenon near Salim, because there was much water there' – evidently these places were not in the well-watered Jordan Valley, since there would then be no point in such a comment. Jesus was on his way into Judaea, according to the preceding verse, presumably by the usual direct route down the watershed ridge from Esdraelon. Disregarding the improbable localizations of later tradition, Salim cannot be separated from the well-known ancient town of that name, south-east of Nablus, nor can it be quite accidental that there is an 'Ainun in the immediate vicinity. The near-by sources of the Wadi Far'ah are extremely well provided with water. Moreover, it was in this very neighbourhood that Jesus met the Samaritan woman of Sychar (John iv, 5 f.). The latter is usually identified with the modern village of 'Askar ('military camp' in Arabic). As long as ancient Shechem was believed to be buried under modern Nablus, two miles to the north-west, the identification of Sychar with the nearer site of 'Askar was tempting. However, Sellin's excavations have proved conclusively that Shechem was located at Balatah, less than a third as far as 'Askar from Jacob's Well (the site of which is certain). Moreover, Balatah was continuously occupied down to about A.D. 67, when it was probably destroyed by Vespasian in connexion with his destruction of the Samaritan temple on adjacent Mount Gerizim. Five years later Vespasian founded a new city (Neapolis, modern Nablus) up the valley, and there was no further object in rebuilding Shechem. It seems thus reasonably certain that the Old Syriac Gospels are correct in reading 'Shechem' instead of the current Greek *Sychar*. The latter form is merely a corruption of the original *Sychem* (as in Acts vii, 16); the final letters are clearly the slip of a scribe who allowed his eyes to wander to the previous line, where the name Sam*a*ria appears twice. After the destruction of Shechem and the building of Neapolis, a narrator who did not rely on old tradition would probably have mentioned Neapolis as the town nearest to Jacob's Well.

These are by no means the only examples of authentic early topographical colouring in the Gospels; together with the strong evidence of an Aramaic linguistic substratum they point inescapably to a date before the catastrophe of A.D. 66–70 for the formation of the Gospel tradition. If the Gospels had been written in Palestine we should doubtless have much more definite localization of many other episodes which they recount; since they were probably all written in other parts of the Roman Empire (Rome, Ephesus, etc.), the compilers were often somewhat vague about the general geographical situation. Where they followed direct tradition they could, however, be exceedingly precise about the location of a given episode. In the writer's opinion there is scarcely a passage in the Gospels which was appreciably influenced in form by the history of the Church in the decades immediately following the year A.D. 70. That the choice of traditions to be employed by the compilers was somewhat affected by the needs of Christians in those decades may, on the other hand, be considered a reasonable supposition.

Archaeological discoveries of the past generation in Egypt, Syria, and Palestine have gone far to establish the uniqueness of early Christianity as an historical phenomenon. In former decades it was often held that Christianity was only one of many different sects of similar type which proliferated in the eastern provinces of the Roman Empire around the turn of our era and the first century A.D. Excavations have not, however, brought to light any documents or buildings belonging to such sects. Egypt has yielded early written evidence of pagan, Jewish, and Christian religion; it has also preserved the recently discovered works of Manichaean and other Gnostic sects, all considerably later than the rise of Christianity. Dura on the Euphrates has yielded pagan temples, a

Mithraeum, a Jewish synagogue, and a Christian chapel; it has yielded scraps of Jewish and Christian writings, but nothing belonging to any other similar sect. Palestine and Syria have disclosed the existence of countless pagan temples, synagogues, and churches – but no other religious structures. Christianity thus appears in the light of archaeology as a unique historical phenomenon, like the faith of Israel which had preceded it.

The Dead Sea Scrolls from Qumran have added vital new evidence for the relative antiquity of the Gospel of John. Many books and fragments of the otherwise lost literature of the Essenes in the century or century and a half preceding the Crucifixion demonstrate the existence of religious circles which were the direct precursors of John the Baptist and Jesus. The Essenes were not 'pre-Christian Christians', as suggested in certain quarters, but Jewish forerunners of apostolic Christianity. The points of contact in phraseology, symbolism, and conceptual imagery between Essene literature and the Gospel of St John are particularly close, though there are also many resemblances between them and nearly all New Testament writers. Among them are: a simple dualistic phraseology, contrasting good and evil, light and darkness, truth and falsehood; the opposition of the Spirit of Truth and the Spirit of Perversity; expressions such as 'the sons of light', the 'light of life', 'walking in darkness', 'doing the truth', the 'works of God', etc. Yet the Essenes remained thorough-going Jews and their basic theology was virtually identical with that of the Pharisees. The supposed cases of Gnostic influence on the Gospel of John actually do not belong in the true Gnostic horizon of the second century A.D. at all, but prove the close relations in time between the Essenes and Jesus.

CHAPTER 12

Ancient Palestine in World History

—

THE extraordinary influence of Palestine on world history has always been a paradox to historians with pragmatic bias. That such a poor little country could produce both Judaism and Christianity, and through them could exercise such otherwise unparalleled effects on the course of man's activity during the last two thousand years, seems absurd to many people who visit it for the first time. To be sure, Greece, from which emerged the intellectual life and the artistic beauty which have conditioned all subsequent Western history, was also little and physically poor – but Greece had become wealthy through her far-spreading commerce before the flowering of the Hellenic spirit, and she remained wealthy throughout her golden age. Palestine, on the contrary, was always a poor country; its periods of even relative prosperity were few and brief. Though no historian can ever fully resolve so profound a paradox, he can at least marshal facts which make it easier to recognize the unusual suitability of the Holy Land for its historical role.

The conventional approach to the problem of a land's destiny through physical and economic geography is futile without careful analysis of its historical vicissitudes, which cannot be really appreciated without essential data provided by the archaeologist. A few illustrations may serve to point our thesis that it is impossible fully to understand the history of Palestine or its role as the cradle of the Hebrew–Christian tradition without the aid of archaeology. In his famous book, *Palestine and Its Transformation* (1912), the late Ellsworth Huntington explained most of the historical vicissitudes of Palestine in accordance with his hypothesis of cyclic oscillations of climate and rainfall. By an uncritical combination of data from literary sources with a superficial study of archaeological remains, then inadequately undersood even by professional archaeologists, he concluded that there had been a series of drastic shifts in the water-supply of the land since the second millennium B.C. Systematic archaeological research has proved that all his deductions were wrong. For example, the Colt expedition has demonstrated that the Roman and Byzantine cities of the Negeb did not flourish simultaneously, as Huntington had assumed, but at different periods; their total population at any one period was, therefore, much smaller than he had inferred from the extent of their ruins. Moreover, the underground water-level was then roughly the same as it is to-day, as was proved soon afterwards by Woolley and Lawrence; and the water supply of these towns came from many cisterns as well as from water impounded by dry dams across neighbouring ravines. On many such erroneous inferences Huntington built up an elaborate superstructure of historical interpretation. The achievements of Israel he attributed largely to the supposed increase of the supply of water and the consequent enlargement of population and resources; the stagnation of Palestine under Turkish rule he ascribed to a prolonged period of insufficient water supply, with corresponding impoverishment. Since these views have been accepted by many historians and sociologists, there has been wild distortion of historical reality.

However, Huntington has been only one of the more prominent interpreters of historical phenomena on the basis of false archaeological and geographical data. In 1928 the greatest ancient historian of modern times, Eduard Meyer, wrote two years after visiting the Jordan Valley for the first time in his life – unfortunately in the early autumn – that the Jordan Valley south of Beth-shan and Pella was absolutely barren, 'burning hot between its mountain walls', and that no attempt had ever been made in pre-Roman times to make the soil productive by systematic irrigation! No one who reads Nelson Glueck's vivid account of the very same district in his book, *The River Jordan* (1946), can fail to see how completely archaeological research has disproved this off-hand impression of the great historian, who would have been much better advised to stick to his literary sources. As a result of this wrong impression, Meyer belittled the enterprise of the Israelites, and failed to recognize some vital factors in their material culture. Another kind of error was made by the famous German economist, Werner Sombart, in his book, *The Jews and Modern Capitalism* (1913). Here, for example, he collected the most inflated estimates of the gold and silver resources of Israel, especially under Solomon, and considered them as characteristic of ancient Palestine, actually stating that the Israelites had a partial monopoly of the precious metals. Since the total amount of gold and silver hitherto excavated in Israelite strata is disproportionately small when compared to earlier Canaanite strata or to contemporary Syria, Egypt, or Mesopotamia, it is certain that Sombart's conclusions are wholly false. No unprejudiced specialist in the field of ancient Near Eastern studies can fail to conclude from a systematic examination of all evidence now available that Israel was a relatively poor country throughout its entire history. Sombart's deductions with regard to the great antiquity of supposititious Jewish capitalism were thus archaeologically absurd, yet they played their part in persuading an influential segment of German intellectuals that Nazi anti-Semitism was historically justified.

Examples like these may easily be multiplied, especially when illustrations from the writings of minor scholars are included. The role of archaeology in providing data for objective evaluation of the history of Palestine is already so great that no student can now neglect it without intellectual disaster. Although twenty years have elapsed since the study of Palestinian archaeology reached a sufficiently stable phase to warrant use of its data by sober historians, it is still very difficult for the non-specialist to pick his way among the conflicting dates and conclusions of archaeologists. It is therefore not surprising that many able philologians and historians are still dubious about venturing into archaeological terrain. Yet their caution is misplaced; Millar Burrows's *What Mean These Stones?* (1941) has worthily replaced S. R. Driver's *Modern Research as Illustrating the Bible* (1909), which was in its time an example of sound evaluation of archaeological data by a good scholar without archaeological training or experience. Thanks to this new synthesis of geographical and archaeological data we can now reconstruct the material environment of ancient Palestine far more successfully than could possibly have been done by the ablest historical geographer of the school founded by Edward Robinson and brought to a climax by the brilliant survey of George Adam Smith (*Historical Geography of Palestine*, 1896).

Situated between the two principal foci of ancient Eastern civilization, Egypt and Mesopotamia, Palestine drew continuously from both. Nearly all important elements of ancient Oriental material culture originated in one or the other of these lands, and inevitably spread from them through Syria and Palestine. The culture of Palestine was more or less mixed in all periods, containing Egyptian and Mesopotamian components as well as elements from other minor sources. Substantially the same is true of the literature, learning, and religion of Syria and Palestine. Thus the people of Palestine became acquainted with all significant developments of ancient Eastern civilization. The higher culture of the Canaanites (known especially from Ugarit) and their Phoenician descendants was profoundly influenced by borrowings and adaptations from Egypt and Mesopotamia. In art and architecture this was equally true of Israel, which followed closely in the wake of Phoenicia. In literature and religion this was in some respects even truer, since the early Hebrews had successively been exposed to much more immediate Meso-potamian and Egyptian influence. The discriminating student is constantly surprised to see how often the finest things in Babylonian and Egyptian literature reappear in transmuted form in the Hebrew Bible.

Accessibility to foreign influences is not in itself advan-tageous, however, since most small countries in such a situa-tion content themselves with more or less docile acceptance of foreign ideas. The hills of Israelite Palestine were just off the main caravan routes which passed through the river valleys and coastal plains skirting the hill-country. Owing to the fact that these hills, though too low to be considered mountains, were separated by deep valleys and often by pre-cipitous cliffs, they were relatively inaccessible to direct foreign influence. This situation, combined with stiff resist-ance to foreign conquest and especially with pronounced national and religious particularism, meant that Israel did not adopt foreign practices and ideas until they had proved their worth and could be assimilated without sacrificing the auto-nomy of the spirit which remained one of Israel's chief characteristics.

The relative dryness of the hill-country of Palestine joins with its elevation to make it one of the most healthful regions of the Near and Middle East, as well as one of the poorest areas occupied by a sedentary population. Under such con-ditions the Israelites became an exceptionally rugged people, whose native good health was favoured by a strict regime of dietary and hygienic regulations, as well as by high standards of social and sexual purity. Moreover, the poverty of their hills forced them to work hard and to struggle unceasingly for the right to eke out a Spartan existence. Ancient Israel was thus a parade example of Toynbee's 'stimulus of hard countries'. During its formative phase, under the 'Judges', it was also a striking example of another principle of his, 'the stimulus of blows'.

No Eastern land occupied by a sedentary population has as uncertain a water-supply as Palestine. Its Mediterranean climate leaves it without any rain for about half of each year, on the average. Since Palestine is at the southern end of the rainy westerly winds, its rainfall becomes progressively more scanty as one goes south towards the Negeb. Winters with inadequate rainfall are both frequent and unpredictable, and disastrous famines have thus been common throughout its history. Moreover, crop failure may also be caused by invasions of locusts and field-mice, as well as by other causes. No man could be sure of owning his land throughout his life; even life itself was at best uncertain. It is not surprising that the Canaanites emphasized the cult of Baal Hadad and other storm-gods, or that this aspect of Yahweh was often dominant in early Israel. Life in the hill-country of ancient Palestine was thus a constant stimulus to religious action, which became more effective in influencing its people as it reached higher ethical and spiritual levels. The career of Israel's first writing prophet, Amos, can be adequately understood only in the light of his economic and geographical background. Given the initial tension of spirit which raised the faith of Israel so far above the pagan religions of that day, Palestine was thus an ideal land in which to develop increasing trust in Providence as against reliance on the magic and divination which were the mainstay of surrounding peoples.

Though archaeology can thus clarify the history and geography of ancient Palestine, it cannot explain the basic miracle of Israel's faith, which remains a unique factor in world history. But archaeology can help enormously in making the miracle rationally plausible to an intelligent person whose vision is not shortened by a materialistic world view. It can also show the absurdity of extreme sectarian positions, from the once reputable doctrine of verbal inspiration of Scripture to the weird vagaries of believers in the divinatory properties of numbers, measurements, and alleged biblical ciphers.

Against these and other modern forms of ancient magic, archaeology wages an unceasing war, and few things are more irritating to the sober archaeologist than to see religious faith confounded with magic by exponents of cheap materialism. To one who believes in the historical mission of Palestine, its archaeology possesses a value which raises it far above the level of the artifacts with which it must constantly deal, into a region where history and theology share a common faith in the eternal realities of existence.

*

A SELECTED LIST OF RECENT BOOKS
FOR FURTHER STUDY

Albright, W. F. *The Excavation of Tell Beit Mirsim*, Vols. I, IA, II, III (*Annual of the American Schools of Oriental Research*, Vols. XII, XIII, XVII, XXI–II, New Haven (Conn.), 1932–43).

Albright, W. F. *The Archaeology of Palestine and the Bible*, New York, 1932 (3rd ed. 1935, now out of print).

Albright, W. F. *From the Stone Age to Christianity*, Baltimore, 1940 (2nd ed. 1946).

Albright, W. F. *Archaeology and the Religion of Israel*, Baltimore, 1942 (2nd ed. 1946).

Badè, W. F. – see McCown.

Barrois, A. G. *Manuel d'archéologie biblique*, Vols I–II, Paris, 1939–53.

Biblical Archaeologist, quarterly, New Haven (Conn.).

Bulletin of the American Schools of Oriental Research, quarterly, New Haven (Conn.).

Burrows, Millar. *The Dead Sea Scrolls*, New York, 1955; *More Light on the Dead Sea Scrolls*, New York, 1958.

Burrows, Millar. *What Mean These Stones?*, New Haven, 1941 (reprinted).

Cross, F. M., Jr. *The Ancient Library of Qumran and Modern Biblical Studies*, New York, 1958.

Crowfoot, J. W., and others. *Early Ivories from Samaria*, London, 1938.

Crowfoot, J. W., and others. *The Buildings at Samaria*, London, 1942.

Garrod, Dorothy, and others. *The Stone Age of Mount Carmel*, London, 1937.

Garstang, John. *Jericho* (published in instalments in the Liverpool *Annals of Archaeology and Anthropology*, 1931–6).

Garstang, John, and J. B. E. Garstang. *The Story of Jericho*, London, 1940 (new ed. 1948).

Glueck, Nelson. *Rivers in the Desert*, New York, 1959.

Glueck, Nelson. *The Other Side of the Jordan*, New Haven (Conn.), 1940.

Glueck, Nelson. *The River Jordan*, Philadelphia (Pa.), 1946.

Grant, Elihu, and G. E. Wright. *Ain Shems Excavations*, Vols. I–V, Haverford (Pa.) 1931–9.

Guy, P. L. O., and R. M. Engberg. *Megiddo Tombs*, Chicago, 1938.

Israel Exploration Journal, quarterly, Jerusalem, Israel (since 1951).

Kenyon, Kathleen. *Beginning in Archaeology*, London, 1952.

Kenyon, Kathleen. *Digging up Jericho*, London, 1957; (with J. W. Crowfoot and others) *The Objects from Samaria*, London, 1957.

Kraeling, E. G. *Gerasa, City of the Decapolis*, New Haven (Conn.), 1938.

Lamon, R. S., and others. *Megiddo I*, Chicago, 1939.

Loud, Gordon. *Megiddo Ivories*, Chicago, 1939.

Loud, Gordon, and others. *Megiddo II*, Chicago, 1948.

Macalister, R. A. S. *Gezer*, 3 vols., London, 1912.

McCown, C. C. *The Ladder of Progress in Palestine*, New York, 1943.

McCown, C. C., and others. *Tell en-Nasbeh*, 2 vols., New Haven (Conn.), 1947.

Maisler (Mazar), B. *The Excavations at Tell Qasile. Preliminary Report* (published in instalments in *Israel Exploration Journal*, 1951).

Mallon, A. *Teleilat el-Ghassul*, Rome, 1933 (continued by R. Koeppel and others in Vol. II, Rome, 1940).

Palestine Exploration Quarterly (continuing *Palestine Exploration Fund Quarterly Statement*), quarterly, London.

Quarterly of the Department of Antiquities, quarterly, Palestine Museum, Jerusalem.

Revue Biblique, quarterly, École Biblique et Archéologique Française, Jerusalem.

Reisner, G. A., and others. *The Harvard Excavations at Samaria*, 2 vols., Cambridge (Mass.), 1924.

Rowe, Alan. *The Topography and History of Beth-shan*, Philadelphia (Pa.), 1930.

Rowe, Alan. *The Four Canaanite Temples of Beth-shan*, Philadelphia (Pa.), 1940.

Sukenik, E. L. *Ancient Synagogues in Palestine and Greece*, London, 1934.

Tufnell, Olga, and others. *Lachish II: The Fosse Temple*, London, 1940; *Lachish III: The Iron Age*, London, 1953; *Lachish IV: The Bronze Age*, London, 1958.

Watzinger, C. *Denkmäler Palästinas*, 2 vols., Leipzig, 1933–5.

Wright, G. Ernest. *The Pottery of Palestine from the Earliest Times to the End of the Early Bronze Age*, New Haven, 1938.

Wright, G. Ernest. *Biblical Archaeology*, London, 1957.

Yadin, Yigael, and others. *Hazor I (1955 Season)*, Jerusalem (Israel), 1958.

ACKNOWLEDGEMENTS

The author wishes to express his indebtedness to the following scholars, institutions, and publishers for permission to reproduce photographs and drawings:

Mr J. W. Crowfoot and the Palestine Exploration Fund for Plates 21, 23, 24 and Figs. 33, 35, 43 from their Samaria publications; Prof. A. H. Detweiler for pre-publication use of Figs. 1, 2, 34 from his *Manual of Archaeological Surveying*; Prof. Dorothy Garrod and the Clarendon Press for Plates 7, 8, 10 and Figs. 6, 7, 8, 9 from *The Stone Age of Mount Carmel*; Dr Froelich Rainey and the University of Pennsylvania Museum for Plate 6 and Fig. 13 from the Beth-shan publications; Prof. C. C. McCown and the University of California Press for Figs. 4, 45, 62 from the Tell en-Nasbeh publications; the Oriental Institute of the University of Chicago for Plates 4, 16, 18, 19, 20 and Figs. 31 and 32 from the Megiddo publications; Mr R. W. Hamilton and the Palestine Museum of Archaeology for Figs. 12, 18, 22, 29, 48 from the *Bulletin of the Palestine Museum*; Prof. E. L. Sukenik of the Hebrew University for Plates 26 and 30, Figs. 11 and 59; the Wellcome Trust for Plates 25 and 27, Figs. 21 and 28 from the Lachish publications.

Nearly all the remaining illustrations have been taken from the author's own publications, especially from the *Excavation of Tell Beit Mirsim*. A number of charts were drawn especially for the present book.

The author also wishes to thank his wife and several of his students for assisting him materially with the preparation of the text and illustrations. The editor of the series, Mr M. E. L. Mallowan, has been most helpful, and M. C. F. A. Schaeffer contributed some valuable suggestions.

*

LIST OF PLATES

(Between pages 128 *and* 129)

Plate 1. Edward Robinson, 1794–1863.

Plate 2. Sir W. M. Flinders Petrie, 1853–1942.

Plate 3. James L. Starkey, 1895–1938.

Plate 4. The mound of Megiddo.

Plate 5. Superimposed stratification of walls at Tell Beit Mirsim
(periods G–B).

Plate 6. The Mound of Beth-shan (from the north).

Plate 7. The Prehistoric Caves of Wadi el-Magharah (Garrod).

Plate 8. Flexed burial of Natufian Period.

Plate 9. Plastic Marl Statue from pre-pottery Neolithic of Jericho.

Plate 10. Carved fawn on end of bone implement from the Natufian Age.

Plate 11. Early Bronze stele from Shihan.

Plate 12. Re-used Early Bronze stele from Balu'ah.

Plate 13. Hall of house from Tell Beit Mirsim G, with F foundations
running across it (*c.* 1750 B.C.).

Plate 14. Battered wall of Middle Bronze Jericho (*c.* 1600 B.C.).

Plate 15. Scarabs of Middle Bronze II from Tell Beit Mirsim (*c.* 1700–
1550 B.C.).

Plate 16. Ivory box with lions and cherubs from Megiddo (*c.* thirteenth
century B.C.).

Plate 17. Libation tray with lion in relief from Tell Beit Mirsim (*c.* 1250
B.C.).

Plate 18. Ivory carving of cherub, Megiddo, early twelfth century B.C.

Plate 19. House altars with horns from Megiddo (tenth–ninth centuries
B.C.).

Plate 20. Israelite stables at Megiddo (tenth–ninth centuries B.C.).

Plate 21. Foundation of city-wall of ninth-century Samaria.

Plate 22. A dye-plant of the seventh century at Tell Beit Mirsim.

Plate 23. Round tower of early Hellenistic Age at Samaria.

Plate 24. Ivories of Samaria: (*a*) Harpocrates on a lotus; (*b*) A cherub.

Plate 25. Reverse of Lachish Ostracon, No. 111 (*c.* 589 B.C.).

Plate 26. Aramaic plaque mentioning King Uzziah of Judah.

Plate 27. Pre-exilic house at Tell Beit Mirsim showing four stone pillars.

Plate 28. Interior of pre-exilic house at Tell Beit Mirsim showing four
stone pillars.

Plate 29. Gezer Calendar (*c.* 925 B.C.). (The Palestine Exploration Fund.)

Plate 30. Ossuary mentioning an Elizabeth in Aramaic and Greek.

LIST OF TEXT ILLUSTRATIONS

Fig. 1. Triangulation for a co-ordinate grid   *page* 15
Fig. 2. Schematic plan of Stratum A at Tell Beit Mirsim   16
Fig. 3. Vertical cross section of a typical mound   17
Fig. 4. Schematic plan of Tell en-Nasbeh   42
Fig. 5. Hand-axes: (1) Chellean; (2) Acheulian (after René
        Neuville)   53
Fig. 6. Upper Acheulian hand-axes (after Dorothy Garrod)   54
Fig. 7. Stratified section through Tabun Excavation   55
Fig. 8. Flint artifacts from Lower Levalloiso-Mousterian (after
        Dorothy Garrod)   56
Fig. 9. Lower Natufian artifacts (after Dorothy Garrod)   60
Fig. 10. Polychrome fresco from Ghassul   67
Fig. 11. House-urn burial from the Chalcolithic of Khudheirah   69
Fig. 12. Early Bronze I pottery in Palestine Museum   73
Fig. 13. Early Bronze III pottery from Beth-shan   75
Fig. 14. Pottery of Stratum H (Middle Bronze I) at Tell Beit
        Mirsim (*c.* 1900 B.C.)   81
Fig. 15. Middle Bronze Gateway and Late Bronze temple at
        Shechem   90
Fig. 16. Patrician house of Stratum D at Tell Beit Mirsim (*c.* 1600
        B.C.)   91
Fig. 17. Middle Bronze villa at the foot of Mount Gerizim (*c.*
        1600 B.C.)   92
Fig. 18. Pottery of Middle Bronze II in Palestine Museum   94
Fig. 19. Running fawns on inlay of Middle Bronze from Tell Beit
        Mirsim (*c.* 1600 B.C.)   95
Fig. 20. Reconstructed Stele of serpent goddess from Tell Beit
        Mirsim (sixteenth century B.C.)   97
Fig. 21. Decoration on bichrome ware of Late Bronze I A
        (Lachish, *c.* 1500 B.C.)   98
Fig. 22. Mycenaean Vases from Late Bronze II (1375–1225 B.C.)   100
Fig. 23. Representation of Astarte on seal-cylinder from Bethel
        (*c.* 1300 B.C.)   101
Fig. 24. Tablet from Beth-shemesh in Ugaritic alphabet   102
Fig. 25. Cuneiform Letter to Birashshena (Shechem, *c.* 1400 B.C.)
        (after F. M. Th. Böhl)   102
Fig. 26. Stele of Sethos I from Beth-shan (*c.* 1318 B.C.)   105

Fig. 27. *Astarte* plaques from Tell Beit Mirsim   *page* 107
Fig. 28. Ivory inlay from Lachish (thirteenth century B.C.)   108
Fig. 29. Philistine pottery in Palestine Museum (1150–1000 B.C.)   116
Fig. 30. Citadel of Saul of Tell el-Ful (*c.* 1000 B.C.), restored 121
Fig. 31. Scene from ivory inlay, Megiddo, early twelfth century
         B.C.   123
Fig. 32. Interlaced ornament on Megiddo ivory, early twelfth
         century B.C.   124
Fig. 33. Israelite masonry at Samaria, showing arrangement of
         blocks   125
Fig. 34. Typical section of Iron Age wall, showing masonry
         elements   126
Fig. 35. Proto-Aeolic pilaster capitals from Samaria (in restored
         architectural context)   127
Fig. 36. Wheel-burnished bowls of seventh–sixth century B.C.
         from Tell Beit Mirsim   131
Fig. 37. Bowl of steatite incense pipe from Tell Beit Mirsim
         (eighth century B.C.)   132
Fig. 38. Amulet figurines of the *dea nutrix* from Tell Beit Mirsim
         (mostly from the seventh century B.C.)   133
Fig. 39. Stele of Mesha, King of Moab (*c.* 835 B.C.)   134
Fig. 40. Hebrew ostraca from Samaria (early eighth century B.C.)   135
Fig. 41. Siloam Inscription (*c.* 700 B.C.)   135
Fig. 42. Seal of Shema, officer of Jeroboam II (*c.* 775 B.C.)   136
Fig. 43. Israelite masonry at Samaria (ninth century B.C.)   138
Fig. 44. West Gate-tower of Tell Beit Mirsim (early sixth century
         B.C.)   139
Fig. 45. City gate of Tell en-Nasbeh (ninth century B.C.)   140
Fig. 46. Typical private houses from pre-exilic Tell Beit Mirsim   141
Fig. 47. Persian palace at Lachish (*c.* 400 B.C.)   144
Fig. 48. Hellenistic Pottery in Palestine Museum   148
Fig. 49. Façade of Mausoleum at 'Araq el-Emir (*c.* 175 B.C.)   150
Fig. 50. Foundations of Hellenistic citadel at Beth-zur   151
Fig. 51. Plan of Hellenistic town of Marisa (second century B.C.) 153
Fig. 52. The Conway High Place at Petra   162
Fig. 53. The Great High Place at Petra   164
Fig. 54. The North Gate of Gerasa, south elevation   167
Fig. 55. The Triumphal Arch of Gerasa, south elevation   169
Fig. 56. The Artemis Temple complex at Gerasa   171
Fig. 57. The Temple of Zeus at Gerasa   173
Fig. 58. The Synagogue of the third century A.D. at Capernaum   174
Fig. 59. The Kefr Bir'im Synagogue, restored   175

Fig. 60. Table of Hebrew–Phoenician scripts, showing comparative date of Gezer Calendar   *page* 191

Fig. 61. Representation of Asiatic visitors at Beni-Hasan (*c.* 1892
B.C.)   209

Fig. 62. Seal of Jaazaniah from Tell en-Nasbeh, showing fighting
cock (*c.* 600 B.C.)   218

Fig. 63. Plan of archaeological remains, around the Lithostroton
(after L. H. Vincent)   246

Table showing development of Hebrew, Greek and Roman
alphabets   192–3

INDEX

Aaron, Tomb of, 25
'Abdeh (see Eboda), 44
Abel, Père F. M., 26
Abusir el-Meleq, 72
Abydos, 74
Accadian cuneiform script, 101, 102, 187
Ader, 8, 77, 78, 82
Aelia Capitolina, 166, 168
Agrippan Wall (Third Wall) of Jerusalem, 26, 158
Ahiram, 106, 188, 190, 191, 194
Ai, 46, 72, 75, 76, 88, 117, 118
Alderson, 158
Alphabets, 101, 185 ff.
Alt, Albrecht, 26, 166
Altars of incense, 144
Amarna tablets, 183, 206
American School of Oriental Research, 41, 44
American School of Prehistoric Research, 37
'Amman, 25, 64, 117, 168
Analysis and interpretation of excavation results, 21
Anthedon, 39
Antiquities, Palestine Department of, 8, 35, 154, 159
Apsidal buildings, 70, 72
Apum, 85
'Aqabah, 44
'Araq el-Emir, 25, 149, 150
Archaeology and biblical tradition, evidence of agreement between, 115, 124, 141, 142, 226 ff.
Archaeology, British School of, 37, 39
Archimedes of Syracuse, 213
Arslan Tash, 123, 136, 137
Ascalon, 38, 111, 114
Asses, Caravans of, 206
Assur, Stele field of, 104
Astarte plaques, 104, 107

'Athlit, 142
'Atlitian' flint culture, 58
Attic currency, 143
'Auja el-Hafir (see Nessana), 44
Avaris, 86, 92

Bab edh-Dhra', 64, 77
Babylonian period, 142, 143
Badè, W. F., 8, 43, 217
Balatah (see Shechem), 45, 247
Balu'ah stele, 79, 186
Baly, T. J. Colin, 44
Band-slip ware, 72
Base-ring ware, 99
Battered walls, 88 ff.
Baur, F. C., 240
Beit Ilfa, 47
Bell, H. I., 239
Beloch, 123
Ben-Dor, I., 129, 150
Beni-Hasan, Tableau of, 207, 209
Bérard, J., 185
Bethel, 7, 44, 46, 91, 92, 101, 108, 109, 111 ff., 117 ff., 142, 228
Bethlehem, 157
Beth-shan, 17, 21, 40, 70, 71, 74, 75, 82, 98, 100, 103 ff., 106, 113 ff., 120
Beth-shearim (see Sheikh Abreik), 48, 176
Beth-shemesh, 32, 43, 77, 101, 111, 118, 122, 187, 190
Beth-yerah (see Khirbet Kerak), 48, 71, 72 ff.
Beth-zur, 44, 87, 89, 114, 118, 142, 150 ff., 228
Bichrome ware, 96, 98
Birashshena (see Shechem), 102
Bittir, 166
Bliss, F. J., 29, 30, 103, 166, 220
Bovier-Lapierre, Père, 49
Braidwood, 62, 76
British School of Archaeology, 37, 39

Brownlee, W. H., 222
Buckingham, John Silk, 25
Bultmann, R., 242, 243
Burckhardt, Johann Ludwig, 24, 25, 160
Burial chests, 68
Burney, C. F., 199
Burrows, Millar, 222, 252
Byblus, 61, 65, 71, 84, 85, 95, 132, 185, 190, 230

Caesarea Philippi, 24
Camels, 206, 207
    caravans of, 210
Canaanite art, 95 ff., 106
    textile manufacture, 96
Canaanites, 109
Capernaum synagogue, 175
Caravans of asses, 206
Carmel, 113, 142
    skeletons, 55
Carnegie Corporation, 10
Carpenter, Rhys, 195
Casemate walls, 121, 122, 137
Cave burial place, 68
Cavern graves, subterranean, 93
Ceramic index to chronology, 33, 117, 118
Chaldaeans, 130
Chariotry, Introduction of horse-drawn, 86, 89
Chester Beatty papyri, 224, 239
Chicago, Oriental Institute of the University of, 41
Chiera, 235
Chinnereth (see Tell el-'Oreimeh), 103
Chorazin, 174
Cist graves, 68, 145
Cistern construction by Israelites, 113, 210
Citadel of Saul, 120, 121
City gates, 89, 126 f., 138 ff.
City of David (see Ophel), 122
City walls, 87 ff.
Clay tablets, 102, 187

Clazomenian ware, 143
Clermont-Ganneau, Charles, 27, 34, 132, 227
Codex Alexandrinus, 239
Codex Petropolitanus, 221, 223
Codex Sinaiticus, 224, 239
Codex Vaticanus, 224, 238, 239
Coffins, anthropoid clay, 115–17
Coins, 142, 143, 151, 152
Colt, H. Dunscombe, 44
Concession required for excavating, 11, 12
Conder, C. R., 27 ff.
Conway, Agnes, 161
Co-ordinate grid, 15
Copper, 65
    refineries, 44, 127, 128
Cotovicus (see Kootwyck), 24
Craters, 115
Cross, F. M., 194
Crowfoot, J. W., 38, 39, 111, 128, 129, 136, 150, 156, 170
Cuneiform alphabets, see Accadian and Ugaritic.
Cuneiform scripts, 101, 102, 187
Cuneiform tab'ets, 102, 103, 187
Cyclopean masonry, 88

Dagon, Temple of, 104
Dalman, Gustav, 158
Dan (see Laish), 86
David, City of, 122
Deborah, Song of, 117, 232
Deissmann, Adolf, 198
Deutsche Orient-Gesellschaft, 32
Dhorme, Édouard, 186
Dibelius, M., 242, 243
Dibon, 48
Dickie, A. C., 30
Dikaios, P., 114
Dolmens, 63, 64, 68, 78
Dörpfeld, 28, 34
Dossin, 236
Drains, stone-lined, 101
    subterranean, 210
Driver, S. R., 252

Dumont, P. E., 183
Dunand, 71, 185, 191
Duncan, J. Garrow, 38
Dura synagogue, 174, 175, 176
Dussaud, René, 194
Dutch School, 240

Ebenezer, 113
Eboda (see 'Abdeh), 44
Egyptian fortresses, 40
Egyptian influence on Canaanite
    art, 85, 95, 106
  on Israelite (Megiddo) art, 137
Egyptian stelae, 40, 103
Ekron, 113
el-Hammeh, 47
Elijah, time of, 208, 212
Elusa (see Khalasah), 44
Epstein, I. N., 160, 172
Equipment, excavating, 13
Esdraelon culture, 65, 70
Essenes, the, 249
et-Tell (see Ai), 76
Excavation results, analysis and
    interpretation of, 21
Execration Texts, 82, 83, 85
Exodus, 237
Eynan, 61
Ezion-geber (see Tell el-Kheleifeh),
    127

Fabri (see Schmid, Felix), 23
Fisher, C. S., 20, 34, 35, 40 ff., 112,
    170
FitzGerald, G. M., 21, 40, 41, 77
Flake tools, 52
Flint artifacts, 37, 49, 53, 56, 59
Flint culture, 'Atlitian', 58
  Natufian, 59, 60
Fortifications, 63, 86 ff., 101, 137, 150
Fortress gates, 89
Fortresses, Herodian, 157
Fosse Temple, 96, 98
Fossil men, 37
Fowls, introduction of domestic,
    217

Frankfort, 71, 72
Free, J. P., 48
Frescoes, polychrome, 67, 68

Galilee, Sea of, 37
Gardiner, Sir Alan, 189
Garrod, Dorothy, 13, 37, 49, 52 ff.
Garstang, John, 7, 8, 21, 35, 38, 61,
    62, 64, 114, 220, 228
Garstang, Mrs, 13
Gateways, indirect-access type,
    138, 139
  Middle Bronze, 89, 90
  Solomonic, 126, 127
Gaza, 14, 113, 114
Georgiev, V., 185
Gerar (see Tell Jemmeh), 39, 127,
    143, 144
Gerasa (see Jerash), 25, 168 ff.
Gerizim, Mount, 36, 92
Germer-Durand, Père, 49, 58, 156
Gezer, 9, 18, 31, 33, 61, 72, 103,
    111, 125, 142 ff., 152, 190, 227
Gezer Calendar, 31, 132, 220
Gezer high place, 104
Ghassul, 66 ff.
Ghassulian culture, 45
  graves, 64
  period, 65 ff.
  pottery, 65
Gibeah (see Tell el-Ful), 111, 118, 228
Gibson, Margaret Dunlop, 201
Ginsberg, H. L., 230, 231, 234
Gizeh, 74
Glacis, 75, 88, 89
Glueck, Nelson, 44, 70, 77, 78, 82,
    127, 165, 251
Goldman, Hetty, 13
Goodenough, Erwin, 240
Grace, Miss Virginia, 152
Grant, Elihu, 43
Greek influence and trade, 143
Grenfell, 198
Grid, co-ordinate, 15
  triangulation, 15
Grimme, 190

Guérin, Victor, 26, 27
Guthe, 28
Guy, P. L. O., 41, 78, 124, 127

Hamath, 80
Hamilton, R. W., 111, 156, 166, 168
Hammer-dressed masonry, 76, 88, 121
Hand-axes, 52 ff.
Haram Ramet el-Khalil, 156
Harbaj, 8
Harding, G. L., 222, 223
Harran, 83
Hauran, 28
Hazor, 7, 18, 85, 86, 125, 228
Hebrew University, 47, 48
Hebron, 43, 156
Hellenistic Age, 147 ff.
Hero of Alexandria, 213
Herodian masonry, 26, 154, 156
    phase, 154 ff.
Hiel the Bethelite, 34
Hieroglyphic (Egyptian) alphabet, 101
High places, 104, 163, 164
Historical Geography of Palestine, 252
Hittite monopoly of iron, 110
Honeyman, A. M., 122
Horites, see Hurrians.
Horse-drawn chariotry, introduction of, 86, 89
Horse-stables of Solomonic Age, 41, 124, 125
Horsfield, George, 161, 168
House-shrines, many-storied, 104
House-urn burial, 68, 69
Hums, 85
Hunt, 198
Huntington, Ellsworth, 249, 250
Hurrians, 86, 183, 184
Huts, improvised, 205
Hyksos, 80, 83, 85 ff., 92, 95, 101

Ibrahim, Sheikh (see Burckhardt), 25
Iliffe, J. H., 145
Improvised huts, 205

Incense, Altars of, 144
Indo-Aryans, 86, 182 ff.
Ingholt, Harald, 80
Irby, C. L., 24, 25
Iron, Hittite monopoly of, 110
    installations for smelting, 127
    introduction of, 110
    meteoric, 110
    Philistine monopoly of, 110
Isbeita expedition, 14
Israelite art, 137
    inscriptions, 132 ff.
    masonry, 125, 138
Israelites, 109
Ivory inlay, 123, 136

Jacob, time of, 204-9
Jar-handles, Byblus, 185
    Rhodian, 152
Jean, 236
Jebel et-Tannur, 165
Jerash (see Gerasa), 25, 167 ff.
Jericho, 7, 17, 21, 30, 33, 34, 38, 45, 61 ff., 80, 87 ff., 103, 108, 109, 111, 113
Jerusalem, 7 ff., 25 ff., 38, 41 ff., 47, 72, 154 ff., 166, 168, 172
    Third Wall of, 26, 158
Jewish Palestine Exploration Society, 47
Johns, C. N., 154, 156
Jordan, 69, 70, 72, 77, 82, 250, 251
Josephus, 146, 150, 154, 156, 158, 168, 213, 228

Kahle, Paul, 221
Kan'an, Yusif, 31
Karge, Paul, 49
Kefr Bir'im, 174
Kelso, J. L., 44, 48, 157
Kenyon, Sir Frederick, 239
Kenyon, Miss Kathleen, 38, 111, 129
Khalasah (see Elusa), 44
Khirbet Kerak (see Beth-yerah), 48
'Khirbet Kerak' ware, 76
Khudheirah, 68, 69

Kings, Tombs of the, 26
Kitchener, H. H., 27
Kjaer, 118
Koeppel, Father, 45
Kohl, 172, 175
Koine, 198 ff.
Koldewey, 34
Kootwyck, Johann van (see Cotovicus), 24
Köppen, 50
Kraeling, C. H., 240
Kyle, M. G., 43

Labour for excavating, 18, 19
Lachish (see Tell ed-Duweir), 14, 39, 40, 86, 96, 103, 106, 108, 116, 127, 130, 138, 190, 230
Lachish ostraca, 136, 221
Lachish, Persian villa at, 144, 145
Laish (see Dan), 86
Languages, 177–85
Lartet, Édouard, 49
Lartet, Louis, 49
Lawrence, 250
Lejjun, 78
Lewis, Agnes Smith, 201
Libby, W. F., 22
Linear alphabet, 101, 187, 188
Literary evidence, parallelism between archaeological and, 117, 118, 141, 142, 152, 226 ff.
Literature, 196–203
Loman, 240
Loud, Gordon, 41

Ma'adeh, 70
Macalister, R. A. S., 30 ff., 111, 125, 142, 145, 156, 220, 228
Maccabaean remains, 150, 151
McCown, T. D., 55, 170
Mackenzie, Duncan, 32, 111
Magharet Abu 'Usbah, 66
Magharet el-Khiyam (G-F), 58
Magharet el-Wad, 63
Mahan, Father, 45
Maisler, B., 48

Mallon, Father Alexis, 45
Mallowan, M. E. L., 236
Mamre, 156
Manen, van, 240
Mangles, James, 24, 25
Mari, 7, 85, 89, 236
Mariette Pasha, 11
Marisa, 152, 153
Marquet-Krause, Mme Judith, 46, 76
Marston, Sir Charles, 10, 39, 220
Masada, 165
Masonry, cyclopean, 88
   hammer-dressed, 76, 88, 121
   Herodian, 26, 154, 156
   Israelite, 125, 138
   polygonal, 88, 89
   Solomonic, 125
Maspero, Sir Gaston, 11
Maudsley, 28
Maundrell, Henry, 24
Mausoleum of Tobiad family, 149, 150
Mayer, Dr L. A., 47, 158, 159
Megiddo, 7, 9, 14, 17, 18, 32, 33, 41, 66, 70 ff., 81 ff., 96, 100 ff., 106, 111 ff.
Menhirs, 63, 78, 104
Merrill, Selah, 28, 158
Mersin, 64
Mesha Stone, 27, 132, 134, 188
Mesopotamian script, see Accadian.
Meteoric iron, 110
Meyer, Eduard, 250, 251
Milankovitch, 50
Minaean commerce, 145
Minet el-Beida, 187
Miriam, Song of, 232, 233
Mishnah, the, 146, 213, 244
Moab, 79, 82, 186
'Moabite' forgeries, 27
Modern Research as Illustrating the Bible, 252
Money for excavating, raising of, 9, 10
Montet, Pierre, 84, 188

Monumental gateways, 89, 90
Mound (*Tell*), shape of Palestinian, 16
Mud-brick walls, 72
Murphy, Father, 45
Murray, Margaret, 161
Mustafa 'Amr Bey, 70
Mycenaean ware, 99, 100, 108

Nabataean ware, 162
Nablus, 9, 46, 247
Natufian flint culture, 37, 59 ff.
Natufians, 61
Nau, Michael, 24
Nebo, Mount, 9
Neolithic Age, 62
Nessana (see 'Auja el-Hafir), 44, 45
Neuville, René, 37, 49, 52, 53, 55, 58, 61
New Testament times, 212–18
Nimrud, 136
Nock, Arthur Darby, 198
Nora Stone, 122, 123

Old Testament Period pottery chronology, 11
Olmstead, A. T., 243
Open-air monuments, 77, 78
Ophel (see City of David), 14, 38, 72, 122, 156
Oriental Institute, 33
Oriental Research, American School of, 41, 44
Ostraca, 39, 40, 129, 132, 135, 136, 220, 221, 228
Ossuaries, 159, 244

Palaestina ex monumentis veteribus illustrata, 24
Palestine and its Transformation, 249
Palestine Department of Antiquities, 8, 35, 154, 159
Palestine Exploration Fund, 9, 14, 26, 27, 30, 32, 37, 154
Palestine Exploration Society, 28

Palestine Museum, 36, 73
Palestine Oriental Society, 36, 159
Papyri, 45, 146, 149
Parker expedition, 11
Parallelism between archaeological and literary evidence, 117, 118, 141, 142, 152, 226 ff.
Parrot, André, 7, 235
Paton, Lewis B., 158
Patriarchal Age, 83, 235
Patriarchs, life of, 205, 206
Patricians and serfs of Canaan, gulf between, 9, 92
    difference erased by Israelite conquest, 119, 120
Pennsylvania, University of, 40, 41
Permanent houses, oldest, 62
Perrot, Jean, 48, 61, 70
Persian Period, 142 ff.
Persian villa at Lachish, 144, 145
Perthes, Boucher de, 49
Peters, J. P., 147
Petra, 25, 39, 104, 160 ff.
Petrie, Sir Flinders, 8, 22, 29, 30, 34, 37 ff., 110, 127, 145, 188, 220
Petrie, Lady, 13
Philistine culture, 114 ff., 184 f.
    monopoly of iron, 110
Philistines, domination of, 113, 114
Phoenician script, see Linear.
Phoenicians, 109
Phythian-Adams, W. J., 38, 111, 114
Pictographs, 185
Pisé fortifications, 75, 86
Pleistocene, phases of, 50
Pococke, Bishop, 24
Polychrome geometrical designs, 67, 68
Polygonal masonry, 88, 89
Posener, G., 83
Pottery as basis for chronology, 19, 29
    replaced by inscriptions and coins, 147
Pottery chronology of Old Testament Period, 111

Pottery, band-slip ware, 72
  base-ring ware, 99
  calciform, 80
  Clazomenian ware, 143
  covered with burnished red slip, 74
  Hellenistic, 148
  impressed by seals, 71
  Ionian and Attic ware, 143
  'Khirbet Kerak' ware, 76
  Mycenaean ware, 99, 100, 108
  Nabataean ware, 162
  painted, 72
  Philistine ware, 114, 115
  wheel-burnished, 131
  wheel-made, 93
  with bichrome painted, panelled ornament, 96, 98
  with envelope ledge-handles, 78
Prehistoric man, remains of, 37
Prehistoric Research, American School of, 37
Pre-pottery plastic statues, 63
Pritchard, J. B., 48
Proto-Aeolic pilaster capitals, 126, 127
Przeworski, 187
'Pseudo-hieroglyphic' script, 185
Publication of excavations, 21, 22

Qal 'at Jarmo, 62
Qatna, 85
Quaresmius, 24
Qumran Scrolls, 222 f., 249

Radiocarbon, 22, 51, 70
Ras Shamrah, 7, 187, 230
Rauchwolff (Rauwolf), Leonhard, 23
Reisner, George Andrew, 18, 34, 39, 111, 128, 129, 150, 220
Reland, Adrian, 24
Rephaim, 49
Revetment, 88, 89
Rhodian jar-handles, 152
Richard, Abbé, 49

Roberts, C. H., 239
Robinson, Edward, 25 ff., 34, 47, 158, 178, 252
Robinson, George L., 163
Rockefeller Foundation, 10
Rockefeller, John D., Jr., 10
Rockefeller, John D., Sr., 10
Roman remains, 165 ff.
Roof-rollers, 215
Rothschild, Baron Edmond de, 10
Rowe, Alan, 40

Sachau, E., 201
Samaria, 7, 30, 34, 39, 111, 123, 125, 128, 130, 142, 150, 152, 156, 170
Samaria fortifications, 137, 138
  ivories, 136, 137
  ostraca, 132, 135, 220
Sanctuaries, 103
  Nabataean, 165
Saqqarah, 74
Sarcophagi, Anthropoid, 106
Saul, Citadel of, 120, 121
Saulcy, F. de, 26, 79, 158
Savignac, Père, 159, 160
Sbeitah (Subeta), 44
Schaeder, H. H., 201
Schaeffer, C. F. A., 7, 104, 106, 114, 187, 197, 231
Scharff, 72
Schiff, Jacob, 10, 34
Schliemann, 28
Schmid, Felix (see Fabri), 23
Schmidt, 118
Schulten, Adolf, 157
Schumacher, G., 28, 32, 33, 125
Scripts, 101, 102, 185-96
Scrolls found in 1947, 203, 222, 249
Sea Peoples, invasion of the, 109, 113, 184
Sebaste, 157, 170
Seetzen, Ulrich Jasper, 24
Seleucid Period, 149, 150
Sellers, O. R., 44, 151

Sellin, Ernst, 32, 33, 45, 46, 104, 111, 219, 247
Serabit el-Khadem, 189
Sethe, Kurt, 83
Seton-Williams, V. M., 64
Sha'ar ha-Golan, 64
Sharon, Plain of, 68, 143
Sharuhen (see Tell el-Far'ah), 39, 87
Shechem (see Balatah), 7, 14, 45, 46, 71, 86, 88 ff., 103, 104, 118, 122, 190, 247
Sheikh Abreik (see Beth-shearim), 48, 176
Shephelah, 30, 82, 114, 118
Shihan stele, 79
Shiloh, 113, 118, 228
Shipton, 111
Shrines, Neolithic, 62, 63
Siloam inscription, 135, 221
Sinai, 188 ff., 201, 237
Siq el-Barid, 163
Site of excavation, contour survey of, 15
   lease to be obtained, 14
   reasons for choice of, 7, 8
Skeat, T. C., 239
Smith, Eli, 25
Smith, George Adam, 158, 252
Smith, Sidney, 204
Solomiac, M., 158
Solomonic Age, 123–28
   masonry, 125
Sombart, Werner, 251
South-Arabian trade, 143
Speiser, E. A., 183
Staff, excavation, 12, 13
Starkey, J. L., 40, 220, 228
Steckeweh, H., 45, 46
Stekelis, M., 64, 66, 68, 72
Stelae, 79, 103, 105
Stele field of Assur, 104
Stele of Balu'ah, 79
   Mesha, 132, 134
   Shihan, 79
Stone-circles, 63

Stone-lined drains, 101
Strabo, 161
Strata, cleaning of, 19 ff.
Subterranean drains, 210
Subterranean cavern graves, 93
Sukenik, E. L., 47, 68, 136, 158 ff., 172, 244
Susa, 17
Syllabic alphabet, 101
Synagogues, 47, 48, 170 ff.

Taanach, 32, 76, 101, 102, 117, 125
Tabernacles, Feast of, 205
Tahunian period, 64
Teleilat el-Ghassul, 45, 65, 68
Tell (mound), shape of Palestinian, 16
Tell Abu Hawam, 111, 114
Tell 'Atshaneh (Alalakh), 89
Tell Beit Mirsim, 8, 14, 16, 18, 21, 43, 74, 77, 78, 81 ff., 107, 108, 111, 113, 118, 119, 122, 129 ff., 138 ff., 230
Tell Djezer, 227
Tell ed-Duweir (see Lachish), 39
Tell el-'Ajjul, 18, 39, 86, 92, 96
Tell el-Amarna, 103
Tell el-Far'ah (see Sharuhen), 39, 46, 66, 70, 71, 87, 106, 110, 116, 142, 145, 221
Tell el-Ful (see Gibeah), 8, 14, 27, 111, 118, 120, 228
Tell el-Hesi, 8, 17, 18, 29, 100, 103, 125
Tell el-Kheleifeh (see Ezion-geber), 44, 127, 128
Tell el-Judeideh, 76
Tell el-'Oreimeh (see Chinnereth), 103
Tell el-Qedah, 227
Tell el-Yahudiyeh jug, 94
Tell en-Nasbeh, 8, 42, 72, 114, 118, 130, 138 ff., 217
Tell Jemmeh, 39, 127, 143 f.
Tell Keisan, 8, 86
Tell Qasileh, 48

Tell Umm Hamad el-Gharbi, 78

Tell Umm Hamad esh-Sherqi, 70

Tempelgesellschaft, 28

Temples, 103, 104

Tertiary Age, 50

Tethys Sea, 50

Textile manufacture, Canaanite, 96

The Four Gospels, a New Translation, 199

The Jews and Modern Capitalism, 251

The River Jordan, 251

Thiersch, Hermann, 32, 147

Third Wall of Jerusalem, 47, 158

Thompson, Gertrude Caton, 13, 144

Tiberias, 9

Tischendorf, Constantin, 239

Tjikal, 113

Tobler, Titus, 25

Tombs, Herodian, 157
  Jewish, 47, 158 ff.
  near Petra, 161
  of Marisa, 147-49
  Persian period, 145

Torczyner, 227

Torrey, C. C., 141, 199 ff., 226, 240

Transjordan survey, 44

Trever, John C., 222

Triangulation grid, 15

Tübingen School, 240

Turville-Petre, F., 37, 49, 59

Ugarit, 85, 89, 103, 104, 108, 120, 187, 230

Ugaritic cuneiform script, 101, 102, 187

Ullman, Berthold, 195

Umm el-Qatafah, 57

Ur, 83

Valle, Pietro della, 24

Variety in objects found in Palestine, 20

Vaux, Père Roland de, 46, 48, 66, 70

Vertical stone walls, 88, 89

Vincent, Père L. H., 35, 155, 158, 245, 246

Virolleaud, Charles, 197, 231

Vries, H. de, 22

Wadi Dhobai, 64

Wadi Ghazzeh, 65, 66

Waechter, J. d'A., 64

Walls, city, 87 ff.

Warren, Sir Charles, 26, 27, 155

Watzinger, Carl, 33, 36, 80, 111, 142, 152, 172, 175, 220

Weidenreich, Franz, 57

Weill, Captain Raymond, 156, 172

Wellcome, Sir Henry, 10, 39

Wellhausen, 229

Welter, G., 46, 104

What Mean These Stones?, 252

Wiegand, 161

Wilson, Captain Charles, 27

Women as archaeologists, 13

Woolley, 250

Wright, G. E., 43, 48, 70

Writing, systems of, 101

Wulzinger, 161

Yadin, Y., 48

Yarmukian culture, 64

Yellin, Avinoam, 160

Zeno Papyri, 149

Zeuner, 50, 51, 52

Zuallart, Johann, 23

Zumoffen, Father, 49